"Aversion to authority seems to increase with each succeeding generation in America, and the Christian community is not immune. Today's young adults raised within the church seem even more allergic to hierarchy than those I taught ten years ago in Christian school, and the erosion of trust seems the undeniable motivator. If Satan used falsehoods to play upon the trust of God's children in the garden, it only makes sense that rehearsing what is true about God's good intentions will lead to a restoration of our trust in authority. Jonathan Leeman takes readers by the hand and walks patiently through God's plan for authority and submission outlined in the Scriptures. He deftly clarifies when the role of authority calls for action or restraint, addressing many of the subtle lies that have eroded trust in the institutions of our day."

Roy Griffith, Headmaster, Rockbridge Academy, Crownsville, Maryland

"In a world where authority is constantly being questioned, Jonathan Leeman reminds us to steward our authority for God's glory. He helpfully examines both good and bad practices and guides us toward better examples of God-given authority."

Gordon Reid, President, Stop and Shop LLC

"Thirty-two years of military leadership and six in industry, and still learning! This is a compelling, convicting, and compassionate discourse. Jonathan Leeman uses powerful anecdotes and stories to drive home the principles, truths, and precepts of authority and frames the context for practical application. A must-read for all in and under 'author-ity'!"

Scott Vander Hamm, Major General, United States Air Force (retired)

"Authority is under attack today because it is deemed to be oppressive. This book is a refreshingly thoughtful study of this theme. It firmly rejects abuse while showing authority to be vital to the proper functioning of society, church, and family. When properly used, authority serves those who are led. This timely book is a sure guide to this contentious subject: biblically faithful, pastorally wise, comprehensive in scope, and full of practical examples."

Sharon James, Social Policy Analyst, The Christian Institute

"With the heart of a pastor and mind of a theologian, Jonathan Leeman offers a timely perspective on a timeless challenge. Using clear prose and compelling examples, he urges all faithful Christians to consider anew the biblical warrant for authority in every domain of our lives."

William Inboden, Professor and Director, Alexander Hamilton Center for Classical and Civic Education, University of Florida

T0270365

Authority

Other 9Marks Titles

Overview Books

The Compelling Community, by Mark Dever and Jamie Dunlop

How to Build a Healthy Church, by Mark Dever and Paul Alexander

Nine Marks of a Healthy Church, by Mark Dever

No Shortcut to Success, by Matt Rhodes

The Rule of Love, by Jonathan Leeman

The Building Healthy Churches Series

Church Membership, by Jonathan Leeman

Conversion, by Michael Lawrence

Corporate Worship, by Matt Merker

Deacons, by Matt Smethurst

Discipling, by Mark Dever

Evangelism, by J. Mack Stiles

Expositional Preaching, by David Helm

Additional titles available

The Church Questions Series

How Can I Find Someone to Disciple Me?

How Can I Love Church Members with Different Politics?

How Can Our Church Find a Faithful Pastor?

How Can Women Thrive in the Local Church?

Additional titles available

Titles for New Christians

Am I Really a Christian?, by Mike McKinley

Rediscover Church, by Collin Hansen and Jonathan Leeman

What Is the Gospel?, by Greg Gilbert

Who Is Jesus?, by Greg Gilbert

Why Trust the Bible?, by Greg Gilbert

Healthy Church Study Guides are available on all nine marks.

To explore all 9Marks titles, visit 9Marks.org/bookstore

Authority

How Godly Rule Protects the Vulnerable, Strengthens

Communities, and Promotes Human Flourishing

Jonathan Leeman

WHEATON, ILLINOIS

Authority: How Godly Rule Protects the Vulnerable, Strengthens Communities, and Promotes Human Flourishing

Copyright © 2023 by Jonathan Leeman

Published by Crossway
       1300 Crescent Street
       Wheaton, Illinois 60187

Cover design: Spencer Fuller, Faceout Studios

Cover image: Shutterstock

First printing 2023

Printed in the United States of America

Unless otherwise indicated, Scripture quotations are from the ESV® Bible (The Holy Bible, English Standard Version®), copyright © 2001 by Crossway, a publishing ministry of Good News Publishers. Used by permission. All rights reserved. The ESV text may not be quoted in any publication made available to the public by a Creative Commons license. The ESV may not be translated into any other language.

Scripture quotations marked NIV are taken from the Holy Bible, New International Version®, NIV®. Copyright © 1973, 1978, 1984, 2011 by Biblica, Inc.™ Used by permission of Zondervan. All rights reserved worldwide. www.zondervan.com. The "NIV" and "New International Version" are trademarks registered in the United States Patent and Trademark Office by Biblica, Inc.™

The Scripture quotation marked CSB has been taken from the Christian Standard Bible®, copyright © 2017 by Holman Bible Publishers. Used by permission. Christian Standard Bible® and CSB® are federally registered trademarks of Holman Bible Publishers.

All emphases in Scripture quotations have been added by the author.

Trade paperback ISBN: 978-1-4335-8763-4

ePub ISBN: 978-1-4335-8766-5

PDF ISBN: 978-1-4335-8764-1

Library of Congress Cataloging-in-Publication Data
Names: Leeman, Jonathan, 1973- author.
Title: Authority : how godly rule protects the vulnerable, strengthens
    communities, and promotes human flourishing / Jonathan Leeman.
Description: Wheaton, Illinois : Crossway, 2023. | Series: 9Marks |
    Includes bibliographical references and index.
Identifiers: LCCN 2022060731 (print) | LCCN 2022060732 (ebook) | ISBN
    9781433587634 (trade paperback) | ISBN 9781433587641 (pdf) | ISBN
    9781433587665 (epub)
Subjects: LCSH: Authority—Biblical teaching. | Authority.
Classification: LCC BS680.A93 L44 2023 (print) | LCC BS680.A93 (ebook) |
    DDC 262/.8—dc23/eng/20230414
LC record available at https://lccn.loc.gov/2022060731
LC ebook record available at https://lccn.loc.gov/2022060732

Crossway is a publishing ministry of Good News Publishers.

To my parents (David and Barbara Leeman),
grandparents (Eric and Helga Newbold, Roy and Amanda
Leeman), pastors (Mark Dever, Thomas Schreiner, John
Joseph), professors (Steve Wellum, Bruce Ware, Shawn Wright,
Greg Wills), bosses (Chip Collins, Matt Schmucker, Ryan
Townsend), and too many fellow elders to name, each of
whom let me experience the creative power of good authority
in my life, and apart from whom this book would not exist

Contents

PART IV: WHAT DOES GOOD AUTHORITY LOOK LIKE IN ACTION?

Tables and Illustrations

Tables

Illustrations

Series Preface

THE 9MARKS SERIES OF BOOKS IS PREMISED on two basic ideas. First, the local church is far more important to the Christian life than many Christians today perhaps realize.

Second, local churches grow in life and vitality as they organize their lives around God's word. God speaks. Churches should listen and follow. It's that simple. When a church listens and follows, it begins to look like the One it is following. It reflects his love and holiness. It displays his glory. A church will look like him as it listens to him.

So our basic message to churches is, don't look to the best business practices or the latest styles; look to God. Start by listening to God's word again.

Out of this overall project comes the 9Marks series of books. Some target pastors. Some target church members. Hopefully all will combine careful biblical examination, theological reflection, cultural consideration, corporate application, and even a bit of individual exhortation. The best Christian books are always both theological and practical.

It is our prayer that God will use this volume and the others to help prepare Christ's bride, the church, with radiance and splendor for the day of his coming.

A Prayer of Confession

THIS IS A BOOK ABOUT AUTHORITY, both the good and the bad kind. Yet I don't want to write an abstract book about an abstract topic. I want to personally engage you and how you use your authority, which requires being personally engaged myself.

To that end, I have written in a more conversational style. More important, I begin with a confession: for me to write about the good kind of authority is to write better than I am.

The good kind of authority is beautiful, like a perfectly symmetrical face is beautiful, or a life in perfect conformity to God's law is beautiful. But spend time staring into that face or into that law and you'll discover, by comparison, your face isn't perfect. And you don't keep all the law.

But I want to help you and me both to gaze into the face of the one who perfectly kept the law and who perfectly exercised his authority, so that you and I might be changed. And the only honest way to do that is with gospel transparency. I'm not a paragon of the good. Nor are you. To think otherwise is to be like the Pharisee who prayed, "I thank you, Lord, that I am not like that tax collector over there."

Our profoundly Pharisaical post-Christian world, which has abandoned all ideas of original sin, teaches us to think that way. It classifies everyone as an abuser or a non-abuser, oppressor or non-oppressor. Those are the only moral categories it has left. If therefore you don't count yourself as an abuser or oppressor, you get to point the finger at the bad people and thank God you're not like them.

The Bible does not let us off the hook so easily. It indicts all of us for misusing our authority. It teaches that Adam's bite of the fruit and Pharaoh's spilling of blood are differences of quantity, not quality. Pharaoh simply swung a much bigger hammer.

To be clear, some sins are far worse than others: murder is much worse than hatred and adultery than lust. Yet Jesus also asks us to meditate on how all these sins are constructed of the same stuff (Matt. 5:22, 28). Here is an unassailable fact: To some degree, you and I have misused our authority by lording it over others. We've used our leadership to serve ourselves rather than others. We have used our God-given stewardships at the expense of others and for our own gain. For us to begin anywhere other than acknowledging and confessing these things would be misguided.

Further, it will cause us to miss the opportunity to stare into the face of the Only One Man who is truly beautiful. It would also cause us to miss the path toward becoming like this One Perfect Man.

> And Jesus called them to him and said to them, "You know that those who are considered rulers of the Gentiles lord it over them, and their great ones exercise authority over them. But it shall not be so among you. But whoever would be great among you must be your servant, and whoever would be first among you must be slave of all. For even the Son of Man came not to be served but to serve, and to give his life as a ransom for many." (Mark 10:42–45)

The path to leading like he leads requires more than a moral lesson, as in, "Do these five things." It requires recognition and confession at the deepest levels of who we are, not just "Lord God, I have once or twice misused my authority. Oops. Sorry for the slipup," but, "Lord God, I am, by fallen nature, a misuser of authority, and I will misuse it repeatedly apart from your grace."

It requires repentance and faith.

For my part, then, I began this project by asking those "above" me (like bosses), "beside" me (like friends), and "beneath" me (like children or employees) whether I use authority well, asking each to especially highlight the negatives. Gratefully, people have said nice things. Yet to share my shortcomings, one person observed, "Every once in a while, you can be really intense. At worst, this can feel a little controlling." Another remarked, "You can be very straightforward, which I enjoy. But I can imagine someone who doesn't know you finding the occasional remark abrasive."

Did you notice the subtext? Ordinarily, I know how to "behave." I know how I should appear in my leadership on the outside. But "every once in a while" or "occasionally" something else slips out, and those little slips reveal the fallen version of me—or the "natural me" apart from God's grace. They reveal something in the deeper waters of my soul.

What would that be? Perhaps a deeper and more chronic overestimation of myself and my ability to control things. And deeper than that, an ongoing tendency to believe the serpent when he said to Eve, "You can be like God." And deeper still than that, a profoundly diminished view of who God is. And together with all that, too little love for the ones I lead, sensitivity to them, and desire for their growth and strength.

Yet what about you? You have authority. Everyone does, even if you're a thirteen-year-old and have rule only over your bedroom or the thoughts inside your head. You have dominion over something—some plot of dirt like Adam and Eve in the garden. Do you view that plot of dirt as a stewardship given by God? Are you using your authority to create life, prosperity, and vitality for others? Or do you look at your domain and say, "It's mine!" and use it for your own purposes and glory? And if we could see into the deeper waters of your soul, what would we find there? Would we find the impulse to say together with John the Baptist about Jesus, "May he increase and I decrease," or just the opposite?

Those are some of the things I encourage you to think about as you read this book. Don't read the stories about people who have used authority well and quickly tell yourself that you're like them. Rather, thank God for their example, but ask yourself how you have not been like them but have been more like the people in the darker stories. Part of what's wrong on this planet is that each one of us assumes, "I'm the good guy in that story," when the Bible tells us over and over, "No, there is only One Good Guy." His name wasn't Adam or Abraham, Moses or David, Miriam or Mary, Peter or Paul. It is Jesus.

If you think you can simply adopt the five moral lessons that I offer midway through the book on how to exercise authority well, you might as well stop now. You will remain proud. And if you remain proud, you will eventually use your authority in a way that hurts or belittles or undermines those whom you lead, even if God simultaneously uses your selfishness for good through his common grace. Insofar as you and I remain anxious or insecure or selfish or boastful or controlling or proud, no tools can finally help us. There is no "how to." We will use our authority wrongly, even if we dress it up with lipstick and nice manners. As Jesus said, a good tree bears good fruit, and a bad tree bears bad. Good authority grows out of good natures, but if you're a bad apple, you're going to taste rotten. We need new natures, so that we can lead out of those new natures.

To gain new natures, we must begin by getting low, confessing our sins, and putting our hope in Christ. Perhaps the best way to begin this book, then, is with a prayer of confession. The goal of such confession isn't just to feel bad about ourselves. It's to name things accurately, so that we can then build a better life on a foundation that's truly good and lasting, namely, on Christ:

Father God,

You have given us authority to give shape to the world around us. You have asked us to image you in how we use that authority, and to demonstrate for the world your own righteousness, love, generosity, and goodness.

Yet we have used our authority for our own gain, our own fame, our own power. We have failed to serve and love those under our care. We have taken advantage of them and their strength for our own purposes.

We've been like all those kings of Israel, who thought they could rule without being accountable to you; and the priests, who forgot your word.

We've been like Pharaoh, who used and even destroyed others for his own gain, instead of using his authority to give and encourage life.

We've been like David, when he refused to discipline his sons, taking the shortsighted and easy path, to the hurt of his family and kingdom.

We've been like the foolish child in Proverbs, despising the counsel and wisdom of others as they try to help us lead.

We've been like Abraham, when he put his wife in harm's way instead of undertaking the risk and burden himself.

We've been like Adam and Eve in the garden, who thought they were equal with you.

We've not been like Christ, who proved himself king by laying down his life for the sake of love. We have not loved.

Forgive us, Lord, both for what we've done and what we've left undone with the authority you have given us. Thank you for your promise that, if we confess our sins, you are faithful and will forgive us our sins and cleanse us from all unrighteousness. We don't stand before you saying, "Look at what a good job we've done," or "We weren't that bad," or "Consider these excuses." We plead not the smallness of our sin but its considerable size. And we plead the Son's perfect and beautiful righteousness, asking that you would mercifully regard us as you regard him.

Thank you for Jesus, who ruled as Adam, Abraham, Moses, and David did not. What a glorious King and Savior, who came not to be served but to serve, and on whose shoulders the government of the world rightly rests. This Prince of Peace is worthy of all our praise and worship. Use this book to teach us to rule like him, for the good of others and the praise of your name.

Amen.

Introduction

Our Angst about Authority

ON A MONDAY IN NOVEMBER 2021, the parents of students at Reynolds Middle School in Fairview, Oregon, just outside Portland, received a three-sentence email from the school district. It told them the school would be shutting down in-person learning for three weeks. The faculty had been unable to stop the streak of fighting. They needed a chance to regroup.

Before the shutdown, students had staged a walkout due to their frustration with the administration's lack of control. "We just decided it was time to do something about it," observed one eighth-grader (age 13) about the grown-ups' failure to address the widespread fist-fighting, name-calling, and inappropriate touching.

"Kids are trying to take action that adults should be taking," said one parent.

"It was very unclear who was in charge," said another.

As the clamor from students and parents over the unsafe environment grew, the school finally decided to take the three-week hiatus in order to develop "safety protocols" and "social-emotional supports" for handling the chaos.[1]

---

1 "Students, Parents Call for District to Rein in Sexual Harassment, Fighting at Northeast Portland Middle School," *The Oregonian* (November 5, 2021): https://www.oregonlive.com/education /2021/11/students-parents-call-for-district-to-rein-in-sexual-harassment-fighting-at-northeast -portland-middle-school.html; "Reynolds Middle School Is Shutting Down In-Person Learning for 3 Weeks to Address Student Fights, Misbehavior"; *The Oregonian* (November 18, 2021): https://www.oregonlive.com/news/2021/11/reynolds-middle-school-is-shutting-down-in

I was staying with friends in Portland several weeks after this happened. Talking about it, we assumed the teachers and administrators cared about education. We assumed the parents did too. Yet for various reasons, the adults lacked the ability to take charge in a building full of eleven-to-thirteen-year-olds. Until the whole thing collapsed. The system shut down.

What was missing? Along with anything else we might say, the school lacked a right understanding of authority. Folks in Portland are angsty about authority. As are most Americans. As are citizens of Western democracies generally.

In the Democratic West

Human beings generally have a problem with authority, not just those of us who live in a Western-style liberal democracy. Yet to speak to my primary audience for just a second, our Western problem is that we don't know what to do with it. We hate it, but we cannot live without it.

So, leave Portland and join me in a trendy coffee shop in the neighborhood of Capitol Hill in Washington, DC, a few blocks from where I work. It's Saturday morning. You're watching a well-heeled DC power couple at another table in their overpriced athletic attire, probably in their late thirties, trying desperately to placate their three-year-old. He's dropped a muffin and is now throwing a fit. The husband pleads softly. The wife desperately offers toys and more treats. They reason with him as if he were an adult. It's as if no one has ever explained that *they're* the parents. That they can draw lines and impose consequences. That they don't need the child's consent, if it comes to it. But now the kid is running around the coffee shop, and they look more desperate than ever. They're neutered. This family might live several economic strata above the world of Reynolds Middle School, but it's the same story. They lack the tools to lead their child and do him good. They don't know how to exercise authority.

To give them the benefit of the doubt, they come by their ignorance honestly. Western culture has betrayed and blinded them. Like the parents and teachers at Reynolds, they are the beneficiaries of several centuries worth of attacks against every authority conceivable. Every human has

---

-person-learning-for-3-weeks-to-address-student-fights-misbehavior.html. Both accessed April 9, 2022.

resisted authority since the garden of Eden, but we in the Enlightenment West have given that resistance moral and philosophical respectability. My public school teachers taught me not to trust the church's authority because the church persecuted Galileo; or the Bible's authority because science teaches us to leave superstition behind; or science's authority because one generation of scientists will disprove the former; or the king's authority because there's no such thing as the divine right of kings; or the democratic majority's authority because majorities can be tyrannical, too; or the authority of the courts because they're also playing politics; or the authority of the philosophers because they're playing language games; or language's authority because some French philosophers observed that people weaponize everyday terms like "straight" and "queer" to normalize our preferences and marginalize people who are different; or the market's authority because capitalism is the conjoined twin of racism; or police authority because they're racists too; or the media's authority because it is biased; or the authority of our XX or XY chromosomes because they don't tell us how we must define our gender; and, of course, Mom and Dad's authority because, well, life is more fun if you can sneak out and party. Haven't you seen *Ferris Bueller's Day Off*?

When all is said and done, there aren't any authorities left to topple. Except the authority of "Me." This is what the writers mean when they describe our day as "individualistic." Individualism doesn't mean I like to be alone or I don't have friends. It means, nobody can tell me what to do or who to be. No one has authority over me.

In Western Churches

Over the last few decades this angst about authority has grown inside churches, too. Christians have been impacted by the politics of the Donald Trump era, movements for opposing sexual assault (e.g., #MeToo and #ChurchToo), episodes of police brutality caught on smart phones, COVID quarantines and shutdowns, not to mention social media's ability to draw geographically far-flung people with shared discontents together into factions. Increasingly, Christians seem more suspicious of authority than ever.

The pile of church abuse cases and the fall of prominent pastors have undermined confidence in *pastoral and church authority*. We cannot trust the elders or even the whole congregation to keep pastors accountable.

Instead, we need academics to tell us what to think and "independent investigations" to solve our church problems.

This same pile of cases, together with the ever-present problem of abusive husbands, have undermined confidence in *male authority*. The label "complementarian," which affirms the two-millennia-old Christian teaching of male headship in the church and home, may have experienced a surge of popularity in evangelical churches in the 1990s and early 2000s. But the tables have turned, aided in part by the leveling power of social media.

Meanwhile, government overreach during COVID provoked Christians on the political right to grow more and more suspicious of *government authority*. Of course, COVID restrictions only added to the suspicion that's been growing steadily on the political right over the last two decades in response to sexual orientation and gender identity laws. A typical example: the governor of Oregon signed the Menstrual Dignity Act, requiring Oregon high schools to place tampon dispensers in *men's* bathrooms! As a result, the rhetoric of an anti-elitist populism increasingly characterizes the political right. Christians on the political left, similarly, increasingly question *police authority*, due in part to the smart phone's ability to film violent police encounters.

Who Are Our Heroes?

Perhaps the easiest place to spot our cultural angst over authority is to go to the movies and notice who the heroes are. As often as not, our movie heroes are the individuals who stand up to authority, because the authority figures are evil.

Luke Skywalker fights against the Empire in the *Star Wars* trilogy, Neo against the machines in the *Matrix* trilogy, Jason Bourne against the US Central Intelligence Agency in the *Bourne* trilogy, Katniss Everdeen against the capitol and President Snow in the *Hunger Games* trilogy, Tris and Four against the Erudites in the *Divergent* trilogy, and on and on we could go.

General Maximus stands up to a corrupt Caesar in *Gladiator*, William Wallace opposes a corrupt King Edward in *Braveheart*, and literature teacher John Keating teaches his class to "seize the day" by casting off anything that hinders their freedom in *Dead Poet's Society*.

And I'm just naming blockbusters. We also love the anti-hero who does things his own way and doesn't quite fit society's conventions: Indiana

Jones, Batman, Dirty Harry, and most cowboy Western movies you've ever seen.

Of course, the anti-authority catechizing begins in childhood with the Disney princess movies. As a man with four daughters, I've seen them all. The Little Mermaid sings, "Bet'cha on land they understand / they don't reprimand their daughters."[2]

So with Queen Elsa, somewhere in Scandinavia, belting proudly, "No right, no wrong, no rules for me, I'm free."[3]

And Moana, on the opposite side of the planet in the South Pacific, harbors the same ambitions as her Scandinavian and underwater counterparts: "What's beyond that line? / . . . One day I'll know / How far I'll go."[4]

The repetition from movie to movie is striking, not to mention predictable and boring. It's as if our moral imaginations cannot conceive of a different kind of hero, so saturated is the Western soul with anti-authority-ism. The hero we cheer on is the person who resists the leadership, the system, the powers-that-be.

When you open your Bible, by contrast, a very different kind of hero emerges. These heroes often resist tyrannical rulers—Moses against Pharaoh, Elijah against Ahab, Esther against Haman, and of course Jesus against the religious leaders. Yet another, more central theme is always present in the Bible's picture of a hero. From start to finish, no matter what story is being told, the biblical hero is the person who is obedient to God.

Noah is obedient, making him a hero. Just ask the kids in Sunday school. So is Abraham, when he follows the Lord even to the point of being willing to sacrifice his son. So are Moses and Joshua and Ruth and David and the prophets, at least when they are obeying. And all this leads to Jesus, the perfectly obedient Son, who speaks only what the heavenly Father tells him to speak and does only what the heavenly Father tells him to do. Jesus is the blessed man of Psalm 1 who doesn't walk in the way of the wicked but whose delight is in the law of the Lord, meditating on it night and day.

2 Alan Menken and Howard Ashman, "Part of Your World" (from *The Little Mermaid*), © 1989, Walt Disney Music Company.
3 Robert Lopez and Kristen Anderson-Lopez, "Let It Go" (from *Frozen*), © 2013, Walt Disney Music Company.
4 Lin-Manuel Miranda, "How Far I'll Go" (from *Moana*), © 2016, Walt Disney Music Company.

Meanwhile, the bad guys in the Bible are always the ones who disobey, from Cain to Pharaoh to King Saul to Queen Jezebel to Herod and Pontius Pilate.

Every once in a blue moon a blockbuster movie will encourage you to root for someone to obey—basically the exception that proves the rule. Viewers want young Anakin Skywalker to submit to his Jedi master Obi-Won Kenobi and not turn into Darth Vader, for instance. We also want Harry Potter to stop lying and tell the truth to Dumbledore. So the instinct to obey is not entirely absent in our culture, but it's pretty unusual.

Interestingly, cheering for someone to obey or submit is more common in Christian movies. In the Christian movies, the plot always centers around the hero coming to the end of himself, submitting to God, and finding redemption, whether the movie is *Ben Hur*, *The Mission*, *Fireproof*, *Facing the Giants*, or *I Can Only Imagine*.

Yet notice, even in these Christian movies, the storylines picture the person wrestling only with himself and God. It's not about submitting to other people. Submitting to God is one thing, but submitting to people? That makes us nervous.

Conflicted and Angsty

So here we are, in this moment in which we all feel both conflicted and angsty about the idea of authority. After all, we've seen authority's abuses, from George III overtaxing the American colonists to parents abusing their children. There are good reasons why the Western modern and now post-modern tradition have cultivated in our hearts a "hermeneutic of suspicion" toward all authority. In one sense, we're right to adopt a default setting of suspicion toward those who have authority over us. Power corrupts, as they say. And abuse, which I'd define simply as misusing authority in a way that harms another person, is common.

Still, strangely perhaps, something instinctive in us keeps reaching out to *other* authority figures to solve the problem of bad authority. During the Civil Rights era, African Americans reached out to the federal government to address the discrimination they were experiencing at the hands of state and city governments. In our own era, the public voices advocating for abuse victims inside churches not only condemn the pastors who handled their cases poorly, they commend the path of reaching out to the police and child-protective services.

We instinctively recognize that the solution to bad authority is seldom no authority, but almost always good authority.

Yet book after book and tweet after tweet in our present moment only highlight the badness of bad authority. Very few attempts have been offered to define, illustrate, and commend good authority. In a world characterized by so many bad authorities, defining the bad strikes me as a necessary job, but the easier job. The harder job is to define and present good authority.

Around the World

On the flip side, it's worth mentioning how context-specific these introductory remarks have been so far. Spend time in other countries around the world, and you'll discover that this contempt of authority is not typical.

In my day job, I work with pastors and have had the privilege of spending time with pastors internationally. Whether I'm speaking to pastors in Colombia, Zambia, India, or other places, often they struggle with teaching their congregations the opposite problem: that the senior pastor should not possess all power and authority. My friends in Hispanic and African contexts, for instance, explain that people like the strong leader. Therefore, pastors struggle with raising up other leaders who will do anything more than rubber-stamp the senior pastor's own preferences. Meanwhile, pastors in southern or eastern Asian contexts, like their African counterparts, feel the challenges that arise within the context of an honor/shame culture. Leaders expect honor; people under them quickly give it.

Every location has its own challenges. A missionary friend in a formerly Soviet Central Asian country, knowing that I was working on this book, wrote me,

> One of the biggest obstacles to seeing healthy churches in our context is the abuse of authority within the church. Our country was part of the Soviet Union until its dissolution in 1991. The Soviet idea of authority continues to this day in the country's government, and that idea of authoritarian leadership has seeped into the church and is the prevailing way most pastors and church leaders view authority. There is a dire need for a biblical understanding of authority and how to use it properly in the post-Soviet, Central Asian context.

To make his point, my missionary friend offered two examples. First, a church member asked his pastor if there was church budget money for helping with evangelism and outreach. The pastor responded by saying that the church member had no authority to ask him about church funds. The money is given to the pastor, and he has sole authority over what happens with that money. Nor did he expect to be held accountable for his handling of the funds.

My friend's second example: in a conversation with other pastors, an older pastor referred to himself as "king" in his church and the members as his "subjects." He encouraged the younger pastors to anticipate the day when they, too, would be kings in their churches with subjects under their authority.

At best, the pastors in these two illustrations will have ineffective ministries, with few people growing in grace and wisdom. People will wander away until the churches shut down. That's what will happen if these two pastors lack charisma or competence. If it turns out they *are* charismatic and competent, their ministries could do great damage in people's lives and Christian discipleship.

This introduction has emphasized an American antipathy toward authority, since I assume that's my primary audience. Still, I have tried to reflect on Scripture and write the rest of this book with both problems in mind—the problem of an authoritarian overemphasis and the problem of an individualistic rejection of all authority.

One Eye on the Good, One on the Bad

A right view of authority must always keep both eyes open. One eye must always be fixed on bad authority. This is Satan's version. It's authority as exercised in the fall. And one eye must be fixed on good authority. This is God's version. It's authority as intended in creation and as exercised in redemption. With both eyes open, we see that authority is a good but dangerous gift.

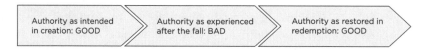

Authority as intended in creation: GOOD   Authority as experienced after the fall: BAD   Authority as restored in redemption: GOOD

Good, godly authority "authors" life, like the root of the word itself: author-*ity*. As we'll discover, it doesn't just work from the top down, but also from the bottom up. Good authority says, "Let me be the platform on which you build your life. I'll supply you, fund you, resource you, guide you. Just listen to me."

Good authority binds in order to loose, corrects in order to teach, trims in order to grow, disciplines in order to train, legislates in order to build, judges in order to redeem, studies in order to innovate. It is the teacher teaching, the coach coaching, the mother mothering. It is the rules for a game, the lines on a road, a covenant for lovers.

It says, "Trust me, and I will give you a garden in which to create a world. Just keep my commandments. I love you."

Good authority loves. Good authority gives. Good authority generally passes out power.

Yet our first parents, and we ourselves, chose not to use our authority according to God's commandments. We stopped asking for God's authorization but relied instead on the serpent's, since he appealed to our desires for supremacy. He promised loosing without binding, growing without trimming, innovation without study.

What has resulted is a rebellious and cursed world. We use our authority selfishly and therefore ineffectually. And since ineffectually then violently, believing violence will achieve our ends. Cain is not worshiped for his "worship," so he kills.

Sin, in other words, is nothing more or less than humanity's misuse of authority. Adam's bite and Pharaoh's bloodshed belong to the same class, operate by the same principles, possess the same authorization. As I expressed it in the prelude, Pharaoh merely swung a much bigger hammer.

Bad authority discourages, cripples, wilts, sucks dry, dehumanizes, snuffs out, annihilates. It uses, but doesn't give. It is political imperialism, economic exploitation, environmental degradation, business monopolization, social oppression, child abuse.

Of course, bad authority doesn't always wear such monstrous faces. Often it charms and persuades. It borrows truth and offers empathy. It says, "I know how you're feeling. I recognize your troubles. Here is the solution. Listen to me. Keep *my* commandments."

Bad authority takes a good and glorious gift that God has given to humanity and employs it for evil. It is a liar and a charlatan. Yet it is so very real, at least for a time.

Ever since the fall, the world has offered a mix of good and bad. The good comes sometimes from God's special grace, sometimes from his common grace. Even apart from Christ's first coming, history offers comparatively good and bad kings. Think of Pharaoh at the time of Joseph versus Pharaoh at the time of Moses.

The first coming of Christ, the perfect king, represents the beginning of the end of the bad. Yet now, in between Jesus's first and second comings, good and bad uses of authority remain mixed together, even among God's people, even in a single person. One day I'm the father I want to be. The next day I'm not.

Wisdom today is knowing how to keep our eyes on both good and bad uses of authority. Just as the Bible tells us there's a time to tear down and a time to build up, a time for war and a time for peace (Eccl. 3:1–8), so there's a time for Luke Skywalker to rebel and for Anakin Skywalker to submit. We must talk about the goodness of authority as God intends, yet we must not have idealized expectations for how well people in this world will use it.

The Bible is acutely aware of both good and bad authority, and it intends for us to study both. Consider an Israelite king. The king is *over* his kingdom. Yet he's a good king only insofar as he puts himself *under* God's law and *with* his fellow Israelites. Look at God's instructions for him, and notice what I have italicized for emphasis:

> And when he sits on the throne of his kingdom, he shall write for himself in a book a copy of this law. . . . And it shall be with him, and he shall *read in it all the days of his life, that he may learn to fear the LORD his God by keeping all the words of this law and these statutes, and doing them, that his heart may not be lifted up above his brothers, and that he may not turn aside from the commandment,* either to the right hand or to the left, so that he may continue long in his kingdom, he and his children, in Israel. (Deut. 17:18–20)

The kings of Israel were supposed to make themselves accountable to God's law, and to acknowledge a basic equality between themselves and the people. "If you are *over others*," says God, "you had better be *under me*, because then you realize you're no better than anyone else, and that you're only a steward, a landlord, a guardian of what's mine!"

The take-away lesson here: Good human authority is never absolute. Good authority is always accountable. Good authority drives inside the lines that God has painted on the road. In fact, good authority is always submissive!

You shouldn't lead if you cannot submit or stay in your lane, because good leadership is always in submission to God and anyone else whom God places over us. Only God's authority is absolute and comprehensive, being accountable only to the law of his own nature. The authority of creatures is always relative, as we'll consider in the coming chapters.

Furthermore, good authority, as set down in Scripture and as I've witnessed it, is seldom an advantage to those who possess it. It involves leading and making decisions, to be sure. Jesus led. But what the godly leader feels day to day are not all the advantages, but the burdens of responsibility, of culpability, of even bearing another's guilt. Good authority is profoundly costly, usually involving the sacrifice of everything. It requires the end of personal desires. Meanwhile, those "under" good authority often possess most of the advantages. They're provided protection and opportunity, strength and freedom. For instance, I would much rather have *my* job than my boss Ryan's job. Ryan has to deal with the tough stuff. He has to absorb blame when things don't go well. He has to pick up the slack when others leave it. Meanwhile, he continually provides me with a track to run on, and I'm free not to worry about the tougher things.

Furthermore, isn't this precisely what we see in Jesus's use of authority, leading up to the cross? He took the hard stuff on himself so that we might have the freedom to grow and run.

When we stop believing authority can be good, we grow in cynicism. We grow incapable of trust. We insist the world operates on our terms, which is another way of describing "individualism." When this becomes widespread, community breaks down, because authoritative relationships teach us how to defer to other people, even in relationships where no hierarchy exists.

When we stop worrying about authority becoming bad, we grow in pride and self-deceit, because we assume we're right. We lack sympathy for the vulnerable, because we assume the decisions of the hierarchy are just. We condone sin in our leaders or sin performed on behalf of the group.

A Tale of Two Coaches

In short, the goal of this book is to understand both the good and the bad versions of authority.

What makes bad authority bad? My friend Anthony's high school baseball coach, Coach Linus (not his real name), was a bad authority.[5] Anthony attended a boarding school for disadvantaged children in Pennsylvania. Like most of the boys in the school, he grew up poor and without a dad. Coach Linus knew how important coaches are to fatherless boys, and he used that knowledge to play favorites and leverage the boys against each other. He would insult them, mock them, and always remind them that he was above them. Anthony recalled one friend named Mike, who was one of the best hitters he had ever seen. Yet Coach Linus continually criticized Mike's weight and character, until Mike quit. "Playing for Coach Linus," Anthony said, "felt like a burden you could never be relieved of." Not surprisingly, Coach Linus got nothing out of his players and never won a game.

Meanwhile, what makes a good authority good? Anthony's high school *football* coach, Coach Guyer, was a good authority. Guyer, too, knew most of these boys were fatherless. Yet, knowing that, he worked to provide what they lacked with strong accountability and care. He made them work hard. He required them to sprint from every exercise to the next and drilled them constantly. Sometimes he did the running and drills with them, and he could convince them he was confident in them. He offered hard words of correction, but he said them in a way that no boy doubted the coach had his best interest at heart. "Looking back," Anthony reflected, "I realized Coach Guyer wasn't the best coach in a technical sense. He had a simple and basic playbook. The other teams could call out our plays before they happened. But the coach got everything out of us. Every guy on the team gave it his all. And we won games!" Guyer now belongs to the Pennsylvania Sports Hall of Fame. Anthony would eventually invite Coach Guyer to attend his wedding and remains in touch with him to this day.

What's the difference between these two coaches? Answering that is the goal of this book.

---

5   Unless specified otherwise, names in this book are real.

The Plan

Here's the plan for doing that. *Parts 1 and 2* ("What Is Authority?" [chs. 1–3]; "What Is Submission?" [chs. 4–5]) look at the biblical basics. We'll consider what authority and submission are, and I'll try to help you stare hard at the good and the bad—both in the Bible and in life. Bad authority steals and destroys life, while good authority creates life. Beyond that, God gave us authority to protect the vulnerable, strengthen communities, and promote human flourishing. If you're a critic of authority, you might try staring hard at the good. If you're an advocate of authority, and especially if you're in a position of authority, you need to stare hard at the bad.

Part 3 ("How Does Good Authority Work? Five Principles" [chs. 6–10]) will focus on five attributes of good authority. If the goal of parts 1 and 2 is to help us to embrace good authority and hate bad authority, the goal of part 3 is to offer five practical handles for practicing good authority. These principles aren't just theories for me. They capture how I've sought to live with my wife, children, employees, and congregation. I haven't kept them perfectly, but they are the principles I strive toward every day.

Part 4 ("What Does Good Authority Look Like in Action?" [chs. 11–17]) begins by distinguishing two kinds of authority: authority of counsel and authority of command. Those with an authority of counsel, like husbands and elders, do not have a biblically assigned enforcement mechanism. Those with an authority of command, like governments and parents of young children, do. We'll discover that this distinction significantly impacts how you will use your authority. From there we'll consider how authority should look in a number of different domains.

Following chapter 17, the Conclusion then offers a final reflection on the idea of equality as well as the beginning of all good authority, which is the fear of God.

The goal of this book is to help every husband, parent, pastor, policeman, politician, officer, and employer understand this good and dangerous gift of authority, and then equip you to handle it with care. I hope to challenge those who use authority excessively, as well as those who abdicate and avoid the hard decisions. Not only that: I hope it helps you reflect a little bit more on God and what he is like. The topic of authority takes us right to the heart of who God is, and how he means for us to image him. What you think about authority, finally, reveals quite a bit about what you think about God.

PART I

––––––

WHAT IS AUTHORITY?

1

Authority Is God's Good Creation Gift for Sharing His Rule and Glory

| Authority as intended in creation: GOOD | Authority as experienced after the fall: BAD | Authority as restored in redemption: GOOD |

"I LOVE TO TALK ABOUT MY DAD."

That's the first thing Angela said when I finally got ahold of her by phone. Several weeks earlier, I had told my church I was writing a book on authority and asked them for stories about their experiences with authority—good or bad. Angela was excited to help.

There's no tension in her story. No unexpected turns or disappointments. You might even call it wonderfully boring. It's just a woman in her early forties with three kids of her own and a great husband praising—or gushing about, really—her dad. I wish you could hear the enthusiasm in her tone.

Immanence and Transcendence

The first thing Angela talked about was how her father, a full-time pastor, worked hard to be *with* her and her siblings:

He always made time for us. He was available. He was at my piano competitions. He coached my basketball team. He was home for dinner. My school was across the street from the church where he pastors, and every other week he'd sign me out to have lunch with me. He was available and wanted to spend time with me. I in turn wanted to be with him.

We enjoy such stories—a father on a date with his daughter or investing himself in her pursuits—because we like the picture of someone *over* us stooping down to be *with* us.

Likewise, we like pictures of God walking with Adam and Eve in the garden or the Son of God becoming a baby in Bethlehem. We want a God who makes himself immanent. Who stoops down. Who draws near. Who attends to our concerns.

Yet don't miss the bigger picture: we enjoy *immanence* because it's set against *transcendence*, which is something we have a harder time liking. To speak of God's transcendence is to refer to the fact that he's over us and possesses all authority. He's high and holy. He can tell us what to do. Earthly fathers, too, possess a measure of transcendence, or author-ity, over their children. They establish the rules and set the boundaries.

You could hear Angela talk about her father's "transcendence"—his over-ness and authority—even in the way she said his name. Right after describing how he spent time with her, she also observed, "He was *daaaad* [she drew out her "a" like that], and what he said, we did. He put boundaries in place for us. If he said be home at ten, I knew I needed to."

Good authorities blend both postures, though they combine them differently depending on the role. A husband should offer his wife mostly immanence, while an army general will lean toward more transcendence. Angela's father, apparently, struck a good balance for a father. Right after referring to him setting boundaries, she continued, "But that was a positive thing, and I trusted him. I knew he set his boundaries in love."

How did you know he did that in love?

> I just knew he was for me. I was really into music. He didn't know music or understand it at all. He was really into sports. Since I was tall, I wondered if, deep down, he wanted me to be a basketball or volleyball player. But in fact he never demonstrated the least bit of disappointment in me for doing what I wanted to do or was good at. Instead, he was proud of me. He supported me and showed up at everything.

In our flesh, we dislike the idea of someone else being "over" us. Yet when we know the authority figures love us, we more easily trust them. We can recognize that having someone over us can be a source of blessing, even in their discipline of us.

To illustrate, Angela told a story from high school of going out with friends. Her father gave her an exact time to be home, but she didn't make it. He called the place where she said she would be, but she wasn't there. When she arrived home, she found a note waiting. It read, "Angela, I tried to find you. You were not available like you said you would be. I'm disappointed. I've taken the family, and we went to the coast." He had planned a surprise trip for the family to the beach, and she missed it. Her reaction?

> I remember seeing the note and feeling crushed. Later, when the family got home, my dad didn't hammer the point. There was no scolding and no lecture. He knew missing the trip would be enough. And he was right: it crushed me to miss out on my dad's blessing, because he had built our family around a trust and a love of receiving his blessings.

That last line challenged me when she relayed the story. Have I taught my family to trust that my use of authority would lead to their blessing? Do my daughters connect *boundaries* and *blessings* like this? The comment also made me think of judgment day. How many people will discover that the very thing they despised—God's law—was given to them for their blessing?

Freedom, Empowerment, and Growth

Why exactly is authority a blessing? Because it grows us. That's the first purpose of authority to highlight in this chapter: *good authority grows and empowers those who are under it.* Hence, the apostle Paul refers to "the authority . . . the Lord has given me for building up and not for tearing down" (2 Cor. 13:10).

Our natural and shortsighted perspective is to equate authority with restrictions and the repression of growth. So say many teenagers to themselves: "Once I'm out of the house, I'll be able to do what I want and become the person I want to be." We think of authority and freedom, or authority and growth, as opposites. And there are more than enough bad authorities in this world to prove the point.

The teenager's impulse, moreover, is not entirely wrong. To possess authority is to possess freedom—the freedom to make decisions or exercise power within a particular domain. And the parent possesses an authority and freedom in the home that the teenager doesn't possess. Indeed, the parent restricts the teenager's freedom in particular ways.

Yet the teenager who bucks the arrangement is being shortsighted. The very purpose of those restrictions is to draw the teenager, little by little, into the parent's own freedom and authority—into mature adulthood. A good parent wants the teenager to experience freedom and to exercise authority, but to employ both of those gifts responsibly and morally.

So it is in every domain of authority and leadership. Your goal should be to lift people up. Human beings don't grow only when freed from restrictions. We also grow when restrictions are placed upon us, like wooden stakes strengthening saplings, or rose bushes sprouting when trimmed. Likewise, children gain wisdom from study. Runners run faster from drills. Employees become managers through training. Obedience, discipline, and boundaries teach. They strengthen. "You cannot learn without obedience," one elementary school teacher said, reflecting on her classroom.

Yet good authority nearly always offers a blend of transcendence and immanence. The one *over* us in wisdom and authority draws *near* to us and says, "Do what I do. Follow me." And by following, we acquire wisdom. We grow to be like the one we're following.

Pretend Michelangelo is your art teacher. How will you learn to paint like he paints? In the beginning, you learn by training and disciplining your brush to do what his brush does. You conform your eye and hand to his. Then, that mastered, you possess all the freedom of the master himself. You can do as he does. Or you can paint in your own style, but with all his skill.

This theme of growth and empowerment ran through everything Angela said. Her dad empowered her, encouraged her, made her strong. This came through especially as she talked about the double blessing of his being not just a dad but her pastor:

Not only was he a humble, strong father, but he did it while being a pastor. It was a double encouragement. His role as father shaped me. And so did his role as pastor. Those two things worked favorably in my life.

As my pastor, he encouraged me in my personal walk with the Lord. I don't know how he did it, but his encouragement never felt like it was for his own benefit or his own renown in the church, as if he were afraid of people saying, "The pastor better have kids who are walking with the Lord." Rather, he simply encouraged us to read our Bibles and be at church.

Then I remember being excited to take the church membership class, which he taught, when I was 16. I was able to ask questions on my own two feet. It felt empowering. I didn't feel compelled to be a certain way because he was the pastor. Yet his leadership was alluring to me. Somehow he provoked in me a desire to know the Lord and to be a part of the church and to know what Scripture says.

It takes skill or wisdom to simultaneously lead people in the right direction, while also letting them figure out their direction on their own. It's hard to know how much transcendence and how much immanence to offer. Does the cookbook call for one cup of each, or a cup of one and half a cup of the other? In fact, different moments call for different ratios. And a wise father knows that the older and stronger and more mature his daughter becomes, the more he will lean toward immanence:

> As I got older, my dad would parent with questions—like Jesus, who asked a lot of questions. By asking questions, he was able to lead me without a heavy hand, letting me put the pieces together myself. And by leading with questions, I never felt like he was overbearing. Instead, he gave me space to process things with him, and I knew it was a safe space to process—safe because he didn't need me to be a certain way or look a certain way. I knew he loved me and was for my good.

In these comments, you hear a theme that's going to surface several times in this book: the generosity of good authority. Good human authority doesn't strive to continually remind you of the hierarchy, but typically aspires for equality, even when the formal hierarchies remain enduring. It exists not to serve itself, but to grant freedom, power, wisdom, and growth in those it serves. It works to draw people up *into* itself—so that they can do what the person in authority does.

"Let me play the piano scale; now you imitate me and do the same."

"I'll swing the golf club; now you hold it and swing it."

"I'll walk in righteousness and love; now you follow me."

Something else you hear in Angela's comments: the person in authority, also, is being trained. As Angela's father exercised authority, he also was learning to be like Jesus. If the first purpose of authority is to grow the one we're leading, the second purpose is *to grow ourselves as we lead.*

Good authority benefits not only the one under it, but the one in it. It gives us the opportunity to be like God—a ruler who rules.

Sharing Rule and Glory

Which brings us back to God's authority. How does God rule? He ruled by giving Adam and Eve rule, so that they might share in his rule. To them he said, "fill the earth and subdue it, and have dominion" (Gen. 1:28). The psalmist, meditating on this creation moment, responded in amazement:

> what is man that you are mindful of him,
> and the son of man that you care for him?
> Yet you have made him a little lower than the heavenly beings
> and crowned him with glory and honor.
> You have given him dominion over the works of your hands;
> you have put all things under his feet. (Ps. 8:4–6)

God has all things under his feet, but he puts them under ours. He deserves all glory and honor, but he shares that glory with us. He crowns us—makes us kings—with glory and honor.

God is nothing if not generous. In fact, his generosity is beyond reckoning. Creation exists because God wanted to share—not just his stuff, but his rule and glory.

By giving us authority, he gives us the opportunity to grow and train and become like him. The Creator teaches us to be creators, the Ruler equips us to be rulers. He created us in his image in order to image him and his rule.

People might hate authority, but God gave authority to humanity precisely so that we might grow to be like him. The devil played Adam and Eve for suckers when he promised they could be "like God" by disobeying. The opposite was true. We learn to be like God by obeying him, which means ruling like he rules.

As Angela watched her dad exercise this kind of generous empowering authority in her life, she couldn't help but want to know God. Her conclusion to our conversation: "One of the greatest gifts I have, one of the kindest things God has done for me, is to give me a relationship with an earthly father who made a relationship with the heavenly Father enticing, who made me long for it."

How I long for my four daughters, now in their teens, to speak that way of me when they're in their forties. And so with my wife. And so with the members of my church as well as anyone who works under me. I hope it's your prayer for your life, too.

King David's Last Words

King David, who knew a little something about authority, captured the life-creating power of good authority in his final words:

Now these are the last words of David: . . .

"When one rules justly over men,
    ruling in the fear of God,
he dawns on them like the morning light,
    like the sun shining forth on a cloudless morning,
    like rain that makes grass to sprout from the earth."
        (2 Sam. 23:1, 3–4)

Picture it. Rain falls on a field of grass. Then the sun emerges and warms the field. Each blade of grass then traps the energy of the sun and uses it to convert the water offered by the rain, together with carbon dioxide, into a sugar. That sugar, once broken down, grows and repairs the grass. Then you and I can look and behold a field of vibrant green. Good authority is like that sun and like that rain, says David. It gives power to the lives of others. It authors growth. Which is what we heard as Angela talked about her father.

This, as I said, is the first purpose of authority—to author life in others so that they might eventually share in that authority. As mentioned in the introduction, you see it in the word: author-ity.

So think: where do you have authority at work? Maybe it's the authority to answer the phone. Or the authority to hire and fire. Or the authority to choose a new logo for the organization. Now ask yourself: what are you using that authority for? To enrich yourself, or to author life in others and teach them to do what you do?

Yet as you seek to benefit others, you, too, grow. "It is more blessed to give than to receive" (Acts 20:35). The second purpose of authority, as I said a moment ago, is to *grow yourself, if you're the person in authority*. Every human being exercising authority will learn and grow in the process of leading. We learn the skills of leading and creating, and perhaps more crucially we learn the skills of giving and sharing. Good authority strives to delegate and to pass out power, which means that exercising authority trains us to share in rule and even in glory, as God does with us. When we use authority like this, we train ourselves to become like God—his priestly kings who mediate his rule over creation.

The third purpose of authority is closely related to the first two: *authority creates groups of people and gives them an assignment*. To have a soccer team, someone has to say, "These people are the team, and this is how to play." To have family, someone has to say, "This is what a family is, and these are its members." So it is with every group, whether a school, a company, a team, a farm, a marriage, a church, an army, a nation. Some type of authority must bind people together, name them as members, and give them a purpose. With a soccer team it might be the coach. With a church it might be every member establishing themselves by covenant. Yet the existence of any group—formal or informal—depends on someone saying, "This is who we are; this is what we do." To hate authority, finally, is to hate creation, and in particular it's to hate the creation of groups of people doing things together. God the ruler creates, and the creator rules. Likewise with us, when we image him.

People think of authority as a zero-sum proposition: more for you means less for me. Yet good authority creates more for everyone. That's what authors and creators do: create!

Defining Authority

We have yet to define authority. What exactly is it?

Distinguishing authority from power helps answer that question. Power is the ability or capacity to do something—the ability, say, to pick up a boulder or solve a math problem or fix a leaky faucet. Authority, on the other hand, is *the moral right* or *license* to make decisions with that power.

It is an *authorization* to do something. What's more, to have authority, someone must *authorize* you to do whatever they want you to do. There must be a granting agent.

At age 15, my daughter had the power to drive a car. She could physically do it. Yet she could not do it legally because she had not been authorized. At age 16, she passed a driving test, and the Maryland Motor Vehicle Authority gave her a driver's license. That license represents her authority to drive a car on public roads.

Furthermore, every authority or authorization has boundaries or limits. These boundaries are tied to the purpose for which the authorization is given. My daughter, for instance, was given the authority to drive a car, not a motorcycle or an eighteen-wheeler semitrailer truck. Both of these would require an additional license or authorization.

In other words, when you're given the authority over something, you have the authority only over that *some*thing, not over *any*thing and *every*thing you want. Your moral right to make decisions or give commands falls inside certain boundaries, or what we might call a jurisdiction. Think of Jesus's reference to "a man going away: He leaves his house and puts his servants in charge, each with their assigned task, and tells the one at the door to keep watch" (Mark 13:34 NIV). God hasn't put anyone in charge of everything, only some things—an "assigned task."

Therefore, when we get to the later chapters on the authority of the husband, parent, elder, and so on, we will need to ask the question each time, "What's the purpose of this authorization? What's the assigned task?" Answering those questions will help us determine each jurisdiction, as well as what is and what is not a legitimate assertion of authority in each case.

For instance, the police have been authorized to enforce the speed limit. They can pull my daughter over if she's speeding, and she's morally and legally obliged to pull over if she sees those flashing lights in her rearview mirror. That's within the policeman's jurisdiction. Yet suppose the police officer walked up to her window and told her she had to marry his son, who goes to the same school as her and has a crush on her. Clearly, that would be well outside of the officer's jurisdiction. I would say to him, "Excuse me?!"

As I said in the introduction, the Creator alone has absolute and comprehensive authority. His authority *is*. He can tell us what to eat, what to wear, whom we can or cannot sleep with, and how to worship. His authority is not subject to judicial review or a job termination because we didn't put him in office. We might ignore him for a while, but we cannot vote him out. He possesses an intrinsic moral right to rule, make judgments, and exercise power. Like an author who writes whatever he pleases, so the author of all creation has all author-ity over what he has made.

Human authority, on the other hand, is always relative. It is not something we *are*. It is something we must *be given*.[1] It's an office we must step into—whether the office of parent, husband, citizen, church member, pastor/elder, policeman, congressman, judge, teacher, airline pilot, tollbooth operator, and so forth.

Authority as an Office

I like the word "office" when talking about authority. It functions like an X-ray machine that helps us see the skeletal or institutional structures that define various kinds of relationships. To say "Michael is Cecelia's father" is to define the relationship between Michael and Cecelia. It shapes the identity of each, and assigns a set of obligations, responsibilities, and powers to each. To speak a little more technically for just a second, the idea of an office communicates the fact that

- authority is not intrinsic to a person but comes from a granting agent;
- one's authority serves a particular purpose or scope;
- it carries certain responsibilities and a code of ethics;
- it is a stewardship possessing a limited jurisdiction and duration;
- it is given to specific individuals and not to everyone.

Insofar as authority exists as an office, we can discern the subtle difference between the ideas of authority and leadership. When we talk about leadership, we're often focusing on an actor, not an office. Hence, I heard my wife, an elementary school teacher, recently say to the parents of one of her students, "He's a natural leader." What she meant was, the boy in question possesses the social intelligence and gifts of charisma which

---

1   Nicholas Wolterstorff, *The Mighty and the Almighty: An Essay in Political Theology* (New York: Cambridge University Press, 2012), 48.

cause other students to follow him, whether on a classroom project or in a game on the playground. It doesn't mean he possesses formal authority. He could possess authority only if my wife were to grant it to him, say, by making him a line leader.

When a natural leader leads, there might be natural consequences for failing to follow, but there is no moral obligation to follow. When a person holds a position of formal authority, however, there are moral obligations to submit or follow. It is wrong not to follow. Which is why I defined authority as a moral license to make decisions or give commands.

The same difference abides between the ideas of authority and influence. Influence is a type of power, which means a person may have it whether or not they possess the moral right to that influence.

That said, I will use the ideas of leadership and authority synonymously for the rest of this book. It's easier to say "leader" instead of saying "person in a position of authority" every time.

Authority Teaches Us about Goodness and God

There's one last purpose for authority, which was implied earlier but is worth making explicit: *exercising authority teaches people what God is like.* I can explain this in one of two ways. I can talk like a philosopher and say that authority teaches us the difference between right and wrong, good and bad, worthy and unworthy, true and untrue, holy and profane. Or I can talk like a theologian and say authority teaches us about God, since God is the source of all that's right, good, worthy, true, and holy.

Let me start as a philosopher. Authority exists because morality and truth exist, and because meaning and value and purposeful-ness and glory and beauty exist. Authority is the moral requirement that comes with the existence of all of these things. In a universe with no universal or shared values or meanings or truths or goodnesses, then we can do away with authority. But if there are values and truths and meanings we wish to protect and uphold, then authority must exist. We have rules about stealing because property is valuable. We outlaw murder because human life is precious. We restrict physical intimacy to marriage because the union of a man and a woman is precious.

To decry all expressions of authority and the rules they enjoin, then, is to decry all meaning, value, truth, beauty, and goodness. Such a dismissal leaves life completely at the whims of every passing fancy that wayward hearts might spontaneously conceive. However, to reserve a place for authority, even amid its dangers, is to step out in faith and to insist that this universe must have meaning and value, glory and beauty, waiting to be fully revealed.

Now let me talk like a theologian. Unlike he did with the animals, God created humans in his image (noun) so that we can image (verb) him as we rule over creation. He made us representatives (noun) so that we can represent (verb). As I said a moment ago, he doesn't just make us kings, he makes us priest kings, because priests mediate. Our rule should mediate or represent his rule. When we rule like he rules, we show the cosmos what he is like. In one sense, human authority is nothing more or less than human choice or agency. God licensed us to make choices, and to make choices according to the principles of his righteousness or law. In that way, as we exercise dominion over the earth, we look like him.

God says, "Watch how I speak—truthfully and lovingly. Now you do it, too." So then we open our mouths to talk. What comes out? Is it truth and love? If so, we represent him rightly, and we tell the world around us that God is a God of truth and love. If instead we lie with our words, we teach the world around us that God lies.

God says, "Watch how I act—righteously and for the good of others." Our actions, too, must then be righteous and for the good of others. If we're selfish, we teach people that God is selfish.

In short, people sometimes wonder if human hierarchies issue from the fall. Yet in fact the issue of authority goes to the heart of your existence and mine. You and I were created to rule, and part of that rule involves shaping and training others so that they, in time, can rule, too. Good authority grows those beneath it. And it grows the person in authority to become more like God. It creates groups of people. Not only that, but every time we use our authority correctly we both teach theology and affirm that good and true things exist in this universe. We're telling the world what God is like, and that he created a good world, even if rebellion exists. When we rule like he rules, we teach. When we pervert his rule, we teach. But we're always teaching. That's what it means to be made in God's image. The very structure of human existence serves this theology-teaching purpose.

Table 1.1: Four Purposes of Authority

1. Grow those under it

2. Grow those in it

3. Create groups

4. Teach what God is like

Conclusion

All these definitions and explanations, hopefully, help explain why Angela's experience of being under a godly, wise, and loving father provoked the desire in her to know her heavenly Father. Her dad wonderfully imaged or represented God's own love and rule in Angela's life. He served as a pointer to the Almighty.

Not surprisingly, Angela's father is himself devoted to God's word. Angela remarked, "My dad is a wise man. He studies Scripture. And out of the overflow of his heart his mouth speaks. His wisdom is from God and God's word." In that regard, he's like the Israelite king we considered in the introduction, whom God commanded "to write for himself on a scroll a copy of this law" and "to read it all the days of his life."

In general, good authority helps lead people to God, while bad authority can cause people to doubt or even despise God. Good authority creates life and more authority. Bad authority kills both life and authority itself. I'd guess that most people haven't had a dad as good as Angela's. Yet God has provided in his word pictures of such good authority that we can all learn from. Before we turn to the bad in the next chapter, take a final moment to reflect on the good. How do you see God exercising his authority in Genesis 1 and 2? Perhaps, before you do anything else, you should stop and whisper a word of praise. Isn't he good?

2

Authority Is Satan's Sinister Scheme for Supplanting God

| Authority as intended in creation: GOOD | Authority as experienced after the fall: BAD | Authority as restored in redemption: GOOD |

"I STILL HAVE A HARD TIME SINGING 'How Deep the Father's Love for Us,'" said Amy (not her real name).

Amy, like Angela from chapter 1, is a mother of three, only she's a single mom. "I can remember standing in the front row of the church, next to my husband, the whole church singing loudly. Yet some part of my body would be aching or burning in pain from where he had beat me the previous night. Then he would walk up on the platform and preach."

Amy was married to this pastor for fifteen years. She had met Rick (not his real name) shortly after converting to Christianity in college. He was charming, charismatic, and a known leader on campus. Amy couldn't believe such an amazing guy would take an interest in her. Her friends were even a little jealous. Then again, since becoming a Christian, many things in her life seemed new and exciting. Around the time she was twelve, she and her sister had been raped by one of the elders in their church. Things weren't much better at home. Amy's father was a highly successful businessman who was absent for half the year. Then he came home for the other half and was physically abusive toward her, her sister, and her mother. Home life was materially comfortable, physically dangerous, and desperate. Her mother had adopted a "keep the peace" posture and had taught Amy, "This is how everyone's marriage works," counsel which Amy took for granted.

Until she met Rick. Everyone expected great things from this promising young man. He was heading into the pastorate, where no doubt he would do great things for Christ. Amy began to think, "Maybe my mother was wrong."

Abuse

"How far into the marriage did it take until you realized Rick wasn't who you thought he was," I asked Amy.

Without a second's pause, she answered, "Three days. Early on the honeymoon he grabbed my hair, hit me, and raped me. I remember crying in the shower that night, realizing that my mother was right. I guess this is just marriage." What followed were years of abuse: being kicked and punched; broken ribs and concussions; perverse demands in the bedroom; a necessary kidney surgery following one beating; being locked in a closet; having her knuckles forced down onto a hot stove; and the list goes on. In good seasons he hurt her monthly, in bad seasons daily.

Rick also taught her not to contradict or question him, even with mundane matters like, "Do you want chicken or beef?" Simple requests threatened his need for total domination, triggering violence. He also cut off her relationships, including with her own family, as well as internet and media. He kept her at home, allowing her out for church and errands. She learned about the news at church.

For her part, Amy looked to the Bible. She read passages like "Do all things without grumbling or disputing" (Phil. 2:14) and would repeat this line to herself over and over. She worked hard at being a good Christian, who was submissive to her husband and submissive to the Lord's will for her life, trusting God's good purposes even in trials. She didn't realize that Satan can use the Bible, too (see Matt. 4:1–11).

Asking for Help

The first time Amy fled from one of Rick's violent tempers, she drove to the house of one of Rick's fellow pastors. She showed up without shoes and a bleeding nose. The pastor and his wife received her, listened, assured her that marriages are always tough in the beginning, and then sent her home.

More physical punishment followed, only now it was worse because of her betrayal.

This pattern continued over the years at several churches. She would keep the abuse quiet as long as she could. Eventually she would talk about it with one of Rick's fellow pastors or a pastor's wife. Sometimes they would believe her and take steps to confront Rick. Yet they would also exhort her to return home and work harder at submitting without grumbling, which in turn allowed his abuse to continue and even worsen.

Finally, Rick's fellow pastors removed him from his role. They required Rick and Amy to seek special marital counseling with a man Amy didn't trust because of how he leered at women. She refused. Around the same time she also separated from Rick. The pastors responded by excommunicating Amy, and her few friends in the church avoided her. Incidentally, that counselor was later removed from his position because of marital infidelity, while the pastor requiring Rick and Amy to see him was removed because of his issues with anger.

Before the divorce, Amy had called the police on a number of occasions, always with little to no effect. Yet following the divorce, she called the police more often, particularly when Rick abused the children. The police arrested Rick a few times. Judges required him to see counselors. But nothing could finally stop him from showing up at the house consistently and continuing in all his old ways.

On one occasion, Amy's lawyer presented evidence in court of Rick's violence toward one of the children. The police officers corroborated the account. Then the child herself testified against her father. The case seemed like a slam dunk for Amy. But Rick's lawyer spun a story about the child being out of control and Rick's need to restrain her to keep her from harming herself or others. Once again, the judge required Rick to seek more counseling, and then he sent the daughter home with her dad—with the angry, violent man against whom she had just testified.

In court, Amy, like many victims of trauma, would forget details, or put events in the wrong order, or sometimes contradict herself. She would easily panic, leading to more confusion in what she was saying. The same thing could happen in a pastor's or counselor's office. Rick's performances, however, were fluid and compelling. The natural people-skills that convinced people he should be a pastor worked to his advantage. He knew how to win a room, as well as which of Amy's buttons to push. The difference between public and private versions of Rick are well described by the psalmist:

> His speech was smooth as butter,
>> yet war was in his heart;
> his words were softer than oil,
>> yet they were drawn swords. (Ps. 55:21)

In public, Rick would finesse and persuade with soft-as-oil speech. In private he would draw out the swords and wage war.

One thing I've learned by watching Amy battle her now-ex-husband for purposes of custody is how complicated even cases of physical abuse can become in the courts. Rules concerning what counts as admissible evidence or reliable testimony, or the gamble of settlement versus pushing through to a trial, will cost a single mom tens of thousands of dollars she doesn't have for legal fees. It's easy to say, "Just call the cops!" to a wife who is being beaten. Yet step inside the complexities of her actual circumstances and you'll discover how elusive justice and protection are. It's also easy to presume that police and the courts behind them are good and honest. But how often is this *not* the case? Could you have said "Just call the cops" to an African American in the Jim Crow South, or to a Muslim wife in Afghanistan today?

Even in the Place of Justice, Wickedness

A single verse that captures Amy's story, and so many stories, is Ecclesiastes 3:16: "Moreover, I saw under the sun that in the place of justice, even there was wickedness, and in the place of righteousness, even there was wickedness." The author goes to the courthouse hoping for justice, but receives wickedness. He walks over to the temple expecting righteousness, but finds still more wickedness.

How fallen the world and its authorities!

Every authority established by God in Amy's life has failed her, either by abusing her or by failing to protect her from abuse. Her father failed her, as did her husband, as did her pastors, as did several churches, as have the courts. Are there any categories of authority left to name that don't fall under this indictment? I cannot think of one.

I once asked Amy by email for a lawyer recommendation for another woman who had been beaten up by her husband. Amy replied, "This woman will end up spending a considerable amount of time (years) and money (tens of thousands) and all she will do will further enrage her husband." Not only that, "Her husband's defense attorney will spend hours on the stand trying to discredit her, attacking her as a person, and making her out to be a liar, insane, a bad mother, and so on. Every single mistake she has ever made in her life will be exaggerated, twisted and blown up before a courtroom of total strangers." She concluded, "Whatever you do, please, please, do *not* offer her any kind of hope that the justice system will protect her. I am not only talking from my personal experience, but from hearing stories at support groups, while living in shelters, and having been through the system."

Amy's experience isn't the whole picture, but it's a part of it. Recall again the sad reality of Ecclesiastes 3:16.

Of course, Amy wasn't the first person to find wickedness in the places of justice and righteousness. God was. When God went for a walk in the garden in the cool of the day, Adam and Eve hid, and God called out, "Where are you?" The garden was to be a place of justice and righteousness, but there God found wickedness.

For a creature to be *in* authority, he or she must be *under* authority. The fall occurred when Adam and Eve, having been placed by God in authority, moved out from under *his* authority. They thought they could come alongside him and be "like God," as the serpent had promised (Gen. 3:5).

For Satan, authority is like the hammer and saw a child finds in the father's workshop, which the father uses to build things but the child then uses to destroy things. And what Satan mainly seeks to destroy is worship. He seeks to supplant God.

When We Think We're God

This is the key ingredient of all fallen and wicked uses of authority: the creature believes he or she stands alongside the Creator as an equal, entitled to all the rights and powers and praise of the Creator. Think of Pharaoh's boast: "Who is the LORD, that I should obey his voice?" (Ex. 5:2). Or Pilate's: "What is truth?" Such is the story from Cain to Saul to Belshazzar to Herod to Revelation's beast, to God's own people when they sinned, like Moses and David and Peter.

We place ourselves alongside God either by taking authority we have not been given (as when a church picks up the sword of state) or by misusing the authority we have been given (as when a pastor uses his flock for shameful gain). In both cases there is the assumption that we get to call the shots, define the rules, do as we please. Call it pride. Call it idolatry. Either way, it's us playing God.

When humans play God, we stop listening to the voices of others. We don't heed counsel. We're easily offended or threatened when corrected. *We presume to be omniscient.*

When humans play God, we strive to maintain control. We fight and lie and manipulate and charm and humor and browbeat and force and do whatever we can to maintain control. *We presume to be omnipotent.*

When humans play God, we trust our own instincts about right and wrong. We honor our own moral evaluations before we listen to our parents, bosses, pastors, and certainly the Lord. We justify our every emotion, defend our every decision. We measure fairness and justice by the standards of ourselves. *We presume to be righteous.*

When humans play God, we demand that others honor us and our decisions. We grow thin-skinned and self-pitying when we don't get our way. We covet what others have and work to steal it. *We presume to deserve glory.*

When humans play God, to summarize, we make ourselves utterly transcendent over other people. We tell ourselves we're entirely *over* them, not at all *with* them. Yet it's not God's transcendence. It's a false transcendence. It's a mockery. We use them as pawns on our chessboard. We require them to conform to our image, as Rick required of Amy. Few things are more dehumanizing, for both the abuser and the abused. If we lose our temper with them, we tell ourselves they deserved it. We congratulate ourselves on any gift of kindness we bestow.

In none of these ways do we actually become like God, even as we play God. God is powerful and never feels threatened. He is good and never petty. He already possesses everything. Every cow on every hill and every star in space is his. Therefore, he exercises his authority with beneficence and generosity, as we considered earlier. He never ever needs to seek something he doesn't already have, including dominion and control and glory. Therefore, his authority is never fear-driven or desperate. It's always and forever exercised in strength and love. It gives and gives and gives, even as it makes demands.

Human authority that moves out from under God, on the other hand, is always stolen. It's a perpetual grabbing for something you don't already possess. Therefore, it's always weak, fear-driven, and desperate. It must commit some form of violence to get what it wants, even if that violence wears a smiling face.

Sure enough, Rick knows how to charm the world on the outside. Yet his entire life has been a shell-game, as he constantly works to hide reality under quickly moving, deceiving hands. He's desperate, wracked by fear, and finally weak, even as he destroys Amy and his own children.

Teaching Heresy

When we presume to be God, we cast a false image about God, like a haunted-house mirror that distorts the face that it reflects. And in that sense, we become heretics.

Those under our authority begin to believe the haunted-house's distorted image. They begin to wonder if the God we're imaging is in fact a liar, abuser, violator, after all.

In other words, the misuse of authority, by definition, is accompanied by deception, coming as it does from the father of lies. It claims to be right in what it does. It's self-justifying.

So the child looks up at the angry father who towers menacingly over her. Something in her soul instinctively knows it's not right: "This should not be." Yet he insists his anger has every right. And so she, hardwired by God to trust her dad, begins to believe him. "Maybe he is right. I am a bad child. I am worthless." If he is a religious dad who invokes the name of God, she is that much more likely to ascribe her father's menacing anger to the heavenly Father. "God hates me, too."

In general, people underneath a bad authority will feel a dissonance between what they hear communicated from those on top and what they experience on a regular or occasional basis.

For her part, Amy remains a Christian, but on many days she wonders if God hates her. I've heard the phrases "I'm a bad Christian" and "I'm a terrible person" from her more times than I can remember. She's divorced now, but the troubles remain ongoing because Rick has the money to keep her in the courts. He wants to win back custody of the children. He's also been able to hurt and violate her, always using the kids as leverage.

Based on police reports, photographic evidence, judges' rulings, the private admissions of Rick's own lawyers, and the apologies of several pastors after the fact, I know that God takes Amy's side against this man. I know that God hates what Rick is doing, and that God's judgment will be terrible. If ever the Bible's imprecatory psalms were appropriate, they're appropriate with Rick.

Yet all this is easy for me to say, right?

Amy remains inside of and under Rick's violence. It's harder for her to see clearly. She has said, "Does God hate me? Is he punishing me? If this is his way of drawing me to him, how does that make him any different than how Rick uses punishment to bring me back to him?" Remember what I said in chapter 1: by exercising authority, you teach theology. And Amy's father, husband-pastor, other pastors, churches, and judges have taught her about God as they've broken her ribs, downplayed the rib-breaking, or sent her back to the rib-breaker. Such theology lessons comprise wicked heresy, but they impress themselves indelibly onto the mind, heart, and soul because they argue that they're right, and you start to believe them.

Amy helped me better recognize this theological connection when I was explaining her history to a counselor. I had quickly named some of the physical injuries to the counselor, but Amy later explained her frustration at my doing so. She remarked, "Words like 'concussions,' 'broken bones,' or 'kidney injury' seem so trivial and in some ways are the 'easier' parts of the abuse." Easier?! That doesn't make sense. What do you mean, Amy? She continued:

> I would 1000 times rather have broken bones and physical injuries that I can recover from than the constant and relentless attack on my soul, from which there seems to be no recovery. I don't lie awake at night thinking about my kidney injury, or have nightmares about broken bones. What keeps me awake is the terror he has managed to create within me and the hatred I feel towards myself.

She continued:

> I understand that I need to use physical descriptors in court, but I have physically healed (mostly) while still feeling miles away from even beginning to heal in my soul. Spiritual abuse—or abuse being done while using Scripture—over decades is by far the most painful and hardest to recover from, and I hope that Christians and churches deal with it as severely, if not more so, than physical abuse.

In the past, I've struggled to understand the label "spiritual abuse" due to how vague it is. Disgruntled members too easily attach the label to pastors who make decisions or take stands they don't like. Yet Amy's description is simple and sensible: spiritual abuse is using the Bible or the name of God to justify your abuses, whatever they are. When a father strikes a child, that's sinful abuse. All by itself it lies about God. Yet when the father invokes the Bible or the name of God to justify his action, he compounds his crime by committing spiritual abuse as well.

Table 2.1: Two Kinds of Abuse

Abuse	using authority to do harm
Spiritual abuse	using God's name or Scripture to justify abuse

The ex-slave Frederick Douglass, in his autobiography, recounts another terrible real-life example of how religion can compound such abuse. When his master attended a Methodist camp-meeting and "there experienced religion," Douglass hoped the man's conversion would make him "more kind and humane." But, in fact, Douglass remarks, "I believe him to have been a much worse man after his conversion than before." Before, he "relied on his own depravity to shield and sustain him in his savage barbarity." After, he "found religious sanction for his slaveholding cruelty."[1] As one example, he tells of a master savagely whipping a young woman while quoting a passage of Scripture.

Here's a side tip for pastors: recognize that abusers love to use Scripture to maintain control. As you're preparing a sermon, ask yourself how an abuser

---

1   Frederick Douglass, *Narrative of the Life of Frederick Douglass, an American Slave* (1845; repr., New York: Penguin, 1982), 97.

might misuse your biblical text, and perhaps include a warning against such misuses in your sermon. Especially include those warnings with the abuser's favorite texts, like "turn the other cheek"; "do everything without grumbling or complaining"; "bear with one another"; "wives, submit to your husbands"; and so forth.

The worst spiritual abusers in the New Testament may be the Pharisees. Sometimes they add to Scripture to get what they want. Sometimes they use what's there for their own gain. Either way, they claim to come in God's name, but they don't seek the good of others. Which means their use of authority violates the third commandment. They take his name in vain. They seek status, recognition, and power for their own sake.

A Universal Indictment

There's no happy ending to Amy's story, at least not yet. Her woes remain ongoing, like life after the fall.

I admit I have wondered about the wisdom of wrapping this chapter around her story because of how extreme it is. The extreme nature of Amy's experiences might tempt you and me to respond like the Pharisee who said, "God, I thank you that I am not like other people—robbers, evildoers, adulterers—or even like this tax collector" (Luke 18:11). I mean, we're not as bad as Rick, right?

The forces of hell want you to think that way—that you're basically good. So do the philosophies of this world. Those philosophies, in the post-Christian West, have forsaken the biblical category of sin, which makes all sin personal by measuring it against God and his law. The trouble is, we keep stumbling over really bad stuff—like Amy's story. The philosophies of this world therefore offer this solution: let's tape laminated placards to the chests of people like Rick that read "abuser," "oppressor," "sexist," "homophobe," or "racist." The wonderful thing about these placards, like the embroidered scarlet "A" from another story, is that they let the rest of us off the hook. If I can avoid being labeled as an abuser or a racist, then I can count myself as good—or "clean," to use an older idiom. I can remain inside the camp. I won't be canceled, excommunicated, or cast outside the camp as unclean.

As I mentioned in the prelude, I don't mean to suggest that some sins aren't much worse than others, or that there is no value in labeling some sins "abuse" or "oppression," the latter of which is biblical. The interesting thing about the Bible, though, is that it uses the extreme stories to indict all of us. The rise and fall of the nation of Israel, narrated throughout the Old Testament, is an extreme story. God calls a people, but they abandon him over and over, prostituting themselves with other gods and sacrificing their children. That's pretty extreme. Yet then Jesus leverages such stories to indict all of us. He says, "Don't just avoid murdering people; don't even hate. Don't just avoid adultery; don't even look lustfully at a woman. Hatred is just a less obvious version of murder, and lust a more hidden version of adultery. So don't say to yourself, 'Hey, at least I haven't killed anyone!' If you've hated, then, yes, your heart is just as wretched and condemned."

The story of Israel's rise and fall, in other words, offers a (true) parable for humanity. Likewise, Rick offers a (true) parable for all of us. By God's restraining grace, few of us have abused authority as terribly as he has. Yet we've all participated in declaring ourselves God's equal. We've all stolen transcendence. We've all dehumanized others for our own gain. We've all lied in order to justify our misuses of authority. We've all hurt others. Rick is a picture of every one of us apart from God's restraining grace: self-deluded narcissists who will destroy everything in our path, even what we say we most love, like our spouses and our children, to get what we want. The philosophies of this world are right to use labels like "abuser" and "oppressor." They just don't go far enough. They fail to look into everyone's heart, where we're all found guilty and deserving of such a label.

Conclusion

Literally dozens of times, I have heard an old pastor friend of mine warn: the abuse of authority is a particularly heinous sin, because of how it lies about God and how he uses *his* authority.

Just a few days ago, in fact, I heard him explain again to someone, "If you really want to mess someone up, take the authority you have in their life and abuse them. It's like you're getting in between them and God, and you're speaking for God in the deepest and most slanderous way you could." He went on to explain that the cases the pastors probably spend the most time on are abused wives. "They're torn between their love for God and their love for their husband. It's so confusing." The same is true of abused children, maybe even more so.

Yet to say it one more time, you've missed the point of this chapter if you walk away thinking about how terrible other people are. You and I both need to be like the tax collector, who beat his breast and cried, "God, be merciful to me, a sinner!" (Luke 18:13). We don't want one shred, one iota, one speck of such wickedness working through our head, heart, or hands as we lead others.

In his mercy, God uses even bad and selfish authorities for good in this fallen world. Yet our perpetual goal must be to repent of any bad whatsoever, and to aspire to a Christlike use of authority, which we turn to now.

3

Authority Is Christ's Claim
to Rescue and Redeem

| Authority as intended in creation: GOOD | Authority as experienced after the fall: BAD | Authority as restored in redemption: GOOD |

LIKE ANGELA AND AMY, TAMMY is in her forties and is the mother of three children. She works at a Christian school. She's a member of a church. She's happily married.

Yet to hear the story of Tammy's upbringing is a punch to the gut. It'll knock the wind out of you. Without retelling everything, here are a few headlines: Tammy born to a single mother, age nineteen. Man marries mother, moves into home, and brings mistress and her children. Step-father teaches hard work with threats. Stepfather beats wife and mistress. Stepfather breaks mother's jaw but forbids her from going to a hospital. Stepfather regularly rapes mother and mistress. Stepfather also beats Tammy from ages eight to fifteen. Uncle and grandfather (stepfather's side) sexually abuse Tammy through these years. For instance: Uncle forces eight-year-old Tammy to join him in bed with his wife. Stepfather requires disrobing for beatings with a switch. School friends see scarring on fifteen-year-old Tammy's face. School nurse cries as Tammy removes shirt. Judges warn stepfather but send Tammy home. Beatings continue. Tammy later discovers stepfather is not her biological father. On and on the headlines go.

As I said, the story took my breath away.

Lord, why?

At age sixteen, Tammy was placed in a foster home, then another foster home, then the home of her maternal grandfather. With aunts and cousins and boyfriends present, this was also a sexually reckless environment, but physically safe.

Finally, she moved into the home of a high school friend whose father was a deputy chief of police. This was the man who had gotten child protective services involved when his daughter told him about Tammy. He and his wife were not Christians, but he was a faithful protector. When Tammy moved in during her final year of high school, he taught her to drive, helped fill out college applications, and became the parent she had never had. "He embraced me as one of his children," said Tammy. "I had lots of emotional issues and was spiritually depraved. I lived a sexually promiscuous life." Still, she looks back on that time and remarks, "I thank the Lord for his sovereign grace to move in his and his wife's hearts to take in a sixteen-year-old with so much baggage."

Authority in Redemption

The protection provided by this deputy chief of police brings us to the topic of this chapter: *authority-in-redemption*. We have considered how life-giving *authority-in-creation* is, as well as how life-stealing *authority-in-the-fall* is. Authority-in-redemption offers all the good of authority-in-creation. It, too, works to author life in others. It is generous. Its goal is to strengthen, equip, and empower. It aspires to draw those in its care up into itself, like a teacher who wants her students to be as smart as she is, if not smarter.

Yet what makes authority-in-redemption unique is that it reaches down into a world of suffering and sin. That is its job and its contribution to this conversation. It must accommodate itself for weakness, brokenness, and guilt, and it expects to bear some of the costs in the process of reaching down. That's a crucial piece: bearing a cost. A teacher of a special-needs child pays the costs of extra time. A business owner with an employee who bungles a job pays the costs of lost resources and labor. A parent of an insolent teenager pays the costs of absorbing an insult without retaliation. And, of course, the Savior of the world pays the costs of his people's sin. Yet the cost in each case serves the purpose of redemption, of repair, of second chances, of renewed growth. Authority-in-redemption employs its powers—spends itself—for such redemptive ends.

If authority-in-creation blends transcendence and immanence, and authority-of-the-fall stands on its toes with a usurped transcendence, authority-in-redemption offers an extra dose of immanence. It stoops. It doesn't go to work in a lush Edenic garden. It descends into Daniel's lions' den or Gomer's brothel.

Authority-in-creation supplies. Authority-of-the-fall steals. Authority-in-redemption sacrifices.

Authority-in-creation beholds beautiful but untaught people and supplies them with resources, directions, and boundaries. "You may eat from all the trees in the garden except one. Now go and subdue the earth."

Authority-in-redemption, meanwhile, rides into the crooked and broken-down town east of Eden. Its sights are set on rescuing the weak, its heart filled with compassion for the condemned. Yet it knows it will have to sacrifice itself in the effort. The town judge may be corrupt, but his indictments against the citizens aren't entirely wrong. The citizens are corrupt too. "Everyone is both a victim and a rebel," my friend Shai Linne has said. So a penalty must be paid if justice would be true. Redemptive authority therefore gets to work tying up the strong man and shooting the snakes. But it also pays Gomer's ransom. She sold herself into prostitution, after all, and not because she had to.

The authority figures who show up with redemption in mind also emerge from the most unlikely places. They're the dark-horse heroes, probably because God loves to sneak up unexpectedly when it looks like the bad guys will win. He uses the weak and foolish things to shame the wise (1 Cor. 1:27).

This father of Tammy's friend, the deputy chief of police, was one of the first agents God would send into Tammy's life to begin his work of redemption. This man took on the expense and drama of housing a troubled sixteen-year-old girl.

The Bible's Broken-Spell Moment

King Solomon offers a beautiful picture of authority-in-redemption in Psalm 72. He points to a messianic king who applies David's last words to the world of exploitation and injustice. Do you recall David's last words, which I quoted in chapter 1? They're worth repeating:

When one rules justly over men,
    ruling in the fear of God,
he dawns on them like the morning light,
    like the sun shining forth on a cloudless morning,
    like rain that makes grass to sprout from the earth. (2 Sam. 23:3–4)

Perhaps Solomon had his father's words in mind when he wrote Psalm 72:

Give the king your justice, O God,
    and your righteousness to the royal son!
May he judge your people with righteousness,
    and your poor with justice!
Let the mountains bear prosperity for the people,
    and the hills, in righteousness!
May he defend the cause of the poor of the people,
    give deliverance to the children of the needy,
    and crush the oppressor! (vv. 1–4)

Here is a king who undertakes the kingly work of judgment and justice. He brings down the oppressor. And he raises up not just the needy but the "children of the needy"—the doubly desperate. He moves into their world, sees the violence, feels the anguish, has compassion, and rescues. His people are precious to him:

He has pity on the weak and the needy,
    and saves the lives of the needy.
From oppression and violence he redeems their life,
    and precious is their blood in his sight. (vv. 13–14)

Remarkable also are the results of this king's rule. Notice first the flourishing and the prosperity:

Long may he live;
    may gold of Sheba be given to him!
May prayer be made for him continually,
    and blessings invoked for him all the day!

May there be abundance of grain in the land;
  on the tops of the mountains may it wave;
    may its fruit be like Lebanon;
and may people blossom in the cities
    like the grass of the field!
May his name endure forever,
    his fame continue as long as the sun!
May people be blessed in him,
    all nations call him blessed! (vv. 15–17)

Grass grows. Crops flourish. Grain abounds. It sways even on mountain-tops, which is striking. Grain isn't supposed to grow on mountaintops. Mountaintops are often barren and covered in rock or ice. Yet so powerful is this king's rule that grain grows even there. It's like he is the sun shining forth on a cloudless morning, to borrow from David, or like the rain that makes grass to sprout from the earth.

The picture in these verses reminds me of a Disney princess movie—the part where a wicked witch's curse is broken and a kingdom is restored. In that magical moment, dark clouds depart. The sun breaks through. Thornbushes wilt. Grotesque gargoyles on enchanted castles transform into statues of heroes on horses. And the prince and princess's true selves are finally revealed. These verses offer the same kind of broken-spell moment. Yet what's the magic? Good authority. A king and his judgments.

Notice, second, the praise that comes to this king, and how countercultural it is. What would prompt a king as powerful as Solomon to say about another king, "May his name endure forever" and "May gold be given to him"? We want to make a name for ourselves. We want to keep gold for ourselves. Yet this king's rule is so good and life-giving that he says, "I don't want my gold. Give my gold to him. He'll do better things with my gold than I will."

Not only that: "I don't want to rule. I want *him* to rule forever and ever." Is it possible there is a king whose rule and authority are this good?

Sin and Guilt

Yet authority-in-redemption doesn't merely enter into the world of the vulnerable. It enters into the world of the guilty. It comes not just for the oppressed, but for the oppressor, because there's an oppressor in all of us. We want power that we don't deserve, and we use the power we possess at the expense of others. If you don't know that about yourself, you don't yet know Jesus.

Jesus's gospel is the good news that the good guy dies for the bad guy, the hero for the whore. And who do you assume you are in that story?

Remarkably, the messiah king to whom Solomon pointed in Psalm 72 came. Yet notice how this king exercised authority: He didn't lord it over his people. He saved them from their sin.

> And Jesus called them to him and said to them, "You know that those who are considered rulers of the Gentiles lord it over them, and their great ones exercise authority over them. But it shall not be so among you. But whoever would be great among you must be your servant, and whoever would be first among you must be slave of all. For even the Son of Man came not to be served but to serve, and to give his life as a ransom for many." (Mark 10:42–45)

Jesus's words are worth reflecting on for a moment. He presents himself as a servant, and tells us to do the same. But does that mean he actually took the job of a servant?

No, at least not according to the record of his life in the four Gospels. Instead, he led. He told men and women what to do. He gave orders, like when he sent his disciples out to preach or when he told the demons to go into pigs. He set the agenda for himself and his followers, whether to travel to one city or another. He sometimes gave people what they asked for, as when a blind man asked for sight. But never does he take orders, as would an actual servant—not even from his mother (see John 2:3–5). Instead, he defied both the religious and civil authorities. He demonstrated authority over people, demons, sickness, the elements, and death. He taught "with authority," said his hearers (Mark 1:22, 27). And when he laid down his life, he did so by his "own authority" (see John 10:18).

What's a little frustrating to me, then, is how Christians point to this Mark 10 passage, equate leading with serving, perhaps use that popular phrase "servant leader," and then say nothing more. They fail to explain what it means to lead or to exercise authority, but only that leaders must be servants. I agree that leaders must be servants, but *servants* should be servants, too. So is there a difference between a servant leader and a "servant servant"?

Servant leaders lead. They exercise authority. They make decisions and set the agenda and all that. They say, "Do this," and people do it. Yet servant leaders lead with the right *purpose* and the right heart *posture*. Their purpose is to serve the good of others. Their posture is humility. They're not "lifted up above" those they lead, as God required of his Israelite kings (Deut. 17:20). They know they need to listen and learn, too. They exercise authority with grace and compassion. They don't despise weakness.

To be clear, the idea of servant leadership doesn't belong to authority-in-redemption only; it also applies to authority-in-creation. The reason Mark 10 belongs in this particular chapter, however, is how and why Jesus said he would serve: to give his life as a ransom for many. Here we encounter the Bible's central picture of *authority-in-redemption*. Jesus paid the cost of his people's sin. He received the penalty they deserved—the wrath of God. He was a sacrificial substitute, who atoned for the sin of his people.

What we need to get our heads around is this: Jesus submitted and sacrificed himself *as an act of authority*—an act of taking charge and giving orders and declaring what's what. His submission and authority were two sides of one coin. By submitting himself to God's will and dying on the cross, Jesus declared, "Satan, you have no dominion over these people. People, you belong to me because I'm paying your ransom. I'm the king." His cross work was *priestly*, say the biblical theologians. Yet it was also *kingly*.[1]

The central picture of authority in the Bible is Jesus offering himself as a substitutionary sacrifice for sins. That's why the central picture of authority in the Old Testament, the king of Israel, points to Jesus by promising that the king of Israel would suffer for the sins of his people. Read Isaiah's Servant Songs, especially chapters 52 and 53. The New Testament Epistles then point back to Jesus's self-sacrifice and even call it a moral example for us (e.g., 1 Pet. 2:21).

Remember, authority-in-redemption reaches down into a world of suffering and sin and bears the cost. It stoops. It goes to where the people are and rescues them. Which is what the true king of Israel, Jesus, did. He stooped all the way down into the domain of God's wrath and death, satisfied the

---

1   See Jeremy R. Treat, *The Crucified King: Atonement and Kingdom in Biblical and Systematic Theology* (Grand Rapids, MI: Zondervan: 2014).

demands of God's justice, defeated every enemy, corralled a people, and brought them back up into the light. The king went, conquered, and brought his people home—*by* the sacrifice of a priest.

People today might fear being under authority because of the abuse they'll receive. Yet a Christian view of authority might teach us to also fear being the one who is *in* authority, because of the abuse you'll receive as Christ did, at least if you're doing it right. As we'll consider more in chapter 10, good authority often places itself into the position of the most vulnerability.

Tammy's Focus: Her Sin

As I said, listening to Tammy's story knocked the wind out of me. Yet something else struck me. You know how, when someone is telling a story and then they start speaking more slowly and their eyes widen? It means, "Pay attention, this is the important part." Tammy did this as her story turned from adolescence to adulthood. She treated the childhood terrors as the back story to the real story: who she became. The girl who left that home, she said, grew into a woman characterized by pride, anger, manipulation, an idolatrous need for control, and sexual promiscuity. If sin begets sin, she became in certain respects like her stepfather. And Tammy was more concerned about *her* sin than her stepfather's.

Honestly, her emphasis was a little disorienting because it wasn't the story I wanted to hear. I had asked for the interview to hear about the stepfather. His sins were far worse. Which she acknowledged. His authority was "demonic"—her word. And she reminded me of how Jesus indicted the Pharisees with being like their father, the devil, because of how they used their authority. Apparently, Tammy was calling her stepfather the child of the devil. Demonic authority, she further observed, "doesn't nourish. It doesn't give life. It promises, but it only leads to death. It oppresses and exercises violence for its own sake. There's a hardness of heart. The person is past feeling."

Still, even with all that, you can't control the devil. You can only control yourself. And that was Tammy's concern.

Like her stepfather, she became a hard worker. She graduated from high school with honors, thrived academically in college, began making good money in the early years of her career, and bought her first house in her mid-twenties. Yet she also lived, in her words, "an evil life in rebellion." She "craved" the attention of men and "would lie and manipulate or use money" to get that attention. She lived in "a sexually perverted environment" with a man.

Around this time, a former boyfriend who had become a Christian invited her to church. She went. And eventually she, too, repented of her sin and put her trust in Christ. She became a Christian.

Her early days as a Christian were rough. Her struggle with anger became apparent, as did her idolatry of male affirmation and patterns of manipulation. She moved from one relationship to the next. Then she met Tommy. He was different than every man she had known before:

> At a church single's event, I shared my testimony and what had happened to me. When Tommy heard this, he knew he wanted to be a dear friend. He prayed and asked God to help him be a good friend, which we were for about three years. He spent a lot of time getting to know me. Then we were in a courtship for a year. He initiated everything. That was not normal. I ordinarily manipulated everything. He was also the first guy to treat me in an honorable and respectful way. It was not about sex. Several of his pastors and friends encouraged him not to marry me because of the baggage. They knew about the past relationships. But he said he was sure. He said he trusted the Lord would be with us.

Eventually they married, and the people who discouraged the marriage weren't entirely wrong. The first ten years were very hard:

> I didn't know how to function in a relationship with somebody like Tommy. I didn't know how to go about this in God's way. Tommy, by God's grace, was very patient. I didn't know how to communicate in a godly way, and I would get angry. I didn't know how to submit. I thought he would leave me like everyone else.

What did Tommy do that was helpful?

> One of the lies I often heard from counselors and friends coming out of high school was, "You did nothing wrong." And, "You only need to worry about your happiness, comfort, and protection." After becoming a Christian, that way of thinking made me angry with God. I didn't understand

why he allowed all these terrible things to happen to me. So I blamed God. "Why didn't you rescue me?" That's why, in my relationships, I became so—the world calls it codependent; God calls it idolatrous. I would become very needy and overbearing emotionally.

Yet Tommy didn't let me do that to him. He wouldn't let me idolize him or our marriage. He constantly pointed me to the Scriptures and prayed for me. At the time, I saw him doing this as being mean. But he was loving me. He wouldn't let me manipulate him to get my way.

I remember waking up early in marriage, even on our honeymoon, and seeing him reading the Bible and praying on his knees. And I think that that has sustained our marriage. The grace of God working through the Spirit of God and the word of God has sustained us.

Tammy's description of her husband Tommy called to my mind the Bible story of Hosea. Hosea marries a woman named Gomer, who soon sells herself into prostitution. Yet the Lord tells Hosea to retrieve his wife and buy her out of the brothel. Tommy, it seemed to me, played the part of the redemptive hero.

The funny thing was, Tommy's version of the story didn't leave that impression. I sat down with Tommy a few weeks after Tammy to get his version of events. Similar to his wife, he focused more on his sin, and I got a slightly different picture than hers. God did wonderfully use him in the ways she described. But Tommy brought his own sin and folly to the marriage, too. And he made that clear. It would seem that God uses crooked sticks to draw straight lines, as folk say.

A Healthy Church

In the early years of marriage, Tommy and Tammy were members of a couple of unhealthy churches. Yet eventually they joined a healthy one and then another. In both churches the elders exercised authority responsibly. Along with her husband, Tammy credits the pastors of these two churches with helping her grow into who she is today.

One of the things that stood out to us in the last two churches that we've attended is the seriousness with which the elders and pastors of these churches lead the body of Christ. This was something that Tommy and

I had not experienced in previous churches. We were used to selfish, domineering leaders who only cared about using their authority to serve themselves and not to serve God and others. They would say things like, "I'm the pastor; you need to do what I say" or "I know the Bible better than you, so you don't get to question what I say or the decisions that I make." This was also the attitude of my stepdad. You could never challenge him without consequences.

What was different in these two churches?

A genuine submission to the lordship of Christ among the leaders. These men take obedience to the word of God seriously. Tommy and I were shocked. They genuinely have cared about us, and it was evident in their acts of service over and over again to our family, often at the cost of their own comfort or convenience.

I remember Pastor P—rearranging his schedule when my husband was working nights and we wanted to be a part of a small group. I remember him driving his daughter to college in another state and then coming home and immediately helping us move. He also helped me understand that biblical submission doesn't mean I don't have a voice, but that I must use my voice to represent Christ as I encourage the leadership of people with authority over me, like my husband, pastor, or government. He also said that anyone in authority who does not listen to and consider the insights of those that they lead is a foolish leader.

I remember Pastor L—talking me through my issues with authority in my marriage by pointing me to the Scriptures and reminding me that my wrath was inconsequential compared to the wrath of God.

I remember Pastor M—being there for us when my maternal grandfather passed away. He was with us from the beginning to the end of the entire process and kept reminding us that he is our pastor and it is his job to serve us.

These are just a few examples, but there are more. This is Christlike leadership—authority that seeks to nourish, protect, love, serve, and sacrifice for the people they are called to lead, and all for the glory of God. They do not lord it over the people but willingly lead and serve the people as a Christlike example.

She concluded:

> While it is true that the Lord has used Tommy and his leadership to
> help me through a lot, I would also point to the Lord's kindness to us in
> providing us with churches that are committed to sound biblical teach-
> ing, to exalting Christ and his lordship, and to leadership that models
> Christlike authority. Tommy and I are the people we are today because
> of these means of grace.

Before and After Shots

As I said, the early years of marriage for Tammy and Tommy were hard.
Yet things began to change around year ten. Tammy started to trust her
husband. She contested less and less. She got control of her tongue more
and more. She also aspired to be gentle with her children, whereas before
she was "verbally abusive." She has been maturing in grace and has become
the woman my wife and I know today: godly, confident, humble, quick
with a word of biblical encouragement. I asked her to describe a series of
"before" and "after" shots. She offered several:

> Before, I didn't trust Tommy's leadership and authority. Now, as I've
> learned about God's sovereignty, I trust Tommy's decisions more.
>
> Before, I was very angry. I expected leaders to say, "I'm the leader,
> be quiet." So I started conversations combatively. Yet Tommy is not
> that kind of leader. Now, I start respectfully, not seeking my own gain,
> but seeking to be a voice to my husband and letting God determine if
> Tommy hears.
>
> Before, I was very competitive with Tommy. Now, I seek to complement
> and encourage his leadership.
>
> Before, I was verbally abusive to my children. They have memories
> of that. Now, I'm very careful in how I communicate. I try not to let any
> unwholesome word come out of my mouth, but only speak to give grace.
> Recently, I felt convicted by a sermon. My daughter leaned over and tried
> to encourage me by saying, "You are nothing like you used to be." What
> I've learned is, my children don't need to see a perfect mom, but a mom
> growing in the grace and the power of the gospel. They don't need to see
> my perfection but my direction.

Before, I was critical and judgmental. Now, I'm still not a great encourager. I'm quick to point out what's wrong. But I strive to be gracious and encouraging. I try not to return evil for evil, but with a blessing.

Before, my parenting was all about getting my children to obey and respect me. Now, I want them to learn to love God and submit to his authority—in part by obeying me, yes, but it's about him, not me.

Before, my mother-daughter relationship with my oldest was difficult, because I never connected with my own mother. My daughter might want a hug, but my response would be cold and mechanical. I didn't know what maternal warmth looked like. Now, my daughter knows this about me and gives me a lot of grace. She likes to do girly things. I don't. But, yes, let's go shopping. And try on makeup! I enjoy watching her do the things I didn't get to do as a child.

Truth and Justice, Mercy and Grace

The challenge of exercising *authority-in-redemption* is that you must always work to accommodate two sets of demands: the demands of truth and justice on the one hand as well as the demands of mercy and compassion on the other hand (see Matt. 6:12; 7:2). One must astutely balance transcendence and immanence, between correcting a person from on high and drawing near to them with grace. Sometimes justice demands that you punish the child or fire the employee. Yet sometimes grace calls you to show compassion. You don't punish or fire, but you overlook, forbear, pass over, even encourage. No doubt, it's tough to know when the demands of truth and justice should win the day and when mercy and grace should win. We need wisdom.

How many times have my wife and I wondered whether we should impose a hard penalty or a light one or none at all with disobedient children. Unlike authority-in-creation, authority-in-redemption must continually ask such questions in the larger project of redemption. It always seeks to accommodate both sets of duties, yet each in due measure for the moment. Plus, redemption doesn't just mean forgiving someone and drawing near. It means doing so in a way that doesn't ultimately undermine the rules of truth and justice, since redemption ultimately includes living by those rules.

Here's a tragic and ironic dynamic I've observed in the fight for truth or for justice: it's easy to overlook the need for extra doses of immanence when correcting people. As such, you can become harsh and even abusive in your authority and activity. Your motives may be redemptive, at least at the outset. Truth people see the destructive force of falsehood, and they burn to lead people toward truth. Justice people see the destructive force of oppression and abuse, and they burn to protect people from further injustice. Yet, too often, that burning means there's no fight we won't pick and no injustice we won't address, like the parent who corrects every conceivable error and makes no allowances for weakness. We slam down the gavel with the full force of the law. We verbally lash the child with a pristine recitation of God's word. We scorn our political opponent with right invocations of justice. We adopt a posture of overly exuberant transcendence with little to no imma-nence. It's almost as if we've become God, only a god who shows no mercy and never draws near. We offer no concessions, like "I understand why you feel that way," or "I admit I could have been clearer in my instructions," or "Yes, you've had a tough week," or "I've done it, too." Rather, we turn into Pharisees, and so our biblically correct truths and our right demands for justice reek of self-righteousness and contempt.

This is the husband who points to the Bible verse as he belittles his wife; the mother who knows just the right words to make her children feel ter-ribly guilty; the Christian college professor on social media whose words drip with condescension as he stands up for justice; the boss who fires the employee, forgetting he made those same mistakes; the pastor who refuses to be questioned because he's the pastor.

Social media, in particular, foments such Pharisaism, since the structures of the medium preclude meaningful relationship (immanence) yet offer every algorithmical incentive to speak *at* people (transcendence).

Let me illustrate the difference between a Pharisaical correction and a redemptive one. Imagine your teenage son cursing at you. Among other possibilities, you might correct him in one of two ways:

"I can't believe you spoke that way to *me*. I'm personally offended. How dare you! I will punish you and insult you in equal measure because you did not honor me. I will make you treat me like I know I deserve to be treated."

Or, you could say,

"You did not honor me, even though God placed me in your life to lead you. I understand how difficult this can be, because I too fail to honor those God has placed over me. Yet the Lord deserves your obedience and mine. Therefore, I want to help you be what he calls you to be—a son who honors his father. I'm going to account for the difficulties you've been going through and show compassion where I can. But I wouldn't be loving you as a father if I didn't impose consequences as well."

The first response comes from a posture of pure transcendence, which amounts to a stolen transcendence and ends up being misshapen. The search for truth and justice, tragically, devolves to the authority-of-the-fall.

The second posture combines transcendence and immanence. It's properly human. I'm not saying the latter offers the right language or balance for every occasion. Sometimes judgment must be more swift and severe than what's illustrated here. Still, authority-in-redemption stoops. It forbears and shows compassion. It expects to find troubles, some of which must be corrected immediately, some of which must be overlooked for a season.

How can we combine truth and justice with mercy and grace in how we use authority? There's no easy answer, other than to know the gospel, recognize your personal dependence on the gospel, and then ask the Lord for wisdom in knowing how to give both justice and mercy to others.

Conclusion

Tammy grew up in a terrible household. She needed rescuing. So God sent both a government agency and a friend's father. She also needed saving and forgiveness. So God sent an evangelist. And she needed training and growth in godliness. So God sent a husband, a couple of churches, and some pastors. Today, she is another example of God's handiwork, created to do good works and show forth his glory.

Her life teaches that the solution to bad authority is not *no* authority but *good* authority. This, too, is the lesson of the gospel, a word which means "good news." It refers to the good news of Jesus dying on the cross for sinners and rising again for our salvation. The thing is, Christians think of the gospel as good, but submission as bad; at least our instincts often feel that way.

Tammy, who knows the terror of bad authority as much as anyone, knows this doesn't make sense. The gospel of Jesus Christ is all about authority and submission. She wrote me in an email,

> I believe that my lack of understanding about authority and submission was not a result of poor examples from my childhood. It was a result of not understanding the gospel.
>
> The gospel of Jesus Christ, at its core, is all about submission. Jesus Christ is Lord and Master. I am a sinner who is commanded by God to turn from my sin and submit to his Son, Jesus Christ, as Lord, and to follow him faithfully by obeying his word in the power of the Spirit. I am a slave to the righteousness of Jesus Christ.
>
> This is why I believe the gospel is hard for many to believe—because sinful human beings have no desire, apart from the grace of God, to submit themselves to God. We like calling the shots. But Jesus calls sinners to humble and deny themselves, and put others before themselves to glorify and exalt him.
>
> So a right understanding of biblical authority and submission is rooted in a right understanding of the gospel. If you have a false gospel or even a watered-down version of the gospel, you will have people who will not and cannot reflect true biblical authority and submission. I heard a dear pastor say, "Submission is the song of love," and I responded that it is a song that I want to learn to sing well for the Lord.

It's hard to think of a better conclusion to this chapter.

PART II

WHAT IS SUBMISSION?

4

Submission Is the Path to Growth, Authority, and Likeness to the God-Man

SOMETIME IN MY JUNIOR HIGH YEARS I became aware of how much my brain bent toward nonconformity. The kids in the youth group were discussing a political matter, and I found myself arguing for a position I didn't believe merely because something in me needed to oppose the room's consensus.

Part of that need to oppose, I believe, is my brain's wiring. To this day, I think dialectically. I look at one side of an issue, then another, and then search for a synthesis. But another part of that instinct was just plain old immaturity and sin. Something in me enjoyed standing alone and standing against. I think my heart found a sense of purpose and worth in thinking of myself as courageous in these stances. So, if I was in a room of Democrats, I would argue like a Republican. And if I was in a room of Republicans, I would argue like a Democrat. To be sure, this nonconformist tendency helped me academically in high school, college, and graduate school. I wrote good papers. Gratefully, I also had patient parents.

In my early twenties, I moved to Washington, DC, and, for the first time in my life, joined a church. Still, I was *that* guy—the guy who asked persnickety questions in Bible study; the guy who pestered the pastor with "what ifs"; the guy who always thought he knew better. I had a high opinion of myself since I did well in school. In fact, the friend who told me about the DC church mentioned that it had a brilliant pastor, and I said to myself—this is sincerely embarrassing to admit—"We'll see."

"Trust Me"

A year or two into my membership, the church voted on a batch of brand-new elders who had been nominated by this same pastor, Mark. The constitution required 75 percent approval from the congregation. Yet all five received somewhere between 69 and 74 percent of the vote, meaning all five failed. The congregation was shocked. We wondered what the pastor would do next. Two weeks later we found out: he announced he was again nominating the same five men.

"What?! Are you kidding me?!" That was my internal response. "The congregation voted, buddy. You lost. And you're the one who taught me to be a congregationalist. Now you want to call a re-do, because you didn't get the result you wanted? Sorry, pal. No way!"

My nonconformist instincts were in full flair. I had voted for three of the five candidates the first time around, but now I would protest-vote against all five. This Pastor Mark was a jerk and a tyrant!

Shortly after the announcement, Mark hosted a question-and-answer time on a Sunday afternoon concerning his renominations. I attended. Standing before God as our one pastor, he said, he could not in good conscience put another slate of men in front of us. Therefore, he offered, "I'm asking you to trust me." He said this meekly and gently. Yet he said it clearly and directly.

You might expect my heart to have gone into rebellion-hyperdrive at that moment. But for some reason, somehow, it didn't. His request . . . made sense. It landed softly on my heart. He is my pastor, I thought. I should trust him.

You might call this my rich-young-ruler's moment. I didn't have much money to give up, but I did have a high opinion of myself. And I sensed the Lord Jesus saying to me, "Jonathan, if you want to follow me, follow Pastor Mark." Yet unlike the New Testament's rich young ruler, I surrendered myself and followed. God's Spirit was at work. A week or two later I voted for all five men. And enough people joined me that all five passed the 75 percent threshold and were affirmed as elders.

Not only that; my life began changing. I changed from nonconformist to team player; from rebel to disciple; from raising-my-hand-to-stump-the-pastor to raising-my-hand-to-ask-a-question-that-might-help-the-group. I began to grow in the faith—fighting sin, reading the Bible, wanting to do good in the lives of my fellow church members. Sometimes I wonder if that whole affair was when I actually became a Christian.

Something else changed. Little by little, I began receiving opportunities to lead in the church. First, it was a Bible study for other single men. Then, co-teaching a Sunday school class. Then, a deacon of member care, tasked with visiting older members and distributing the church's benevolence fund. Finally, I became a pastoral intern and was sent to seminary, paid for by the church, and became an elder at that same church after seminary.

Before heading off to seminary, I remember reflecting back on what God had done in my life over the previous few years. This thought struck me: submission to Mark and other men in my life had led to my growth. Not only that, nobody had ever told me how powerful submission is for spiritual growth. Why hadn't I heard a sermon on that? "Evangelical Christians in America are missing this amazing gift," I concluded.

To understand that reaction, it's important to understand that I had not grown up in anything closely approximating authoritarian churches. I grew up in a stream of evangelicalism that, if anything, erred toward permissiveness. So while I still believe today that many evangelicals don't recognize the power of submission, I also recognize that some Christians have grown up in churches where the call to submission is a front-burner issue every Sunday. And people are harmed.

Another Interpretation

Speaking of harm, I've given you my interpretation of those years. There is another interpretation someone could offer. Rewind the tape to that Sunday afternoon meeting and tell the story like this:

Pastor Mark is a man who loves control, and so he nominated five men whom he knew would allow him to maintain control—what they call "yes men." When all five got voted down the first time, he knew he had to lean in. So he called for a church meeting where he employed all his power of intellect and charisma to emotionally manipulate the church. "Trust me," he said. "Don't you know I'm your pastor? Don't you know I represent God? Don't you know that making me pick another batch of men is going to cause me to sin, and you don't want to do that, do you?" Then, poor Jonathan, he drank the Kool-Aid. He got sucked in. But don't feel too sorry for him. He joined the system. He became a "yes man" and was rewarded accordingly. Maybe he used to be a nonconformist, but then he discovered an easier path to power: just play along. So he did what he was told and began to move up in the system because the leaders knew he was loyal. He joined the party of oppressors and exploiters and abusers, and now he's writing books for them.

You can look at all the data I've given you and offer that interpretation. It's an internally coherent and intelligent interpretation. Not only that, it rightly describes many pastors and churches and aspiring young people, at least if we're listening to the Bible's warnings. Ezekiel indicts the wicked shepherds who ruled "with force and harshness" and who fed themselves instead of the sheep (Ezek. 34:2, 4, 8). Peter warns of false teachers who "in their greed . . . will exploit you with false words" and who "promise . . . freedom" but are themselves "slaves of corruption" (2 Pet. 2:3, 19). Those guys exist. They're out there.

Yet whether you decide my story is better explained by the first interpretation or the second, exonerating me and Mark or not, doesn't finally matter for our purposes here. I hope you'll acknowledge, both interpretations are hypothetically possible. Meaning, you recognize that people sometimes grow by submitting, and learn how to be good leaders by submitting. And the whole process is healthy.

You know this if you've ever had a good coach, teacher, boss, commanding officer, or parent. You learned that submitting to them made you stronger, faster, smarter, better, even when submission was a tough pill to swallow at first. Today you thank God for that person. You laugh and tell stories about how hard they were on you, but that you always knew they loved you, and that you're a better person because of them.

Or we might think of the biblical story of Joseph. He submitted to Potiphar and ended up ruling his house. He submitted to the jailer and ended up ruling the prison. He submitted to Pharaoh and ended up ruling a kingdom. In God's design, submission is the pathway to authority.

I admit the word "submission" is scary. It can feel dehumanizing. For instance, what do you think of the biblical requirement for wives to submit to their husbands? Does it seem dehumanizing to women? Are you tempted to explain the biblical commands away? I argued in chapter 1 that we image God by exercising authority. Therefore, it seems like giving authority only to men and not to women inside the marriage relationship diminishes the woman's humanity, doesn't it?

Authority and submission are the two sides of one coin, and understanding one helps us understand the other. Since most of this book is devoted to authority, it's worth taking a couple of chapters to meditate on the coin's other side. This chapter will describe submission in the ideal. The next will consider submission's limits.

According to God's design of the world, everyone submits, particularly if they mean to rule. We simply occupy different stations.

Submission Involves Deferring to Another Person's Judgments

Submission, as I will define it in this book, involves two things: *deferring* by moral constraint to another person's judgment and *deploying* your resources for the sake of fulfilling that person's judgment. We'll take those one at a time.

A little girl is playing on her backyard swing. She hears the backdoor open and her mother call out, "Sweetheart, time to come inside." This makes her a little sad, because she would prefer to continue swinging. But she recognizes her mother's authority, and so, as an act of submission or obedience, she defers by moral constraint to her mother's judgment. She runs inside.

What are we doing when we "submit" or "obey"? We're deferring by moral constraint to an authority figure's judgments, even if we don't immediately share those judgments.

When I agreed to vote for all five elder candidates, I was deferring by moral constraint to Pastor Mark's judgment. I was submitting.

You probably noticed that I keep saying "moral constraint." A moral constraint, of course, is different than a physical constraint. An act of submission, as I'm defining it here, involves our free agency. You're not being physically forced to defer. You're choosing to defer, even if those choices involve external pressure, such as the threat of consequences. The speed limit sign requires me to drive fifty-five miles per hour. I know there are possible consequences for driving faster. Still, I can either obey or disobey. I possess the ability to choose. I possess agency. However, were I to be placed in handcuffs and thrown into the back of the police car for driving one hundred miles per hour, I would lose the ability to submit because I would be losing my agency. To be forced to do something, in other words, is different from choosing to submit to something, at least as I am using the word in this book. In that sense, submission also involves an act of judgment. When the daughter chooses to come inside at her mother's call, she makes the judgment that listening to her mother is *better*, in light of the moral nature of her mother's command, than continuing to do what she initially prefers to do.

Insofar as submission involves our freely chosen (not forced) judgments, the opportunity to submit is an opportunity to train. Submitting trains our judgment-making faculties to make better judgments. You're still *choosing*. But you're practicing choosing by holding it up to a ruler or a standard. It's like learning to swing a golf club. The first time you pick up a golf club and swing it, your arms, shoulders, and hips will swing the club in a gangly and awkward fashion. But what happens when you submit your body to a golf pro's instruction? Little by little, your arms, shoulders, and hips will move more naturally. So it is with deferring to a parent's judgments. By submitting, the child learns to exercise her conscience, desires, and decision-making faculties in better, self-controlled, moral, and neighbor-loving fashion.

Insofar as submission involves our freely chosen judgments, the act of submitting also involves making a declaration. When we submit, we declare, "This is better," or "This is worthy or righteous or true." So it is when we submit to God's law. We declare him and his law to be good. As the psalmist puts it, "I find my delight in your commandments, which I love" (Ps. 119:47).

When we submit to God, we are being trained to do something very godlike. It's not right to say that God "submits," because he never defers to another's judgment. Yet he does submit himself to the law of his own nature, and that's what I mean when I say we're doing something "godlike" by submitting to him. Just as he submits himself to the law of his nature, so we should submit ourselves to the law of his nature.

Furthermore, the incarnate Son submitted himself to God's will. The human nature and will of Christ submitted to the divine nature and will. Jesus in the incarnate flesh judged God's will to be most worthy. Therefore, he remarked, "My food is to do the will of him who sent me and to accomplish his work" (John 4:34; see also Phil. 2:5–11). And this act of submission began with a judgment: "my judgment is just, because I seek not my own will but the will of him who sent me" (John 5:30).

Submission to God is the prizing and valuing of God's righteousness, love, and glory above all things, even as God most prizes his righteousness, love, and glory above all things. Ironically, we are most godlike and Christlike when we submit ourselves wholly to him, because it involves us in doing what he does—ruling in submission to his character and nature.

Submission Involves Deploying Your Resources

So, submission involves deferring to someone else's judgment, but it also involves deploying your own resources to that same end. I once heard a preacher—I don't remember where or when—illustrate the word "submit" with the picture of troops on a battlefield. One platoon comes under heavy fire; another platoon redeploys to reinforce the first, submitting themselves to them by order of a commanding officer. It's a good picture of what happens when we submit: we redeploy our resources and strength in order to reinforce a weakness in the battle line.

And make no mistake, moving in to provide reinforcement requires strength. My friend Jeff, a pastor and college professor, described the strength of his wife with his own battlefield reinforcement story. Jeff was midway through a PhD in Old Testament. After a couple of discouraging years, he reached the end of himself and decided to quit. He announced this to his wife, Angela (not the same Angela as in chapter 1). Her response? "The children and I have followed you to this school. We have given ourselves to trusting you. You need to finish it." She also reminded him of his obligation to provide for his family and to follow through on his commitments.

Jeff then summarized the moral of the story: "Would you say she was submitting? You bet she was. And it demanded her strength. She drew me out. She helped me be the man I could never be by myself—the best possible man I could be."

Jeff's story made me think of God creating Eve to be a "helper" for Adam in their joint project of ruling the earth (Gen. 2:18).

Jeff continued: "The fact that Angela challenged me like this is what allowed the first church I pastored to become what it became. And the second church. And the 9 percent of church members we sent to the mission field. In that moment, Angela helped me become the man I needed to be, which in turn has impacted many others."

Submission involves deploying our resources and strength to reinforce a weakness on the battle line. A company needs help in their IT office. They examine resumes in order to determine whose training and experience will best provide the necessary help. The person whom the company hires then submits him or herself to the company's direction, authority, and need. Parents teach children to work hard, so that those children will submit their hard work to the household's upkeep. A pastor instructs a young man to apologize to another member for an insensitive remark. The young man submits by giving careful attention to the apology so that he can rebuild what he tore down.

The training and life-giving operations of submission work even when a formal authority is not present. Other than on social media, for instance, I scarcely publish a word without first showing my writing to friends for feedback. And whenever I believe a social media post might be controversial, I share it first, too. And then, as much as possible, I defer to the judgments of my friends, so that I might deploy my writing wisely.

Submission Always Follows Faith

What's also interesting in the Bible is how closely related the ideas of submission and faith are.

We learn this in a Roman centurion's encounter with Jesus. The story starts with a centurion making a straightforward request of Jesus to heal his servant: "say the word, and let my servant be healed."

The centurion then illustrates the very thing we've been talking about—how authority and submission involve deference to judgment and the deploying of resources: "For I too am a man set under authority, with soldiers under me: and I say to one, 'Go,' and he goes; and to another, 'Come,' and he comes; and to my servant, 'Do this,' and he does it." Following his own lesson, the centurion then submits himself to Jesus. He knows that Jesus, too, has the authority to move troops around the battlefield. Jesus can fix whatever needs to be fixed, including a sick servant.

What's interesting is how Jesus then characterizes the centurion's submission as exemplifying *faith*. "When Jesus heard these things, he marveled at him, and turning to the crowd that followed him, said, 'I tell you, not even in Israel have I found such faith.'" Then Jesus healed the centurion's servant (Luke 7:7–10). Did you catch that? Jesus calls the centurion's submission faith.

To submit to someone's authority—to defer to their judgment—requires faith. If faith is a posture of trust, that trust then shows itself inescapably and necessarily in an act of submission. Faith comes first, but faith always comes with submission. If you don't see submission, you know there is no faith.

By submitting to Pastor Mark's nominations for elders, I exercised faith in Mark, or, more precisely, I exercised faith in the God who calls me to submit to my pastors.

Yet let's go back to the question of whether or not submission is dehumanizing. It is, only if you think *faith* is dehumanizing.

Is Submission Dehumanizing?

There are a few more reasons to resist the charge that submission is necessarily dehumanizing: submission involves agency; submission is the pathway to growth; and submission is the pathway to authority because all good authority involves submission.

First, submission involves agency, that most precious of human commodities, as we've considered. To entirely remove a person's agency can indeed be dehumanizing. There is something less than human about a prison cell, for instance, even if it is necessary. But the call to submit does not do away with agency.

Second, submission involves training and is the pathway to growth. What happens when a coach asks an athlete to submit to a drill, or a parent asks a child to mind her table manners? The authority figure is asking for an exercise of agency, but agency that's being trained in a particular direction, like a wooden stake for a sapling or braces for teeth. The moral nature of the command applies pressure on the person's choice, to be sure, but, ideally, that pressure possesses a training and shaping function. If you don't think people need training or growth, or if there are no standards of goodness and truth, then, sure, people should never submit. It is hardly surprising, therefore, in a culture where all truth and standards of righteousness are contested, that the idea of submission would strike us as infantilizing at best, dehumanizing at worst. But if there is room for people to grow, and if there are standards of truth and goodness, then submission is not just good: it is necessary. By submitting to Pastor Mark, I grew. By submitting to her father, Angela from chapter 1 grew up to become like her father—a woman who fears the Lord, loves his word, and instructs and disciplines her own children as her father did for her. By submitting to her husband, a wife, who may be more competent and spiritually mature than her husband, grows in trusting God even when her earthly head disappoints her.

Third, submission is the pathway to rule or authority. This is what the serpent in the garden never wanted us to see: to obey God is to share in his rule. Walking in God's ways, for Adam and Eve, meant ruling over the earth with a crown of glory (see Ps. 8). By submitting to the heavenly Father, Jesus, ironically, assumed the authority of the Father. "To be *in* authority," theologian Oliver O'Donovan has remarked, "you have to be *under* it, and if you are under it you are in it."[1]

People must learn to submit before they can rule, and the best leaders are the best submitters. Unlike a narcissist, a good ruler or leader recognizes the world outside of himself, including the forces and structures to which he is accountable. He can then lead with sensitivity and conscientiousness. He realizes he's neither omniscient nor omnipotent. Narcissists, on the other hand, only hear and submit to the demands inside their head.

One of the things I appreciate about Pastor Mark the most is that he's always passing out authority. Among other things, that meant he was adamant about appointing five other elders. And he wanted men whom he could trust because he knew that he, too, would be called to submit to them. To this day, Mark loses votes in nearly every elder meeting. When this happens, he remarks, "I just assume the majority is showing me God's will."

By the same token, one of the criteria the elders of my church consider in deciding whether to nominate another man for elder is whether he demonstrates a pattern of submitting to the elders. Is he teachable? Can he be entreated or corrected? Does he ever back down or change his mind or at least happily defer to others?

The larger lesson here is, you cannot lead if you cannot submit. And rebellion is not the only way to gain authority. Submission is, too. By putting

---

1   Oliver O'Donovan, *Desire of the Nations: Rediscovering the Root of Political Theology* (Cambridge: Cambridge University Press, 1999), 90, emphasis original.

yourself under authority and emulating it, you participate in that authority. The path to leadership or authority as God intended it in creation is through submission and obedience. To jump ahead in the Bible's storyline, Jesus perfectly obeyed the heavenly Father while on earth, and he was given all authority in heaven and on earth as a result (Matt. 28:18).

Submission is not dehumanizing, at least not necessarily, because obeying leads to leading. And every human leader must simultaneously submit to the one who has placed him or her in a position of authority.

Submission Depends on a Moral Obligation to God and Only God

This brings us to the last thing we need to do in this chapter, which is to dissect the ingredient of moral obligation mentioned above. Where does that moral obligation come from?

Let's start with where it doesn't come from. No human possesses inherent authority—the moral right to exercise power—over another human. No person can walk up to another person, young or old, rich or poor, educated or uneducated, and simply issue a command that bears any moral obligation. Try walking up to a stranger on the street and commanding him to buy you a soda. See how that goes. Instead, every human, like Adam in the garden, possesses by creation what John Locke called an "executive authority," as in, were we living in the garden, we'd all be executives running our own countries. The command to fill, subdue, and rule over the earth belongs to everyone.

What creates a moral obligation between two equal creatures is nothing more or less than a word from the Creator. The Creator alone can create moral obligations, since, as Creator, he has both the moral right and the power to do so. Furthermore, he can create a moral obligation to submit either directly or indirectly. Directly, he can command us to do or not do something, as in "You shall not murder." Indirectly, he can put another person into a position of authority over us with certain prerogatives or rights to rule, which I've called an office. He has established offices like mother, father, husband, governor, church, and pastor or elder.

In other words, all human authority comes from God and only from God. Paul primarily has civil authorities in mind when he says, "there is no authority except from God, and those that exist have been instituted by God. Therefore whoever resists the authorities resists what God has appointed, and those who resist will incur judgment" (Rom. 13:1–2). Yet the point stands for every kind of authority established by God. Authority comes from God, and apart from God, no authority exists.

Typically, we read that text and consider the burden it places on those *under* authority, which is Paul's primary meaning. Yet almost as quickly a second application applies to those *in* authority: the authority figure's authority is not his or hers, but God's. We are merely stewards. As such, the general call to submission applies not just to those *under* authority but also to those *in* authority. We must rule only and precisely as God means for us to rule, in full and complete submission to him, lest we earn his judgment for ourselves. Husbands must submit no less than wives, parents no less than children, pastors no less than members, governments no less than citizens. To the person who might complain, "It's not fair that I have to submit," the answer is, "And the one over you doesn't?!" Bad authority exists whenever an authority figure insists on holding others accountable but refuses to be held accountable. This might be the husband who domineers his wife but refuses his church's accountability in his life, or the organization founder who fashions a board that cannot keep him or her in check. That sin of omission soon leads to sins of commission.

In short, to be human, a creature created in the image of someone else, means we are most ourselves when we submissively image the Image Maker, whether our particular job or station in life is to lead or to follow. Submission is dehumanizing, in other words, only if being fully human is dehumanizing.

Sometimes people say things like, "It's not the office that I respect and follow, but the man." I've heard church members say this about their pastors, for instance. I understand the point they are getting at: a pastor should demonstrate that he is truly qualified to that office through his character and competence. And there's something right about that comment, which I'll explain in chapter 11. Ironically, however, the offhanded remark treats authority as if it were inherent in people, not God. In fact, we should not submit to the person, but to the office, because submitting to the office is submitting to the one who established the office.

Conclusion

It is hard for sinners to recognize this if they want to be "like God" in the way the serpent tempted Eve (Gen. 3:5), but submission is actually a good thing. It serves our growth. It teaches us to rule. Not only that, it helps others to grow and rule.

Submission, like authority, goes to the very heart of what it means to be a human creature. You and I are created in God's image so that we might be conformed to the image of God's love and righteousness. By submitting our lives to the pattern of his love and righteousness, we declare the judgment, "God is most worthy!" By submitting to God and to those he has placed over us, we become most like the God-man.

5

Submission Is Never Absolute
and Always Has Limits

THIS CHAPTER BEGAN ITS LIFE as a series of paragraphs at the end of chapter 2. I was anxious to explain immediately all the ways in which a woman like Amy should *not* submit to an abusive husband and pastor like Rick. Yet as more and more paragraphs began to pile up, I myself had to submit to the demands of the topic: I needed a whole chapter on the limits of submission.

Should Amy have submitted to such a wicked husband? Should children submit to abusive parents? When should citizens rebel against an oppressive government? Should you work for a terrible boss or company? When does the wrong use of pastoral authority warrant leaving a church? On and on the questions go. I offered a definition of submission in the last chapter as something that leads to growth and even to authority, but for simplicity's sake I assumed the presence of good authority. Yet what if you are under a genuinely bad authority?

Gratefully, people still grow under bad authorities since God can use bad for good. You can still learn a lot by submitting to someone who doesn't have your best interest at heart.

Yet the narrow question I want to ask in this chapter is, what are the limits to our moral obligation to submit when someone possesses an ostensibly legitimate authority over us, like a parent over a child?

Certainly there are limits. Remember, no human authority is absolute. Authority is always relative to the assignment given by the Authority Giver.

When Paul says, "there is no authority except from God," and "whoever resists the authorities resists what God has appointed" (Rom. 13:1, 2), he doesn't mean that human authority is unlimited, and that every action of every authority is morally legitimate, and that every act of resistance is morally illegitimate. Rather, he's describing the government's job description and presenting several basic principles: human authority comes from God; we cannot randomly assert authority over one another; we should generally submit. But this does not mean that everything a human authority says or does, without exception, must be obeyed. All God-given authority has limits, and the fact that authority has limits means that our call to submit to authority has limits, too. The limits of authority and submission are correlates. Sometimes, therefore, we can legitimately say "no" to an authority figure, as other passages of Scripture teach.

As such, the call to submit to God-given authority figures is always *prima facie* (at first glance), never *ultima facie* (as a final consideration).[1] That's a concise Latin way of saying, our initial duty and instinct should be to submit to those whom God has placed over us. Yet that duty is never ultimate or final.

God is interested in being God and forbids us from thinking we're God. Therefore, he's an equal-party opposer of oppression. When the Egyptians oppressed his people, he heard his people's cry: "I have also seen the oppression with which the Egyptians oppress them" (Ex. 3:9). And he punished the Egyptians with a ten-plagued fury. Yet when his people turned to participate in oppression themselves, he turned his fury onto them. "For thus says the Lord of hosts: 'Cut down her trees; cast up a siege mound against Jerusalem. This is the city that must be punished; there is nothing but oppression within her'" (Jer. 6:6; also 9:6; 22:17).

Meanwhile, God lifts up the oppressed. We saw this in chapter 3. The messianic king who cares not just for the needy, but the children of the needy: "From oppression and violence he redeems their life, and precious is their blood in his sight" (Ps. 72:14 [cf. v. 4]; see also Ps. 10:18; 82:3; 140:12). Elsewhere, he pronounces, "Woe to those who decree iniquitous decrees, and the writers who keep writing oppression" (Isa. 10:1).

---

1   Nicholas Wolterstorff, *The Mighty and the Almighty: An Essay in Political Theology* (New York: Cambridge University Press, 2012), 61; cf. Abraham Kuyper, *Lectures on Calvinism* (Grand Rapids, MI: Eerdmans, 1931), 61.

If we want to be like God, therefore, we must have hearts disposed toward opposing oppressors, lifting up the oppressed, and protecting the vulnerable. That means Christians should be very interested in a conversation about the limits of authority and submission.

Here are three limits on our call to submit to God-given authority figures.

Limit 1: When an Authority Requires Sin

The easiest limit to discern: we don't need to submit when *an authority figure requires us to sin.*

God commended the Hebrew midwives for not obeying Pharaoh's command to kill the baby boys (Ex. 1:15–22). He rescued Shadrach, Meshach, and Abednego when they refused to worship Nebuchadnezzar's image (Daniel 3). And when the Sanhedrin commanded the apostles Peter and John to stop preaching Christ, they asked, "Which is right in God's eyes: to listen to you, or to him?" (Acts 4:19 NIV). The answer to their rhetorical question is, God.

That we should disobey when commanded to sin is a fairly noncontroversial point among Christians. It features prominently in conversations about civil disobedience against the government.

Limit 2: When an Authority Drives outside Its God-Assigned Lanes

A second reason might be a little more contentious. Yet I'd argue that we don't need to submit when *an authority figure requires us to do something God has not authorized that particular authority figure to require.* Call this driving outside the lanes, or stepping outside one's jurisdiction.

Churches should not wield the sword. Governments should not decide who gets baptized. Politicians generally should not tell pastors which doctrines to hold. Parents generally should not forbid children from seeking morally legitimate and necessary medical treatment. And schools generally should not undermine a parent's authority concerning what to teach their children. "Generally" is an important word in each of these sentences, because one can nearly always envision certain exceptions.

I don't have an easy proof-text to employ for biblically proving this second category of justifications for disobedience. But I think the suggestion shows up in a number of biblical texts. For instance, no punishment comes to Jonathan for eating honey when his foolish father Saul promised divine judgment upon anyone who did (1 Sam. 14:44–45). Or think of Esther going before the king to plead for her people, which was against the law (Est. 4:11). This enabled her to save her people. Maybe we could even consider Jesus telling the disciples they were free to eat heads of grain from the field even though the Pharisees declared it unlawful to do so on the Sabbath (Mark 2:23–28). In each case, someone broke a human law. The law wasn't commanding those under it to sin. It's not sin to eat a head of grain when walking through a field, for instance. Yet the Pharisees did not have God-given authority to forbid what they forbade, therefore the disciples were free to disobey them.

The story of Rehoboam might also exemplify limit 2 (1 Kings 12). From one angle, the people are properly subjects of their king and must submit to him. But Rehoboam clearly rejects his kingly responsibility to care for and unify the nation, and instead insists on the people being his slaves. Israel abandons him, and God never condemns Israel for doing so.[2]

Whether or not these biblical case studies fit perfectly, I admit the argument here is more theological than strictly exegetical. It's built on inferences. And the theological argument is that God gives no human beings unlimited authority to command whatever they want. Parents cannot demand whatever they want of their children. Nor can pastors, princes, or policemen, in their respective areas. God gives people only narrowly defined authority for specific purposes. Any commands given outside God's authorization is, strictly speaking, unauthorized. To say I can require you to do something when God hasn't authorized me to do so is to make my authority absolute, because now I'm "authorizing" myself.

This basic justification for disobedience appears to show up in the Southern Baptist Convention's statement of faith. Article XVII reads, "God alone is Lord of the conscience, and He has left it free from the doctrines and commandments of men which are contrary to His Word or not contained in it" (Baptist Faith and Message, 2000). That is, our consciences are free from a moral burden with commandments which are contrary to God's word (limitation 1, above). And they are free from commandments which are not contained in his word, presumably

---

2   Thanks to Samuel James for this example.

including those commandments which fall outside an authority's jurisdiction (limitation 2).

It's not always easy to discern whether something falls inside or outside an
authority's jurisdiction. Does the government have the right to require certain kinds of clothing of its citizens? If that citizen is a soldier, yes. But does
the Taliban have the right to require women to wear burkas? One Christian
friend of mine says yes. I say no. If I were a missionary in Afghanistan, and
my daughter asked me if she could shed the burka for a secret Christian
wedding ceremony, and I was confident she would not be caught, I would
say, "Of course." Whatever you might think of the burka example, I don't
think it's difficult to see that there is a line or an edge somewhere, where
everyone's ground of authority drops off into the ocean.

Limit 3: When Protecting Oneself from Wrongful Harm

Related to this second reason to disobey is a third one: *we're not required
to submit to an authority who is acting to wrongly harm us.*

Admittedly, the word "harm" needs clarifying. And why would I say
"wrongly harm" and not just "harm"? Because there's a sense in which
any act of discipline causes "harm" in some vague sense of the word.
When I ground my teenager, I "harm" her plans for the weekend. Yet
somewhere a line exists between a legitimate act of discipline and an
illegitimate one. It's possible for my discipline to "exasperate" or even
abuse my daughter (see Eph. 6:4 NIV), and that is sin. We don't need
to debate where exactly the line is between legitimate discipline and
illegitimate discipline for every authority figure. That would take vol-
umes of case law. The point is, we all know that a line exists. And what
I'm saying here is, a person is not morally bound to submit to an act
of discipline that crosses the line—that's sinfully excessive or unduly
severe. If a father swings his fist at the ornery child, the child should
duck, run, and find help, even if he wrongly spoke back against his
father. Two wrongs don't make a right.

Admittedly, a Christian might decide to submit to sinful harm—say, a
decision to endure persecution for the sake of witness. But they are also
free not to do so, if there's a way of escape. To put it another way, I think
human beings possess the right of self-defense even from someone placed
by God over them.

A biblical text I can imagine someone asking about, which might seem to undermine my point, is 1 Peter 2:18–19: "Servants, be subject to your masters with all respect, not only to the good and gentle but also to the unjust. For this is a gracious thing, when, mindful of God, one endures sorrows while suffering unjustly." Is Peter saying we should submit to harm? Not if we can get out of it. Instead, Peter is envisioning a situation in which slaves are "stuck"—Bible scholar Thomas Schreiner's word to me over the phone—and have no choice about whether to endure unjust treatment. Or as Schreiner put it in his commentary: "Believers could not opt out of obeying masters who were wicked and disreputable." "Ordinarily," says Schreiner, slaves who are stuck should "do what their masters dictate." Meaning, the master might sin against you regularly, but you should still work to do a good job for him. That's what Peter means by "Be subject." That said, Peter is not saying "masters wield absolute authority over slaves" or that "Christian slaves should participate in evil or follow a corrupt master in an evil course of action." Rather, Peter is counseling people in these kinds of "stuck" situations, which would have been quite common in the ancient world, and encouraging them to look to Christ's example of "entrusting himself to him who judges justly," even as the world around them judged them unjustly (v. 23).[3]

Even as Peter counsels people who are stuck, Paul tells slaves to get their freedom if they can (1 Cor. 7:21). If a person can avoid harm, he or she certainly should. People need not submit to the abuse and harm if they can remove themselves from it. Moses likewise commanded the Israelites to not return a slave to his master when he has escaped (Deut. 23:15–16). David fled from Saul again and again. Jesus asked an officer, "Why do you strike me?" (John 18:23). And Paul contested his public beating and asked for an apology (Acts 16:37, 39). In each one of these scenarios, someone—including Jesus—was either challenging or abandoning an otherwise "legitimate" authority because of physical violence.

As I mentioned above, there are times when Christians will choose to stay and endure harm or persecution for the sake of their gospel witness. Cyprian fled for safety during the Decian persecution in 250. Yet he decided to stay during the Valerian persecution in 256, and it cost him his

3   Thomas R. Schreiner, *1 and 2 Peter and Jude*, Christian Standard Commentary (Nashville: Holman, 2020), 151.

life. I believe both were potentially legitimate moral decisions, meaning he was free to do either. People have also willingly submitted themselves to harm to great effect for other causes, as with the civil rights protesters submitting to police clubs on the Edmund Pettus Bridge in Selma, Alabama, on "Bloody Sunday" in March 1965.

Yet all this is quite different from saying that people under various kinds of formally legitimate authorities *must* submit themselves to harm from those authorities. I don't believe the Bible teaches that.

There Is No "Final" Authority on Earth

To say there are limits to how far we should submit to God-given authorities over us is to say there is no "final" authority on earth. God is always and only our final authority.

To make this point in seminary classes I teach, I sometimes ask the students who has "final" authority over a child—the parents or the state. Typically, they quickly say, "Parents." Then I ask, "What if the parent is beating the child?" Then a brief pause will ensue, followed by some tilted heads, until someone says, "Well, then, I guess the state." That's right. God gave governments the responsibility to physically protect its citizens from other citizens, which means it has every right to intervene if a parent is beating a child.

Yet the lesson isn't over. I'll then ask, "What if the state said, 'You may not teach your children Christianity'?" Or: "You must affirm your child's chosen gender." The students quickly affirm that this would be a tyrannical state, and the parents would be justified in disobeying it.

The point is, all human authority is to some measure relative, as is our obligation to obey. God's authority alone is absolute, which means, he will judge all our obediences and disobediences on the last day. With some decisions we make, God will say to us, "You should have obeyed." With others he will say, "You should have disobeyed." And with still others, "You would have been free to disobey, but it was wise that you didn't." The point is, his final judgment is always the final standard.

How to Handle the Complex Dilemmas

Many real-life situations throw us into these kinds of complex dilemmas, which don't offer easy answers. When does a parent's discipline of a child cross the line into abuse? What do we do when two different legitimate authorities recommend opposite courses of action? Which sins should we expect and can overlook in our pastors, and which sins should cause us to leave the church? On the spectrum between "unkind tone" and "threatening my life," where exactly is the line between something we can overlook and not overlook?

Churches struggled with these complex dilemmas during the COVID-19 outbreak. When civil authorities barred churches from gathering in order to slow the disease's spread, some churches responded by saying, "Christ is Lord, not Caesar." After all, the Bible commands churches to gather. Other churches replied, "Yes, but Christ has given Caesar authority to protect our lives, which means that defying Caesar when lives are at stake is defying Christ." Who is right?

Most Christians would concede that civil authority has the right to stop a church gathering in the face of an imminent threat, such as an armed assailant entering the building. Most Christians would also affirm that at some point the government's right to head off physical threats stretches too far and becomes a usurpation of the church's jurisdiction. Just ask Christians in China or Iran who are permanently barred from gathering. We would all agree that they are right to rebel. Yet, as with the question of harm, there is quite a spectrum between closing down for one week and being forced to close permanently. Should we rebel after two weeks? Ten? When? What if the disease isn't COVID but the bubonic plague and one out of three members dies after every gathering? Would we grant the government more space to forbid our gatherings?

When faced by these complexities with the authorities over you, what should you do?

(1) *Keep your eyes fixed on the day of judgment.* That's the first and most important step, because God's judgment is the evaluator and decider of all things. Fearing him is the beginning of wisdom.

(2) *Study Scripture.* God will judge us on that last day according to the principles he's set down in Scripture. More specifically, work to understand from the Bible what jurisdiction God has assigned to each authority at play in your situation. Is the authority asking you to do something that reasonably falls within its jurisdiction to ask?

(3) *Mind your own conscience.* A matter might not be clear in Scripture, but God has still given each of us a conscience, that internal sense or judge

of what we believe to be right and wrong. When you're faced by competing claims on your moral allegiance or by a tough ethical question, ask yourself, what does your conscience say? To do something your conscience is forbidding makes it sin, even if it's not inherently sinful (Rom. 14:23).

(4) *Inform your conscience.* Your conscience could be wrong, after all. Protestants often rehearse Martin Luther's famous declaration that, "to go against conscience is neither safe nor right." Yet would we heap the same praise on the heretic Arius when he denied the deity of Christ, had he appealed to his conscience like Luther did? Of course not. We praise Luther not just because he appealed to his conscience but because he was right. In other words, our consciences can be warped or hardened or just wrong, which is why we must continually form and reform them according to God's word.

(5) *Seek the counsel of your pastors and fellow church members.* Beyond reforming your conscience through God's word, seek the counsel of those charged with teaching you God's word: your pastors or elders. Of course your pastors are not all-wise. We all need the whole church body, with its many different parts and different gifts (1 Cor. 12). Other godly and mature members of the church may offer helpful counsel as well.

(6) *Ask the Lord for wisdom.* Wisdom in the Bible is the God-given skill for understanding the fallen but God-designed world around us, discerning true from false, weighing the options, and making good choices. It is the tool he gives us for the gray areas and times of uncertainty.

The good news is, God delights to give his wisdom when we ask (James 1:5).

Addressing a Leader

One last thing you might do—number (7), by the count above—is to either address the person in authority directly, or work to see that authority removed. This can be scary, and it's certainly not always the right step, especially when it promises to cause more harm than good. But it might also be the most loving thing to do because it serves both the leader and everyone else in the leader's care.

If you do confront the person over you, do it respectfully. Treat that person as you would want to be treated. Remembering that the person over you is just a person and not God helps to take some of the fear out of it, and it allows you to speak with respect rather than panic. Wrongly fearing someone, ironically, can cause you not just to speak too softly; it can also cause you to speak too loudly, angrily, or forcefully, like a cornered dog. And that typically just hardens people's hearts.

What if you feel like your leaders won't humbly receive challenges? It may be that your counsel is wrong. Part of good leadership is sorting through good and bad counsel, and they may rightly discount yours.

Or, it may also be that your counsel is reasonable, but you've overestimated your relationship with the leader. Frankly, it's not reasonable to expect the leader of any organization to hear everyone equally, especially the larger the organization gets. Leaders are human, too, and need *some* allowance for deciding whom they do and do not listen to. My guess is that you don't listen to everyone in your life equally.

Yet, finally, of course, it may also be the case that a leader is unteachable, vindictive, or proud. Your years of experience and position might make you the ideal person to offer a loving challenge, but the person is unwilling to hear correction. Perhaps he or she is simply foolish or immature, which means confronting the person will incur a negative, potentially harmful reaction. Confrontation always involves risk, and wisdom must determine your course. Sometimes you take that risk. Sometimes you realize that a leader's pride is unassailable, that nothing but harm will come from a challenge, and that walking away is best—or doing what you can to see that leader removed. Think of a woman in an abusive marriage, for whom fleeing is the only option. If you are in a situation where the leader is unassailable, you might rethink your long-term prospects there (see 1 Cor. 7:21). Or you'll work to have him or her removed.

I cannot offer counsel for every situation. Yet here's a take-away for everyone: insofar as God allows, we should all aspire to join churches, work for organizations, and (for women) marry men with a healthy understanding of authority—people or organizations who use leadership to strengthen and raise us up. It is in these churches, organizations, ministries, and marriages that we will most grow and flourish. If we can, that's where we want to be.

Yet what do you do if you are genuinely stuck with a leader who is only out for himself? Ask God to (1) change the heart of the leader; (2) change your circumstances; or, if you're stuck in the situation, (3) ask the Lord to do what he so commonly does in our trials: make you look more and more like Jesus, who suffered, and was then exalted (Phil. 2:5–11; 1 Pet. 2:18–25).

Conclusion

In the final analysis, submission to the people whom God has placed over us is the ordinary pathway to life, growth, authority, and even likeness to the God-man, Jesus Christ. Yet our submission is never finally owed to other people. It's exclusively and uniquely owed to God. We owe it to others only when God says we do. This means our submission should never be absolute. It's always relative to God's assignments, and the particular demands of every assignment will need to be worked out on a case-by-case basis.

Remembering that our submission is finally and exclusively owed to God should defang what we might otherwise fear (see 1 Pet. 3:6). It should also keep us from worshiping or making too much of people. I praise God that, from a young age, my four daughters demonstrated a seemingly innate predilection to honor me (except when they didn't!). Yet one of my primary jobs as their dad is to teach them that God is the one who deserves all their honor and hope.

The book of Hebrews, similarly, tells Christians to imitate their leaders and submit to them (Heb. 13:7, 17). Yet in the same breath it reminds us that it is Jesus who is the same yesterday, today, and forever (v. 8). Our pastors might change, die, stumble, or move on. Jesus won't. Pastors deserve our submission only because Christ does, which means our submission to them is always contingent. Yet that submission to them, when appropriate, is an act of worshiping our Lord.

Chapter Appendix: Examples of Not Submitting

Here are two historical examples of people not submitting. What I'm interested in here is how slowly and judiciously both go about the decision not to submit. They set a good example for us.

First, Jeremiah Burroughs, a seventeenth-century Congregationalist pastor, explained the prayerfulness and reluctance of heart that should accompany the decision to leave a church to which you can no longer submit:

> Suppose there are some godly and conscientious men in a church, but there is something done in the church that they cannot believe to be the mind of Christ. After all examination, after prayer, after seeking to God, they cannot see it to be the mind of Christ, but they should sin if they should join them. They can testify to God, their own consciences

witnessing for them, that they would gladly join with their church in all the ways of God's worship, but in such and such ways they cannot join with the church without sin to their own consciences. They labour to inform themselves; they go to the elders; and they go to others in all humility to show their doubts in this thing. After hearing what others have said, they depart and, in conscience to God, examine between God and their souls what was said, and they pray over these things. They pray that God would reveal these things unto them if they be his mind. Now after all this is done, if they still cannot agree, what would you have these men do? Suppose there be a hundred such men; they cannot communicate, yet they are not presently to rend from the congregation, but to wait a while to see whether God will convince them. Now if after all using every means to find a common mind, they cannot be convinced, shall these men live without the ordinances of the Lord's Supper all the days of their lives? Hath Christ so tied a member of a congregation that he must never join with another congregation, even if remaining with his church causes him to believe he sins against Christ? Truly there had need be clear warrant for this if any one shall affirm it.[4]

Second, in March 1775, famous American patriot Patrick Henry, then a delegate to the Second Virginia Convention, offered his famous "Give Me Liberty or Give Me Death" speech. While that famous line valorizes liberty and rebellion, the speech itself takes pains to demonstrate how far he and others went to work within the system. Rebellion was a last resort:

Sir, we have done everything that could be done, to avert the storm which is now coming on. We have petitioned; we have remonstrated; we have supplicated; we have prostrated ourselves before the throne, and have implored its interposition to arrest the tyrannical hands of the ministry and Parliament. Our petitions have been slighted; our remonstrances have produced additional violence and insult; our supplications have been disregarded; and we have been spurned, with contempt, from the foot of

---

4   Jeremiah Burroughs, "The Difference between Independency and Presbytery," in *The Reformation of the Church: A Collection of Reformed and Puritan Documents on Church Issues*, ed. Iain H. Murray (Carlisle, PA: Banner of Truth, 1997 repr.), 287. I have attempted to simplify the language of this quotation in several places.

the throne. In vain, after these things, may we indulge the fond hope of peace and reconciliation. There is no longer any room for hope. If we wish to be free, if we mean to preserve inviolate those inestimable privileges for which we have been so long contending, if we mean not basely to abandon the noble struggle in which we have been so long engaged, and which we have pledged ourselves never to abandon until the glorious object of our contest shall be obtained, we must fight! I repeat it, sir, we must fight! An appeal to arms and to the God of Hosts is all that is left us!

PART III

HOW DOES GOOD
AUTHORITY WORK?
FIVE PRINCIPLES

6

It Is Not Unaccountable, but Submits to a Higher Authority

Nathanael answered him, "Rabbi, you are the Son of God! You are the King of Israel!" (John 1:49)

The Son can do nothing of his own accord, but only what he sees the Father doing. For whatever the Father does, that the Son does likewise. (John 5:19)

I do nothing on my own authority, but speak just as the Father taught me. (John 8:28)

JESUS IS KING. JESUS OBEYS. How do we hold those two truths together? And what does it teach us about any authority we've been personally given?

Passages like these three in John's Gospel offer us far more than "principles of good leadership." We should be careful about merely trying to draw moral principles from passages that focus on the identity of the incarnate Christ and his relationship with the heavenly Father. Still, these passages do offer us such principles. For instance: good authority is never unaccountable, but always submits to a higher authority.

Jesus, the God-man, came to be declared king. Yet throughout his ministry on earth, he submitted himself perfectly to his Father in heaven. He spoke only what his heavenly Father taught him to speak, and did only what his heavenly Father taught him to do. Or as the apostle Paul put it, "the head of Christ is God" (1 Cor. 11:3).

Does Jesus Christ's submission demean him? Only if righteousness and rule are demeaning.

As we've seen, authority and submission are two sides of one coin. To be *in* authority you must be *under* it, and to be *under* it is to be *in* it. Furthermore, we exercise authority in order to uphold something that is righteous or true, and when we submit we render the judgment that that something *is* righteous or true.

Jesus's submission to the heavenly Father was the declaration that God is righteous and true. For Jesus to rule, furthermore, he had to conform himself perfectly to the rule of the heavenly Father. He could rule like Adam was supposed to rule by submitting in a way Adam and Israel never submitted. By submitting, then, he ruled together with the heavenly Father in perfect righteousness.

Another Illustration: A Symphony Orchestra

Let me offer a less exalted illustration of how good authority always submits to a higher authority. My friend Susan offered me this one. Susan has played viola in a number of orchestras over the years. Generally speaking, a standard symphony orchestra has ten first violins, ten second violins, ten violas, eight cellos, and six double basses. Typically, the most skilled player plays the "first chair" of each section, also called the "principal," and everyone in the section follows that principal. All the viola players follow the principal viola player, all the cellos the principal cellist, and so on. The principal of each section, in turn, follows the first chair of the first violins, called the "concertmaster," who follows the orchestra conductor. The concertmaster tunes the entire orchestra before a concert, and then leads every string section when it comes to matters like timing, bowing, and so forth.

String players can adjust their bowing in a multitude of ways, each of which gives a piece of music a different interpretation. When do you bow up? When down? What style? How hard onto the strings? How lightly off? A piece written by Bach might call for one kind of bowing, Beethoven another, Debussy still another. But the point is, all the strings must bow together. And it's up to the concertmaster to make this judgment, based on his or her understanding of the conductor's direction. The principals of each section follow the concertmaster, and the players in every section follow their principals.

Everything in an orchestra, in fact, works according to such a hierarchy. People sitting in the even-numbered chairs (2, 4, and 6) turn the pages for people sitting in the odd chairs (1, 3, and 5), who rank slightly higher. If someone in a lower ranking chair has a question, she doesn't raise her hand and ask the conductor. She asks the person in the chair in front of her. If that person can't answer, the question is passed forward person by person until it reaches the principal of that section. From there, a question would go to the concertmaster, and if the concertmaster cannot answer it, only then does it go to the conductor.

If an orchestra tried to operate like a democracy, with all the members having their own say and choosing their own tuning, timing, and bowing, the music would sound terrible. Only by working within a strict hierarchy does an orchestra sound unified and glorious.

Susan recalled a rehearsal in which she played principal violist, and the man sitting in a chair behind her kept playing his notes early. She tried to signal with her body language when to come in, but he didn't pick up her cues. Finally, she turned around and reminded her entire section that they needed to watch her body language and come in when she came in. The speedy offender replied, "But you're coming in late."

Susan responded, "I'm coming in with the concertmaster."

The man again replied, "The concertmaster is coming in late."

Susan then explained, "You might be right, but we need to be together. If you want to be the principal, you can, and I'll follow you. But as long as I'm here, you need to follow me. You cannot keep asserting yourself and coming in early." Another violist quietly thanked her, and shortly later the conductor himself said something similar to the whole orchestra.

As the principal violist, Susan had authority over the violas, and she exercised that authority by calling this man to account. Yet she also knew that her authority meant submitting to the concertmaster, who in turn submitted to the conductor. Susan's authority was only as good as her submission. And this is how orchestras make beautiful music.

Merging the Two Illustrations

At the risk of getting a little messy, I wonder if we can merge the illustration of the divine Father and the incarnate Son together with the illustration of the orchestra. Suppose the orchestra of humanity were tasked with playing a symphony entitled "The Love and Righteousness of God." In the first attempt, each of us decided that, on our own, we would act the part of player, concertmaster, conductor, and even composer. You can guess the result. The music would be cacophonous and discordant.

But then suppose the composer sends his son to conduct this piece. The son knows precisely what his father means by love and righteousness, and so he submits his conducting to it entirely. He radiates with his father's love and righteousness and in turn conducts the orchestra according to that love and righteousness. The concertmaster, in turn, submits and leads. The principals of every section, too, submit and lead. And the orchestra, playing the notes as intended by the composer and as transmitted through conductor and concertmaster and principals, participates with the composer in the glory of the music. Every one of them, down to the tenth chair of the second violins, proves through submission that he or she can lead still others if called upon. He or she knows and can play the notes of love and righteousness penned by the composer.

To be sure, the illustration of a symphony orchestra playing has its limits for describing what God intends for humanity. God doesn't mean for all of us to be playing the same symphony. He intends, remarkably, for each of us to be composers on our own, some of us writing classical, some jazz, some bluegrass, some rock 'n' roll. He does not intend mass uniformity. Where the illustration applies, however, is in the call to live and apply God's own principles of love and righteousness. Here Jesus calls us to be perfect, even as our heavenly Father is perfect (Matt. 5:48). We're to submit as Jesus the second Adam submitted.

Unaccountable Authority

Now let's consider the flip side. Can you think of an unaccountable leader? Maybe you've known one or have been under one.

My friend Tony (not his real name) worked on the pastoral staff of a megachurch pastor who wasn't accountable to anyone—not to his fellow elders and not to his congregation. Through intimidation, mockery, and strength of personality, this pastor managed to make his elders his minions. He taught them to do his bidding—or be removed. He'd scream and curse at people privately. When a few of the elders tried to place limits on him and keep him accountable, they found themselves publicly denounced before the church.

Tony remarked, "As a staff member, you learned what got pats on the back and what didn't. The closer you were to the center of power, the more loyalty you were expected to have to him over everything."

"But loyalty can be a good thing," I responded. "What's the difference between good and bad loyalty?"

"With unhealthy loyalty," he replied, "you cannot be honest and push back on the person. The person doesn't welcome or invite questions or critique. Just the opposite: you walk around on eggshells, because you know you'll get yelled at, mocked, or fired. Plus, it's really hard to get a straight perspective from people who are closer to the center than you. They just give you the company lines." He summarized: "On the church staff there was a culture of fear, and in such an environment you're trained to be more loyal to the person than to the Lord. You ask, 'What will please this man,' instead of 'What will please God?'"

A leader who doesn't view himself as being inside an accountability structure effectively becomes a law unto himself. He teaches everyone under him to fear him, when it's only God whom we should fear.

Loyalty to a leader is indeed a good thing, but good loyalty is loyalty to his leadership *under* God and anyone else under whom God has placed him, like fellow elders or a congregation. Good loyalty says, "I'm committed to you and your success as a leader, and that means I *cannot* follow you into folly or unrighteousness, because it's bad for both you and us."

Increasingly, this pastor used this church for his own glory. On one occasion, Tony found himself sitting on a private jet with the lead pastor to rush back to the church after a conference. "We see tithes go way down if I'm not preaching in the pulpit," the pastor said. "So the elders allow this." While on the plane, he also offered Tony tickets for a professional hockey game back home, with seats in the skybox. "They're cutting prime rib!" the pastor said. Tony thought to himself, "What an alternative universe this is." He also felt like he was being bribed.

It's hard to say it loud enough: good authorities submit. If you cannot listen and follow, you should not lead. At all. Every person on earth, from the highest to the lowest, should assume a posture of submission to other authorities established by God. Even the president of the United States must submit informally to the counsel of his cabinet and formally to other branches of government, the voters, and the Constitution.

To act otherwise is to make yourself God, like so many Egyptian Pharaohs and Roman Caesars did explicitly, and that we all do in varying degrees. And those who make themselves God by discounting all accountability, if they go unchecked long enough, eventually destroy whatever they lead, whether a family, company, school, nation, army, or church. They also set themselves up for a terrible judgment.

Submitting in Discipline

Here's one more illustration that I think helpfully draws out this chapter's lesson: A pastor in another part of the country called me a few months ago. A mother in his church, in a fit of anger, had slammed her argumentative thirteen-year-old daughter into a brick fireplace. The girl ran out of the house and to another church member's house. She was physically fine, but emotionally traumatized. And the pastor wanted counsel on what to do.

We discussed a number of things, yet here's the one thing I said that's relevant for right now. This pastor needed to help the mother understand this: if she wanted her daughter to respect her authority again and to emotionally heal from the sin against her, the daughter would need to see her mother willingly submit to the authorities placed over *her*, even at cost to herself. Would she, the mother, submit to the pastors of the church as they responded to her violence against her daughter? And would she submit to Child Protective Services, if the pastors decided to contact them? I hardly mean to suggest that we can guarantee that the pastors and CPS would offer good authority themselves. Still, I hope you take my point: the people "under" us need to see us submitting to those "over" us if we expect them to trust and follow us. Our submission to those "over" us gives life to those "under" us.

The take-away lesson here is, authority figures need to submit even to their own discipline. If you won't do that, you're not genuinely submitting.

Shortly after this phone conversation, in a moment of my own anger, I sinfully raised my voice with one of my teenagers. I felt justified in the moment, but you know how that goes. The anger passes, and you know you need to apologize. Reflecting on the counsel I had given to this pastor, I also knew it would serve my daughter to do more than just apologize. First, it would serve her if I would confess my sinful anger to the Christian brothers with whom I meet regularly for accountability, men who are elders and who exercise a form of authority in my life. That would give them the opportunity to ask me hard questions about how bad it really was, or whether it was a pattern.

Second, it would serve my daughter to tell her that I had confessed it to those men. It might make her feel awkward in the moment, but in the long run I hoped it would give her the opportunity to see that I welcome authority, too, and that I submit even the ugly parts of myself to it.

Remember what I said in chapter 2: you know you're under a bad authority when you feel a dissonance between what you hear communicated from those on top and what you experience on a regular basis. This creates trouble for anyone in leadership, of course, because we all sin. We're inconsistent and don't do exactly what we communicate should be done. A crucial practice for those in leadership, then, is confession and transparency. When leaders confess and submit themselves to discipline, they begin to rebuild trust. I'm not saying a leader should confess every shortcoming or peccadillo. Discernment is required. Yet we probably need to confess more than our flesh will want to. Confession forces a posture of immanence and equality when our flesh yearns wrongly for transcendence and hierarchy.

What about You?

Now let's bring all this back to you. The first thing for you to do is to meditate on the Scripture passages at the beginning of this chapter and consider what they teach you about Jesus Christ. He who was in the very nature of God did not consider equality with God something to be grasped, but emptied himself and submitted himself, even to death on a cross, so that others might have life (see Phil. 2:5–7). Before we draw out the moral lessons of that act, it's worth meditating on the person and character of Christ for its own sake. This should draw your heart to worship. We can worship Jesus for many reasons, but one of them is his submission to God the Father. He submitted himself fully to God's righteousness and love and rule. In this way, he did what no other son or daughter of Adam and Eve did. He kept the law entirely and exhaustively. Praise to the Lord Jesus.

And there is a moral lesson for you, too. Where has God given you authority? List all the areas. Do you view those domains as places where you have absolute control, or do you recognize that, even if you're the highest authority in that particular organization, you should be living submissively to other authorities over and around you, whether they're formal or informal?

Would your spouse or friends characterize you as possessing a submissive posture that knows how to listen and reconsider, or as strident, always certain, and unteachable?

Part of being a good authority figure is knowing when to ignore counsel or correction and to proceed with your original plan. Yet if that is always your pattern, you might not be as good a leader as you think. You might be good at forcing things to happen in the short term, which will look like you're accomplishing something. But if you're not careful, the good people around you will all leave or wilt, which is something you'll discover—and regret—only over time.

Remember what I said in chapter 4: people must learn to submit before they can rule, and the best leaders are the best submitters. This is why you should always be reluctant to place someone in a position of authority who doesn't know how to submit. Pray, then, that as you grow in authority, you would also grow in the ability to listen, hear, and submit.

7

It Doesn't Steal Life,
but Creates It

*Moses: God blessed them. And God said to them, "Be fruitful
and multiply and fill the earth and subdue it, and have dominion
over the fish of the sea and over the birds of the heavens and
over every living thing that moves on the earth." (Gen. 1:28)*

Paul: If we endure, we will also reign with him. (2 Tim. 2:12)

*John: . . . by your blood you ransomed people for God from
every tribe and language and people and nation, and you
have made them a kingdom and priests to our God, and they
shall reign on the earth. (Rev. 5:9b–10; see also Rev. 22:5)*

GOD CREATED ADAM AND EVE to be a king and a queen. To rule. That's
what the first verse above says.

As it turned out, however, they didn't rule on God's behalf like they were
supposed to. But fast-forward to the end of the Bible and we discover that,
somewhere in between the bad beginning and the good end, God makes
sure his people turn into the right kind of kings and queens. That's what
the second and third passages above say.

The Greek word translated as "reign" in those latter two passages is the
verb form of the word for "king." A slightly more formal translation of
these verses would be, "we will also be kings with him" and "they shall be
kings on the earth."

These latter two verses are talking about Christians. Christians in the new
heavens and the new earth will be kings and queens together with Christ.

If you're a Christian, this is your destiny. Amazing, no?

The principle to observe here is that good authority doesn't steal life, it creates it. It's a principle we learn by looking at God himself and how he uses his authority with us. He created us to be kings, yet even when we failed God spent thousands of years preparing our coronation ceremony anyway. And then he wrote a book about it.

Passages like 2 Samuel 23:3–4 and Psalm 72, which we examined at length in chapters 1 and 3, articulate this chapter's principle even more explicitly. Good authority, said David, is like the sun and the rain that cause grass to grow. It lifts up the needy and crushes the oppressor, said Solomon. The apostle Paul, too, referred to "the authority that the Lord has given me for building up and not for tearing down" (2 Cor. 13:10). And the psalmist says that God "is the one who gives power and strength to his people" (Ps. 68:35).

Yet it's hard to think of a better illustration of this principle at work than by peering into the structure of human creation (he created us kings!) and the goal of redemption (he will re-crown us as kings!). The life-giving goodness of good authority is hardwired into our existence, our ontology, which in turn exposes how intrinsically and bounteously generous God is.

Not only that, but the very first command in the Bible is a command to use our kingly authority to create life: "Be fruitful and multiply," says the Lord. People today might bemoan parenting. Yet the Bible presents bearing and raising children as a paradigmatic picture of being a king like God.

In all this, God's generosity is difficult to fathom. God would have done a far better job of ruling over creation by himself in the first place. He never would have made mistakes. He never would have misstepped. He never would have exploited or abused people. We often wonder why bad things happen in this world. The answer, in part, is that God decided not to do the whole job of ruling the world himself. Instead, he delegated. He shared. And he continually trains us in the work amid all our failures.

Staring ahead into eternity shows the same thing: a God who will share his rule with his people, world without end, forever and ever.

God is a giver, and his authority is for giving. He says: I want to share my glory. So I will create a people, love them, and share my rule with them so that they can enjoy the pleasures of my glory. So create. Build. Plant and grow. Manufacture. Compose. Design. Govern.

We give God nothing he doesn't already have. Instead he gives to us. His authority is life-giving.

Stealing Life

If you take only one thing away from this book, I hope it's either the main point of the last chapter or the main point of this one. I'm not sure which is more important. Last chapter: whatever authority you have is under the authority of God and others. And this chapter: whatever authority God has given you, he's given it to you so that you might in turn give life to others. Do you have children? Your goal is to train them and build them up. Do you have authority at work? Your assignment is to strengthen those under and around you. Do you have authority in a church? The only reason you have it is to give life to others.

Let me start with a reverse illustration: former Venezuelan president Hugo Chavez. After two failed coup attempts, Chavez won the Venezuelan presidency in a fair democratic election in 1998. Yet between 1998 and his death of cancer in 2013, he managed to accrue dictator-like power to himself. He convinced voters to increase the presidential term to six years, expand presidential powers, reduce the National Assembly (congress) from two houses to one, and eventually remove presidential term limits altogether. His party increased the number of judges on the supreme court and filled the slots with his allies. He tried to do away with all political parties but his own, and when it looked like his party would lose its two-thirds majority in congress, they granted him the ability to rule by decree for eighteen months and they redrew congressional districts allowing them to retain a majority. He seized complete control of the state-owned oil company, and he nationalized or expropriated companies in the electricity, telecom, aluminum, cement, gold, iron, steel, farming, transportation, food production, paper, and media industries. He expelled the Human Rights Watch organization when it reported that he was manipulating the country's courts and intimidating the media and labor unions. He alternatively favored and opposed churches, according to whether they demonstrated allegiance to his "socialist revolution," including expelling one American missions organization from the country.

My friend Alejandro worked as a supervisor in a Mexican-owned cement factory in Venezuela up until 2008, when Chavez expropriated and nationalized the cement industry. "Overnight, I became a state worker," Alejandro told me. The Mexican company in turn sued the government, which responded by sending the wife of the minister of infrastructure to meet with the supervisors of different factories. She brought a retinue of soldiers with her. In an unscheduled, off-the-record meeting, she told Alejandro and all the other supervisors, in so many words, "You have to say that this machinery is worth nothing. You also have to say that you've been sabotaging cement production over the last few years and preventing the government from building houses for poor people." That would give the government a rationale in court for expropriating the factories. Some supervisors signed her statement. Most did not, including my friend Alejandro, and he left his job.

Like his friend Fidel Castro, Chavez championed the cause of a socialist revolution and promised radical democratization. Yet despite the rhetoric, he never distributed power. He hoarded it. Every decision and every year left him with more. He didn't use his authority to create life, but to steal it, as in Alejandro's factory, which today produces almost no cement at all. Throughout Chavez's presidency, inflation averaged 23 percent per year. The murder rate quadrupled. He undermined the oil industry by firing 18,000 highly skilled workers who couldn't be replaced, while also making the economy more dependent on oil than ever before. When the price of crude oil dropped from $100 per barrel to $30 in 2014, the Venezuelan economy collapsed. By 2018 inflation hit 130,060 percent. Food shortages became a regular occurrence with Chavez's imposition of price controls. Within a year of his death, food shortage rates reached a record high of 28 percent, at which time the government stopped recording them.

Giving Life

Let's compare Chavez with another world leader, incidentally one who died in 2013 like Chavez: Nelson Mandela.

Mandela assumed the South African presidency in 1994, but he gave it up after one five-year term, even though he could have run for a second. During those five years, Mandela believed his primary task was to promote racial reconciliation and take the nation from apartheid to a nonracial democratic system. Other post-colonial African nations had started race wars and scared away wealth-holding and educated whites, destroying their economies. Mandela therefore sought to build bridges with the wealthy white minority, even as he led an administration that was largely black and that undid apartheid structures. For instance, he asked the white former president F. W. de Klerk to be deputy president. He rallied both blacks and whites to support the South African rugby team in the rugby World Cup, even though the rugby team represented white authority for many blacks. He also helped initiate the Truth and Reconciliation Commission, which offered the possibility of amnesty in return for truthful accounts of crimes committed under apartheid.

Many, including his estranged wife, accused Mandela of catering too much to whites. Yet most people credit his emphasis on forgiveness as holding the country together at that time and preventing bloodshed. A pastor friend of mine in Johannesburg, South Africa, recalls the assassination of one black political leader by a white right-wing extremist, together with a riot in a township near him that left many dead. "People stockpiled groceries, left the roads empty, and sheltered in their homes," he told me. "My wife and four young daughters stayed at home while I carried on some essential ministry. I remember driving on the highway one day and thinking, 'Why is no one else on the road?' Hearing of threats against the power stations, he bought a gas camping stove in case the lights went out. It's as if the nation walked right up to the brink of chaos and looked over the edge. Yet Mandela addressed the nation several times and insisted on pursuing justice through the system. Eventually, temperatures cooled and South Africa transitioned successfully to a truly democratic government. My pastor friend concluded, "He used his authority to promote forgiveness. Having lived here through those harrowing days, I am grateful."

South Africa continues to face slow economic growth and high poverty among blacks, yet the constitutional structures are in place for facing such challenges. Some say it's one of the best constitutions in the world. Unlike Chavez, Mandela used what authority he had to strengthen and empower others. He worked to help people and the nation grow.

Something else is worth noticing when comparing these two figures: Both sought to raise up an underclass—Chavez the poor; Mandela blacks. Both sought to dismantle structures that perpetuated unjust hierarchies and abused that underclass. Yet Chavez's left-leaning socialist ideology, called Chavism, focused on power. His goal was "revolution," upending the hierarchy, and destroying the oppressors.

Mandela, on the other hand, faced a cultural landscape arguably more ravaged by long-standing abuses of power, yet his focus wasn't on power but on human dignity. His work and speeches were imbued less with the rhetoric of Marxism and more with the themes of Christianity.

Those different emphases are worth reflecting on. When our focus is on power, we will treat power as a scarce commodity and a zero-sum proposition. More power for you means less for me, and more for one group means less for another. We're more likely to demonize our opponents. We don't treat them as a mix of good and bad like all God-imagers, but as wholly bad—like a demon. They wear the black hats; we wear the white hats. Cheers erupt when a member of our posse un-holsters a revolver and shoots a member of the other side off his horse. His destruction feels justified.

When our primary focus is human dignity, on the other hand, we still want to address unjust power differentials, but now we'll want to do so in a way that doesn't undermine our opponents' dignity. Forsaking their dignity means undermining our own. Therefore, we move more surgically, tread more carefully. We recall that both they and we are a mixture of good and bad, and so we constrain ourselves to the rules of due process, always suspicious of our own propensity to injustice. We do what we can to honor the full humanity of our opponents, even as we oppose their injustices.

As such, the life-giving impulse of good authority is finally magnani-mous. It doesn't soak in bitterness or dream of vendettas. Instead, it loves the enemy. It is willing to give the enemy a second chance and restore the enemy's power if it will be used for good, not evil. The life-giving impulse is a redemptive impulse.

Several weeks after the tragic events of September 11, 2001, I invited an agnostic Jewish friend to church. She was someone with whom I had had many open and friendly conversations about the gospel. Yet on that day, she replied, "No, Jonathan, I'm not really in the mood to talk about religion right now. How can you be a friend of religion after what happened at the Twin Towers?!"

I replied, "That's fine. I understand. Just keep in mind, the terrorists on those planes took the lives of others so that they might gain their own, while Jesus sacrificed his own so that others might gain theirs." How differently Jesus used his authority.

Good Authority Authorizes and Passes Out Power

It's not enough, however, to simply say that good authority gives life. The more precise point is that good authority aspires to authorize others to exercise authority, even if it takes years. It works to pass out power.

"Good authority always generates liberty," said my friend Stu, by which he meant the liberty to lead. "A good authority," he continued, "creates room for new leaders to execute on the authority they've been given, not prescriptively tell them how to do it." Before he retired, Stu served as managing director for Accenture, then the largest consulting firm in the world by revenue. During his tenure as managing director, the region led by Stu grew from 2,300 employees to more than 6,000. Apparently, he knows a little something about raising up leaders.

Stu knows, for instance, that it's not enough to place people in positions of authority. You have to supply them with the resources and tools and training they need to succeed. He observed,

> To put someone in a position of authority without the support and equipping needed to perform the duties is—in a business-world sense—sinful. You're setting the person up to fail, and you're going to create downstream issues. Whoever grants the authority has an accountability to make sure that it's being appropriately granted. You can lose before you start by granting a person authority that they're not equipped to handle.

It's laziness and selfishness that puts people in positions of authority and then leaves them to fend for themselves. Good leaders teach and resource other leaders.

The lessons here apply to every domain. More than a decade ago I wrote an article called "How Pastor Mark Passes Out Power." What prompted the piece was watching a gifted pastor, Mark Dever, do the opposite of Chavez—not hoard power but pass it out. I listed twenty ways, over a decade, that I had watched him do this:

- establish a plurality of staff and non-staff elders, each of whom possessed one vote on the board, just like he does;
- limit the number of times a year he's the main preacher in the church's main service, giving other men the opportunity to preach;
- create more venues or opportunities for men to preach or teach, like a vigorous Sunday school program, Sunday night sermons, or small groups;
- give young teachers the chance to make mistakes;
- let others steal his ideas;
- be willing to lose elder meeting votes;
- be slow to speak, and speak sparingly in elder meetings;
- ask other men to be the chairman in elder meetings and church member meetings;
- ask other elders to lead the congregation through tough cases in member meetings;
- use an "invitations committee" for his outside speaking requests, letting it turn down invitations if members of the committee see fit;
- be devoted to only one or two things in the church (like preaching) and give freedom elsewhere;
- avoid micromanaging;
- create a weekly service review, where he will give feedback to others involved in preaching or leading a service;
- invite input into his sermons and invite criticism;
- pray for other churches and denominations;
- be quick to forgive;
- rejoice in the victory of others;
- work to build the church on the gospel, not his large personality.

When the leader "on top" is characterized by generously giving authority to his lay elders and others in the church, he shapes the church's culture in wonderful ways. It helps to keep the gospel uppermost, focusing the church members' eyes on gospel purposes rather than on the leader.

Passing out power promotes "real" relationships. In an environment where authority is jealously guarded, relationships are characterized by politics and strategy. Guards remain up, vulnerabilities are not exposed, and transparency diminishes. But when people feel empowered, they are more likely to be transparent and honest.

It keeps a church from being tribalistic. A man who continually gives away authority teaches those around him that he is most interested in the success of the gospel, regardless of who's leading (see Phil. 1:12ff.).

It encourages church members to share resources. When I see the leader is not out for himself, I too become inclined to give to others.

It destroys natural social hierarchies. Members interact as equals. Why? Because the gospel is kept in the center. We're all sinners saved by grace.

It cultivates trust. When I see the leader is not out for himself, it's easier to trust his motives, even when he is asking me to make a sacrifice.

It cultivates teachability and the willingness to receive criticism. Again, if I trust the man, I become more willing to listen to his criticisms of me. I trust they are rooted in love rather than one-upmanship.

It promotes a willingness to forgive. When the leader is quick to forgive the faults of others, he will be more willing to entrust others with authority. That in turn will help others to do the same.

It encourages the church to be training-minded. A church that sees a pastor continually work to train and empower others will have a hard time not catching the vision and sharing it. They will see all the fruit.

It helps a church to be outward focused.

The take-away for all readers: analogous lessons apply to every group and organization.

Bottom-Up Leadership

The life-creating nature of good authority means it's not just top down, but also bottom up. What do I mean?

When people talk about leadership, we typically refer to the person in authority as the person on "top." There's talk of the "highest" authority, the "top" of the organization, the "pinnacle" of power, the "top dog," the "top of the food chain," moving "up" the ladder, being "over" others, and so forth. Meanwhile, everyone else is said to be "under" authority. There is the "low man on the totem pole," the person on the "bottom rung."

Scripture, too, speaks in this way. "God reigns over the nations" (Ps. 47:8). His throne is "high and lifted up" (Isa. 6:1; 52:13). And New Testament elders possess "oversight" (1 Pet. 5:2).

Using these spatial metaphors of up/down and high/low to describe leadership makes sense. To lead, you need a view of the whole landscape. You need to be propped up in an umpire's chair where you can see whether the server has stepped on the line, or if the ball has bounced out of bounds.

But here's the thing: being a good leader also means learning how to lead from the bottom up. It means being a *foundation*, a *buttress*, a *platform* for the activity of others. You employ the authority you've been given to enable others to run, to work, to minister. You become the platform on which they live, the stage on which they dance.

After all, God is not only over us; he sets himself under us as well. He is our rock, giving us a sure place to stand (Ps. 18:31).

Likewise, leadership is not about running after all your dreams and ambitions; it's often about getting on your hands and knees and making your life a stage on which those you love can pursue their ambitions, hopes, and ministries. It's about building up as much as it's about moving up. It's about equipping and enabling and empowering.

Listen to what the psalmist says immediately after calling God his rock:

> And who is a rock, except our God?—
> the God who equipped me with strength
>   and made my way blameless.
> He made my feet like the feet of a deer
>   and set me secure on the heights.
> He trains my hands for war,
>   so that my arms can bend a bow of bronze.
> You have given me the shield of your salvation,
>   and your right hand supported me,
>   and your gentleness made me great. (Ps. 18:31–35)

God equips. God trains. God secures. God supports. God makes great. How good is God! He gives us a place to stand, like a deer in the heights. He gives us strong arms that can bend a bow of bronze.

When my daughters were little, sometimes they would melt down after a long day, unable to do basic things like get ready for bed. On those occasions, they didn't need an anxious, high-pitched response from me. They needed my calmness. My steadiness. My gentle sureness about where a pajama arm goes, how a toothbrush works, where dolly can be found.

When they got older, they needed that same calm steadiness, but now they needed it for a larger domain. They didn't want help into pajamas, but into the driver's seat of a car. When they were learning, I was tempted to reprimand every slightest infraction. "You're too close to the line . . . that turn was too fast . . . slow down . . . why didn't you begin breaking sooner . . . are you checking your mirrors . . ." Yet too much correction could be crushing and actually make them worse drivers. They needed some space to self-correct and grow.

I remember one outing with a daughter when she had her learner's permit. It wasn't a good day for her. I had to say her name three or four times as she barreled toward a red light, oblivious to it. Later, at home, I remarked to my wife, "That girl *will* crash our car. Prepare yourself now." We briefly wondered if we were being irresponsible to let her get her license. Yet almost as quickly, we also realized, this is how helping someone to grow works. You can't cage them up. You have to take risks. You have to be willing to sacrifice yourself (and maybe your car!) for their growth.

Yet this is where leading top down and bottom up come together. To be a platform, a stage, a foundation in the lives of those whom the Lord has given you, you have to set yourself *over* them.

You have to set the boundaries. Drive like this, not like that, you say. Walk here, not there. Trust these people, not those. This is how you swing the racquet, conjugate the verb, flee the sin, show the care, invest the money, design the circuit board, play the scale, warn the brother, exegete the text, prepare the sermon. You explain which paths lead to life, and which lead to death.

Yet you also provide the space, the platform, the runway, the gas money, the encouragement, the office title, the chance to lead, so that the one you're leading can grow into their own leadership.

You want their success. You pour yourself out. From first to last, you love.

I'm not a man without ungodly ego and ambition. Yet it occurred to me when my daughters were young, if there was anyone on this planet for whom I would naturally and gladly get down on my knees so that they could stand on my back and rule as queens, it was my four daughters. Somehow, the competitiveness that can rise up in my chest toward others didn't with them. This restraint doesn't come from any maturity or magnanimity in me. I think God has hardwired the impulse into creation itself, so that every parent can sometimes feel this way. He gives us all a glimmer of what unselfish, life-giving authority feels like. And what he himself is like.

The trick is to take that impulse, grow it, and transpose it into other domains, where the natural love of a father for a daughter or son isn't assisting us.

What about You?

So, again, what authority has God given you? In the home? At work? In the church? Somewhere else? Think through each domain. Now ask yourself, how are you seeking to create life in others with that authority?

Can you imagine viewing yourself as a platform for the growth and success of those you lead? Are you willing to sacrifice some of your own ambition to see them succeed?

That doesn't mean you discount the mission of your workplace or organization. My friend Paul Miller, a political science professor at Georgetown University, teaches his students, "A leader who loves the mission but not the troops is a tyrant, while a leader who loves the troops but not the mission is ineffective." That's wise. Still, with that caveat, is your goal to win the war in part *by* promoting others? If not, why do you think you have authority?

Some diagnostic questions that might help you ascertain whether you're using your authority to promote others include

- Do the people under you seem reluctant to propose their ideas? And never mind the socially brazen ones who always tell everyone what they think—what about the socially normal ones?
- Do they seem nervous about making any tiny decision without your head-nod even after you've delegated authority to them? Do they turn to you again and again with questions when you've given them an assignment, or do they show a healthy and balanced measure of independence in completing the task that you've asked them to do?
- Would those under you say you make them feel confident and strong?
- If you were unexpectedly removed from your present office through an unforeseen accident, would the family/group/organization im-

mediately fall apart? Or would the lessons you've taught, the equipping you've done, and the strength you've installed in others enable them to soldier on and complete what you began?

- When you're not in the room, do you assume folk under you spend an inordinate amount of time talking about you, or about the work of the family/group/organization?
- Do you verbally encourage people on a regular basis? And do you "gossip" positively about people to others when they're not around?
- Do you give people a chance to do *your* job and then offer careful feedback?
- Do you celebrate with them when they're promoted outside of your jurisdiction, i.e., to work for another company at a higher position?

The work of raising up your lessers to be your equals is inherently risky. It means taking a chance on the young young whippersnapper, giving him the microphone, or letting her drive, even though you know you could do a better job and make less mistakes. You would get it right the first time. He will bumble through and leave a mess.

Yes, you must also maintain a discerning eye for immaturity and folly. You must draw boundaries and keep it contained so that it doesn't harm the body. Still, how can you give the benefit of the doubt? Maybe do what Paul says: consider others better than yourself—as a general posture of heart. Then, use your leadership position to do what Jesus said: don't look to be served but to serve. This doesn't mean you don't lead. Jesus led. It means not clinching your leadership with a tight fist. Instead, you're always preparing to give it away, to let it go, even to the point of your death. You know God will raise you up in due time, and so in the meantime you give yourself entirely to raising others up—to be your equals, or even your betters.

8

It Is Not Unteachable,
but Seeks Wisdom

Fools despise wisdom and instruction. (Prov. 1:7)

*The way of a fool is right in his own eyes, but a
wise man listens to advice. (Prov. 12:15)*

*A fool despises his father's instruction, but whoever
heeds reproof is prudent. (Prov. 15:5)*

Pharoah in the time of Joseph: *"Let Pharaoh proceed to appoint overseers
over the land and take one-fifth of the produce of the land of Egypt during
the seven plentiful years. . . ." This proposal pleased Pharaoh and all his
servants. . . . Then Pharaoh said to Joseph, "Since God has shown you all
this, there is none so discerning and wise as you are. You shall be over my
house, and all my people shall order themselves as you command. Only
as regards the throne will I be greater than you." (Gen. 41:34, 37, 39–40)*

Pharoah in the time of Moses: *The magicians tried by their secret arts to produce
gnats, but they could not. So there were gnats on man and beast. Then the
magicians said to Pharaoh, "This is the finger of God." But Pharaoh's heart was
hardened, and he would not listen to them, as the* Lord *had said. (Ex. 8:18–19)*

*And Jesus increased in wisdom and in stature and in favor
with God and man. (Luke 2:52; see also Isa. 50:4)*

THERE ARE MANY LESSONS FOR LEADERSHIP we might learn by comparing Pharaoh in the time of Joseph with Pharaoh in the time of Moses.
A crucial lesson is that, a leader who seeks wisdom gives life to his people;
a leader who doesn't, destroys both himself and them.

Joseph's Pharaoh didn't just listen, he listened to a lowly prisoner and a foreigner. He recognized the wisdom of God in Joseph's counsel. He submitted to that counsel. And both Egypt and the surrounding nations were saved from the ensuing famine. Not only that, but God's people and the line of Christ would be preserved. This Pharaoh was wise.

Four centuries later, Moses's Pharaoh listened neither to Moses nor to his own magicians nor to the Lord. His early boast, "Who is the LORD, that I should obey his voice," revealed the essence of the man (Ex. 5:2). He was wise in his own eyes. He thought he knew better. He was proud. He gives us the dictionary definition of a fool, and few things are more destructive than a fool in a position of highest authority. Eventually, they will ravage everything in their path, just as Pharaoh's land and people would be ravaged by plague after plague. With each plague, Moses gave Pharaoh an opportunity to listen. Each time, he refused. Soon the land would lie decimated. His son and every other firstborn son in his kingdom would be dead. And he and his army would be swallowed by the Red Sea.

Bad authority despises instruction. Good authority seeks it. It's teachable and therefore wise. Even the young, incarnate Jesus sought wisdom and grew in it (Luke 2:52).

Launching Astronauts

Someone who illustrates this lesson well is my friend and one-time fellow church member Patrick, or "Pat." Pat served as the chief of the astronaut office at NASA for several years. While the head of NASA is a political appointee who may or may not have a background in engineering, math, or human space flight, the chief astronaut must have these credentials. He runs the astronaut program and can serve as an interface between the political world and human space flight. His job is to oversee the astronaut office's resources and operations. He makes flight assignments and ensures that astronauts are trained and prepared.

Pat, a United States Military Academy (West Point) engineering graduate, was an army test pilot and has flown more than 50 types of aircraft. As an astronaut, he took three trips into space, twice on the Space Shuttle *Discovery* and once on the *Atlantis*, each time to help build the International Space Station. He has spent over 39 days in space and has taken 4 space walks, the longest being 7 hours, and totaling more than 25 hours.

The strangest thing about a space walk, he said, is the feeling one has of continually falling toward the earth. Moving at about 17,500 miles per hour in orbit around the earth, you are in fact in a perpetual state of falling.

Without a doubt, Pat is an expert when it comes to space flight. If any pilot or astronaut has the right to think he "knows better," it's Pat. Still, his leadership was characterized by listening:

> I made it a point to try to understand where everyone was coming from. I wanted them to be heard and feel heard. I was always open to changing my decision. I remember saying to one astronaut, "As long as I'm the chief, I'll probably never fly you. But come and convince me otherwise." I wanted to offer more than an open-door policy; I tried to recognize that I could be wrong. Maybe my opinion on a matter was based on some anecdote I had heard, and I wanted to give people a chance to correct any misperceptions I had.

What benefits did you see as a result?

> I believe everyone felt heard and appreciated. Everyone felt known—from administrators to secretaries to everyone—because I would ask about them and their families. Sometimes people would call me from home in tears. They knew I would care about whatever they wanted to talk about. Not that I would always give people what they wanted. Yet even then I worked to help people understand why I wouldn't. One saying I had was, I might not be able to make you happy, but you'll know why you're not happy. I'll sit here and talk as long as it takes. Transparency was key when I made decisions.

As Pat explained all this, I was struck by how much his posture combined both transcendence and immanence. Here is a man who isn't afraid to make the tough decisions that incur anger, like pulling astronauts off of flights. Yet his more fundamental posture was one of immanence: he treated people as he would want to be treated, which is to say, as equals. He honored them as God-imagers by working hard to hear them and to take their perspectives into account in his decisions.

In the same vein, Pat described how carefully NASA conducted its Flight Readiness Reviews (FRRs). The 1986 Challenger and the 2003 Columbia

Shuttle disasters humbled the agency. "Before the Challenger launch, engineers determined that the solid rocket boosters on the shuttle weren't designed for the frigid temperatures being experienced on launch day, and told leadership as much," Pat observed. "A crew died because we didn't listen as carefully as we should have." Leadership therefore devoted countless hours to learning from their mistakes, which included a more robust approach to FRRs:

> The FRRs could take days. I didn't lead the FRR, but I was co-chair for some of them. Every leader of every board which I observed or participated in listened *ad nauseum* to everyone before making a decision to launch a rocket with a human being on it. There were times when I would have said, "I believe we've heard enough." Yet the chair would just keep listening. The agency wanted to do the right thing. One time the crew said, "We need new parachutes." So the NASA administrator insisted on new parachutes. He made sure it happened. I've seen lots of good decisions made by people listening. The whole concept of the FRR means listening hard. We learned this lesson the hard way with Challenger and Columbia. But I've also seen the listening process grow.

When the goal of your leadership is to promote yourself, you will be less interested in listening and seeking out wisdom. After all, you already know what you want and what you think. Why ask questions!

If, however, your goal is the good of the agency, the office, the school, the church, the home, or the brigade and all the members of it, you'll feel burdened to ask questions. To seek wisdom. You will intuitively recognize that this thing you're leading is bigger than you. It has lots of complicated parts and personalities. You won't presume to be a master of it all; you'll instead be a servant of its success and work hard to learn as much as possible.

Long-Term Thinking and Managing Risk

Pat exemplified such a servant-hearted, wisdom-seeking posture, and he tried to help others do the same. For instance, colleagues were surprised when Pat became chief but didn't assign himself to flights. "When an astronaut is the chief, they have the ability to assign themselves to the best flights. I wouldn't do that," he remarked. Why not? "My goal was always for the good of the office." He wanted to build a deep bench of competent astronauts who could successfully complete a mission. To that end he would usually pick an inexperienced astronaut and pair him with an experienced one. "Experience is key to leadership out in space," he told me. "Yet how does the experienced guy get to be the experienced guy if no one gives him a chance in the first place?"

What clarified in my thinking while listening to Pat was that, a central part of exercising leadership and authority is managing risk—as well as the difference between short-term and long-term thinking. It's risky to make decisions in the face of an upcoming rocket launch, a year-end production quota, or a war-time battle. In such moments, self-centered leaders often seek to mitigate risk by trying to control every lever they can get their hands on. It's a short-termed way of thinking, but it often works in the moment. The rocket launches. The quota is met. The battle is won. "Success!" everyone says.

The trouble is, the organization as a whole is ever so slightly weaker, because it's slightly more dependent on the skill and knowledge of the one person. Number-crunchers won't be able to detect this shift in the short term, but people in the organization will have been trained to lean back in their chairs ever so slightly, taught that "success" depends on the leader, not on them.

Others-oriented leaders manage risk by doing things that don't always make sense in the short term. In the short term, it doesn't make sense to spend hours talking to everyone in your agency—from astronauts to secretaries. More generally, it doesn't make sense to rely on people less skilled or knowledgeable than you are. You will do a better job than they. I'm reminded of this every time an older pastor steps out of the pulpit in order to let a younger, inexperienced man preach. The young man fumbles his way through the sermon, and the congregation is asked to exercise a measure of patience. Yet what's better for the church, the organization, or the space agency in the long run, as well as for every member of it? What builds a deeper bench, more committed workers, or a stronger machine that can survive and thrive even when the leader steps aside?

These four factors tend to operate together: a primary interest in the good of an organization and all its members; the conviction that you're not the source of all wisdom and competency, leading you to seek wisdom wherever you can find it; a willingness to take short-term risks by putting less experienced individuals into the pilot or copilot's seat; and a long-term perspective. No doubt, doing all this well takes good judgment and balance. Pat didn't fill rocket ships only with inexperienced pilots. He positioned the older to disciple the younger.

After all, that's how he learned. "Before my first space walk, I remember talking to an experienced space walker," Pat stated. "I said to him, 'Tell me what I don't know. What didn't they teach me in the training, in the classroom, in the Neutral Buoyancy Lab? What do I not know?'" That seems like a pretty wise question when you're about to step outside of a space station.

The Risk of Age and Experience

Pat is no longer the younger man who asked the older astronaut what he needed to know. He had just turned sixty when he became the chief astronaut. That's part of why I'm grateful for his emphasis on listening and seeking wisdom. In some ways, age has a way of humbling people by teaching them they don't know as much as they thought they knew. In other ways, however, it can become harder to maintain a posture of listening as you age, because it's so easy to become proud.

When you're thirty and new to a career, it's comparatively easy to ask older colleagues for counsel. This is socially normal, and there's little threat to your ego. When you're sixty, however, you're supposed to be the expert. Not only that, you may feel like the expert, at least in your own little domain. You've learned a few things over the years. You know what works in your field and what doesn't. You know how people will and won't respond. With every passing year the gap between you and the young folk keeps widening, because twenty-one is always twenty-one, even as your own clock ticks upward and the doctor appointments become more frequent. The young keep getting younger, as they say.

Not only that, your stature may have grown, especially if you're good at what you do. It's easier for you to get your way. People trust you, and rightly so. Like the valleys and ridges of topography carved out by wind and water over decades, so the natural accumulations of clout and capital will accrue to you, and more so with every passing year. More and more, your words will carry the day because you are you.

Such accrual of clout is not all bad. Let the proven leader lead. My point is, the higher your mountain of clout rises, whether through age or talent or both, it becomes easier for a sense of privilege or entitlement to set in, and harder to maintain a posture of listening and learning. Plus, you're a little tired. It's easy to get your way with the wave of the hand. You reason, "Why not stay home from the battles this summer?" as old King David did. Or think of the last few years of the very successful King Uzziah's reign: "And his fame spread far, for he was marvelously helped, till he was strong. But when he was strong, he grew proud, to his destruction" (2 Chron. 26:15–16).

There's a lesson here from these old men's downfalls: the higher that mountain of clout rises, the more you must strive for humility. If you pumped two gallons of fuel into your fight for humility at age forty, pump four gallons in at age sixty. After all, you will have double the authority, and if your growth in humility doesn't keep up with your growth in authority, Satan will find it much easier to trip you off the mountain into the yawning canyon below, like he did with Uzziah.

Here's my point as an epigram: the more talented the man, the more humility he needs. The longer he serves, the more dangerous his pride can be.

What about You?

Other battles in life might grow easier, and other realities of age may let you slow down. But not the fight for humility. If you would presume to continue leading, your fight must not slacken but increase. Don't be like David or Uzziah. Both were godly and talented men. But both grew complacent with age, to the hurt of their nation.

One way to fight for humility is to ask lots of questions, including from those "beneath" you. Work to be teachable. Are you? One way to avoid teachability is to accuse the giver of counsel with an error in how they give the counsel, like throwing a case out of court on a technicality. Maybe their motive was wrong or their tone was off. Yet the only one who loses when this happens will be you. You'll miss any good that might have come from their counsel, even if it was given for wrong reasons. Imagine Pat dismissing the instruction of the older astronaut before his first space walk because the older man gave him an unkind look. Talk about foolish!

I am teachable in theory. That is, I'm conscious of my need to be teachable. Yet too often I'm not. A younger man recently said to me, "I know you've written on this topic, but I really think we should at least give this group of writers a hearing because they might be seeing something we aren't." He was correcting me, and my flesh didn't like it. Yet do I stand to gain anything by discounting his counsel? I can only grow by receiving it.

Yet the battle for humility and a posture that listens is rooted in an even deeper question: whose glory are we seeking?

9

It Is neither Permissive nor Authoritarian, but Administers Discipline

For a parent: Whoever spares the rod hates his son, but he who loves him is diligent to discipline him. (Prov. 13:24)

For a church: Let him who has done this be removed from among you. (1 Cor. 5:2)

For a government: But if you do wrong, be afraid, for he does not bear the sword in vain. For he is the servant of God, an avenger who carries out God's wrath on the wrongdoer. (Rom. 13:4)

Regarding the Lord: For the Lord disciplines the one he loves, and chastises every son whom he receives. It is for discipline that you have to endure. God is treating you as sons. For what son is there whom his father does not discipline? . . . For the moment all discipline seems painful rather than pleasant, but later it yields the peaceful fruit of righteousness to those who have been trained by it. (Heb. 12:6–7, 11)

WITHOUT THE POWER OF DISCIPLINE, authority is toothless, even substance-less. Take away someone's power of discipline and you effectively take away their authority.

Authority, remember, is the moral license to make decisions or give commands. Those decisions or commands mean little if the authority can't enforce the decision or command. The threat of discipline gives authority its power, its teeth.

Parents who don't discipline their children, for instance, evacuate their own authority of power. If a mother says to her three-year-old, "Don't touch that vase," but then, as a typical pattern, does nothing when the child touches it, the child will begin to view such commands as the suggestions of a peer. The remarkable gift given by God for growing the child toward maturity—parental authority—will have been squandered.

It is not without reason, therefore, that Proverbs observes, "Whoever spares the rod hates his son, but he who loves him is diligent to discipline him."

More than once, the Bible connects love and discipline in this fashion. "The Lord disciplines the one he loves," says Hebrews 12:6. That's a tough truth to swallow in the moment of discipline. Discipline always seems "painful rather than pleasant." Who wants it! Yet apparently discipline is loving. It's how we grow. Imagine a math teacher who teaches the lesson but never corrects the student's errors. Or a doctor who prescribes good vitamins but won't cut out the cancer. Such is discipline. When practiced rightly, it is loving. It corrects against the bad and harmful, and it points toward the good, healthy, and holy.

The author of Hebrews further explains, discipline produces "the peaceful fruit of righteousness." Like plucking an apple off the tree to enjoy its sweet flavor, so discipline in a person's life produces the fruit of peace and righteousness. And peace and righteousness taste even better than apples.

Discipline's volume can be turned down to a 1 or up to a 10. At one end of the dial, the teacher leans over a student's shoulder and gently observes, "Oops, you forgot to carry the 3." At the other end, a judge declares, "For the act of murder I sentence you to death." Yet in every case, discipline serves to affirm or reinforce the good and the holy. With her admonishment, the teacher reinforces the good of math. By his punishment, the judge affirms the holy image of God in the victim (Gen. 9:6).

Two exceptions exist to the intrinsic connection between authority and discipline: the authority of a husband and a pastor. Both possess authority, but God has given neither the power of discipline. He reserves that for himself. Without the power of discipline, their authority must be exercised differently. It is purely a "spiritual" authority. We'll consider this further in chapters 11, 12, and 17.

What Do We Most Fear?

Discipline is a difficult topic because it's easy to err toward too little or too much. Good discipline strikes the balance between permissiveness and authoritarianism, between moral laxity and abuse. Yet the right balance changes from context to context. It's different for a three-year-old and a thirteen-year-old. Yet in every case, finding the balance requires love and wisdom, two goods that are in short supply for all of us.

Wisdom begins, says the Bible, with the fear of God. So consider what happens when fear of man motivates our discipline. We will err toward whatever we most fear. Do we most fear moral laxity? We'll probably err toward authoritarianism. Do we most fear abuse? We'll probably err toward permissiveness.

The Problem of Permissiveness

Abuse and authoritarianism are perennial problems. We must forever guard against them because abuse—or selfishly using our authority in a way that harms others—comes so naturally to human beings. Yet I assume I don't have to convince most readers of this book that abuse and authoritarianism are bad. Plus, I have addressed these matters in chapters 2 and 5 and in several other places.

The more publicly acceptable error in the West today just might be permissiveness, by which I mean a lack of discipline. It might be harder for some of us to see. My goal in this chapter, therefore, is to meditate on this harm—and it is a harm. If you think back to this book's opening illustration about the middle school in Portland that could not control its students, the problem was permissiveness. And so it was with the power couple in Washington, DC, who could not control their toddler.

Back in the 1990s, I spent one year teaching second grade in a public school in an economically depressed neighborhood of Washington, DC. One of the most difficult aspects of my job was figuring out how to implement classroom discipline without any real tools. Sending notes home to parents, mostly overworked single moms, made no difference. Sending a child to the principal's office didn't either. She would keep a student for half an hour and then send him (it was always a "him") back, none the worse for wear. In fact, I suspected one or two of my students welcomed the break from the classroom. I technically had "authority," but that authority felt useless.

Part of the problem with discipline in public school classrooms is a couple of Supreme Court decisions that, while they may have accomplished some good, also undermined a teacher's ability to discipline.[1] Another part of the problem is the American education system's preference for therapeutic language over and against moral language. One program instructs teachers "to reduce impulsive and aggressive behavior in children, teach social and emotional skills, and build self-esteem." It encourages the use of role-playing games, breathing exercises, and anger management techniques to help students "identify feelings" and "solve problems." Poor behavior is said to be rooted in a lack of skills, not in bad moral decisions.[2]

When discipline leaves the classroom, everyone loses. A troublemaking student doesn't learn to correct his or her ways and grow. In fact, he gets worse. The other students suffer as well. They don't learn their math or history. They do learn how to misbehave, and the whole classroom environment deteriorates.

To be clear, I'm not encouraging teachers to cultivate a harsh culture of discipline and punishment, like we see in movie scenes where Catholic school nuns slap hands with rulers. Good discipline occurs in an environment of encouragement and affirmation.

Contrast my classroom from almost three decades ago with my wife's previous second-grade and now first-grade classrooms. She has had several unruly students, to be sure. Yet she also has a principal and parents who back up her efforts to maintain discipline in the classroom. They give her authority teeth. Simultaneously, she works hard to show those particular students love and favor, so that they feel confident that she is *for* them. By the school year's end, you should see the hugs and construction-paper thank-you cards she receives—from the tough ones!

The problem of permissiveness besets not only classrooms but workplaces as well. Rebecca, who leads a task force for a federal law enforce-

---

1   *Tinker v. Des Moines School District* (1969) asserted students' rights of free speech in the classroom, even if it disrupted classroom order. *Goss v. Lopez* (1975) ruled against a principal who witnessed a fight and expelled the students, for failing to give the students a fair hearing complete with notice and witnesses. See Kay S. Hymowitz, "Who Killed School Discipline?" (Spring 2000), https://www.city-journal.org/html/who-killed-school-discipline-11749.html.
2   Hymowitz, "Who Killed School Discipline?"

ment agency, dealt with this problem recently. A seventeen-year veteran was transferred to her team from another department. Rebecca soon discovered that the woman was both insubordinate and made racist comments. Therefore, she began the paperwork to fire her, only to discover that the same problems had occurred several times when this woman was working in other departments. Her previous supervisors had taken the easy path by passing the problem to someone else. As a result, the woman had been shuffled from department to department, spreading her poison to more people every time. Rebecca admits she sympathizes with the instinct to take the easier path: "My life would be a lot less stressful if I didn't hold people to account. Firing someone takes a lot of paperwork and gumption, and people won't like you. No one wants to be held accountable or hold others accountable." Yet Christians must "fear the Lord," she went on. "You have to shake off fear of man and not sweep things under the rug."

Transferring this woman to department after department hurt not only each department; I'd say it hurt the woman herself. Every time supervisors failed to fire her for cause, or even failed to have a tough, confrontational conversation with her, they allowed her sin to get a little worse, the patterns to run a little deeper, her conscience to get a little harder. They denied her the opportunity to repent and grow.

Sadly, I've seen this often. A boss or parent, a pastor or principal doesn't want to have a hard conversation. Who likes confrontation! So they find a way to avoid it, leaving the troublemaker unaddressed. As a result, the troublemaker troubles more and more people. The whole group suffers, and the troublemaker is denied the possibility of redemption. He remains in his rut.

I know of one Bible study that decided to stop meeting rather than confront the one member who dominated the group every week. The leader's failure to discipline one man kept a dozen people from studying God's word and sharing their lives together.

Discipline is a crucial part of discipleship. Indeed, notice how "discipline" and "disciple" are etymological cousins. We disciple, in part, through discipline, like a math teacher correcting errors or a coach running a team through drills. Those corrections and those drills teach and strengthen. To deprive people of discipline weakens them.

A Nation Divided

A story in the life of that Sunday-school-hero king, King David, illustrates the destructive potential of permissiveness. David heard that his oldest son, Amnon, had raped his half-sister Tamar. The Bible then says of David, "he was very angry" (2 Sam. 13:21).

That's it. He got angry and then . . . nothing.

The Greek translation of the Old Testament, the Septuagint, adds a sentence that attempts to fill in what the original Hebrew left unstated: "But he would not punish his son Amnon, because he loved him, since he was his firstborn."

Talk about a terrible miscarriage of justice!

If we let Proverbs 13:24 be our guide, however, we would say that David refrained from disciplining Amnon not because he loved him but because he hated him! And David's abandonment of Tamar was hateful in another way. The kindest thing we can say about David is that he was a muddied spring: "Like a muddied spring or a polluted fountain is a righteous man who gives way before the wicked" (Prov. 25:26).

And the dominos continued to fall. David's son Absalom steps into the vacuum of justice left by David. He shelters Tamar in his own home and then kills his brother Amnon. Again, David takes no decisive action. Emboldened, Absalom begins to offer justice to the people of Israel by addressing their individual concerns. He does what the king should have been doing. This wins many hearts to Absalom. Emboldened still again, he leads a coup d'état against his father, which leads to a civil war and eventually to Absalom's own death.

Now step back and watch the whole sequence: David doesn't discipline his son or protect his daughter, leading to a murder of vengeance, then the usurpation of his own power, then a revolution, then a civil war, and then the death of a second son. A household and a nation are torn apart.

Love and justice require discipline. And when discipline doesn't come, injustice and destruction fill the vacancy.

Showing Kindness through Predictable Outcomes

Consistent discipline is also kind, because it is kind to offer predictable outcomes. Or rather, consistently enforcing the standard is kind, assuming it's a reasonable standard.

In the previous chapter, I introduced you to my friend Pat, who served as the chief of the astronaut office at NASA. Among his duties was selecting who flew on space missions and who did not. During his early years as an astronaut, the astronaut office did not consistently define or enforce rules and ethical standards. The astronaut corps sensed they could ignore various office rules or training protocol and still be selected for space flights, which are always coveted opportunities. This hurt office morale. "Astronauts might spend years training, following the rules, and hoping to fly in space, but then watch someone who didn't follow the rules or successfully complete all of their training get selected for a spaceflight, while they didn't," Pat observed. "I told myself, if I was the chief, I would do it differently."

In the Lord's providence, he became chief. He enforced the rules. And morale improved. "People began to understand, 'Oh, following the rules does matter. It makes sense to do my best work.'" Discipline was hard. He didn't like it. "I was miserable because I was making the hard decision of pulling people off spaceflights or sending them home for not meeting training standards or breaking various rules. But in the end, morale improved. People were happier in the workplace. We had to have standards. Or else what kind of organization would we be?"

When you establish a standard and then consistently enforce it, you affirm people's agency. Consistent enforcement makes the structures of reward and discipline predictable. It allows people to make plans and then follow through on those plans with a predictable set of outcomes. When enforcement is unpredictable, on the other hand, you undermine people's agency. You teach them, "You can make your plans and act accordingly, but the result might or might not accord with your actions."

I remember learning this lesson with trying to get my daughters into the car on time for school. My wife and I had set a departure time: 7 a.m. Yet we didn't consistently enforce it. Sure enough, they began to make it to the car at 7:02, then 7:05, then 7:07, and so forth. I remember getting angry one morning at a daughter, and saying something like, "I've told you '7' over and over! Why are you always late? Are you thinking only about yourself?"

In fact, I had spent weeks, maybe months, letting them get into the car later and later. I had failed to demonstrate that my words and my authority had integrity. I had failed to give them a predictable set of incentive and disincentive structures by which they could operate. And then, when my

failures produced the predictable fruit—daughters getting to the car late—
I became angry at them. And that wasn't fair. Yes, they were responsible
for their actions. Yet my failures made it easier for them to fail. In all this,
I was unkind. The kinder action would have been to enforce my instructions earlier and consistently.

Consistently enforced discipline is kind. That's not to say you should
never make exceptions, or offer grace from time to time, or forbear with
weakness. The question to ask yourself is, are you setting general and consistent patterns of discipline?

An Environment of Encouragement and Affirmation

A moment ago I said that good discipline occurs in an environment of
encouragement and affirmation, which brings us to the last thing worth
meditating on a minute longer. Discipline works best in the right kind of
environment, and the right kind of environment includes at least three
things. First, it includes a leader who demonstrates a pattern of willingness
to hear corrections, including from people "beneath" him or her in the hierarchy. I'll more easily trust your corrections of me if you're a leader who
demonstrates a general pattern of teachability yourself. If, however, you're
impervious to correction, you're teaching me to keep my guard up, too.
You're teaching me that you are more interested in organizational politics
and being on top than you are in real growth. You're teaching me how to
play the game where we're all competing for power rather than pursuing
real discipleship and growth.

Second, a good environment for discipline includes a greater emphasis
on affirmation and encouragement than it does on correction. This might
not always be true, as with a drill sergeant's job at army boot camp. He
probably doesn't need to hand out a lot of silver-star stickers. Yet it's true
in most organizational environments. I will more easily trust your corrections if I know you love me, because you've found ways to affirm the gifts
God has given me and to encourage me for the things I've done well. Then
I know you have my best interest at heart and that you're not just using my
skill and labor for your own gain. One friend of mine, with a chuckle, likes
to say he hugs hard so he can hit hard.

Third, putting these first two points together, a good environment is one
of general transparency, honesty, and love. I can think of work environments,

even Christian ones, where people have not been taught to be lovingly honest. Therefore, they complain about one another in the shadows and they put on fake smiles when they're in the light. Little by little, bitterness and broken trust spreads quietly through the organization like black mold in the walls.

On the flip side, I think of a pastor friend of mine who holds a "service review" for his staff and everyone who participated in Sunday's service. The surface-level goal of that review is to help improve Sunday services. But the deeper and more important goal, he says, is to train people to *give* and *receive* godly *encouragement* and *criticism*. All four of those things are difficult and require maturity and skill:

- It's difficult to *give encouragement* and not just flattery.
- It's difficult to *receive encouragement* without succumbing to pride.
- It's difficult to *give criticism* in a way that doesn't foolishly discourage or anger a person.
- It's difficult to *receive criticism* without becoming proudly discouraged or angry yourself.

Yet, little by little, his staff has learned how to have these conversations lovingly and gently, in part because he leads the way in maturely receiving criticism from his staff. As a result, bitterness and resentment don't fester in the shadows. Instead, staff members know how to work through disagreements and hurts when they occur. They also know how to joke and laugh together. And a general culture of trust and affirmation pervades their interactions. Not only that: this maturity and skill spreads to the church, its elder meetings, its small groups, and among friends.

In short, discipline is crucial. Yet lots of preliminary environmental work needs to be done before we can discipline well. The right culture needs to be in place, a culture marked by humility on the top, affirmation and love, and general transparency.

What about You?

There are times to show mercy when discipline is due. Yet for you to neglect discipline altogether is to say yes to evil and folly. It's selfish, and it shows a kind of hatred for the person requiring discipline, as well as everyone impacted by the undisciplined individual.

Typically, when we fail to discipline, we're prioritizing short-term ease over long-term health. Maybe we're trying to be compassionate, but we aren't. Maybe we don't want to cause unnecessary hurt, but we are. Really, we're trying to protect ourselves from trouble, from backlash, from possible fallout. And we're undermining our own authority.

Yet discipline is loving, at least in principle. There's no doubt it can be done harshly or abusively. But that's no reason to abandon it altogether. That's throwing the baby out with the bathwater. God loves perfectly, and his love is shown in part through discipline.

So think once again of any place where you possess authority. How are you doing at discipline—at trimming the rose bushes, pulling the weeds, and killing the slugs?

Are you willing to say no to your kids and offer consequences when they disobey? Are you willing to take away opportunities from people under you at work when they don't follow the guidelines? Are you willing to confront people in their sin, if you're a pastor?

If the Lord disciplines the ones he loves, let's not presume to be wiser and more loving than God.

10

It Is Not Self-Protective,
but Bears the Costs

*Then Judah said to his brothers, "What profit is it if
we kill our brother and conceal his blood? Come, let
us sell him to the Ishmaelites." (Gen. 37:26–27)*

*About three months later Judah was told, "Tamar your
daughter-in-law has been immoral. Moreover, she is pregnant
by immorality." And Judah said, "Bring her out, and let her be
burned." As she was being brought out, she sent word to her
father-in-law, "By the man to whom these belong, I am pregnant."
And she said, "Please identify whose these are, the signet and
the cord and the staff." Then Judah identified [these three items
which he had given to her as a pledge after sleeping with her]
and said, "She is more righteous than I." (Gen. 38:24–26)*

*And Judah said to Israel his father, "Send the boy with me, and we
will arise and go, that we may live and not die, both we and you and
also our little ones. I will be a pledge of his safety. From my hand
you shall require him. If I do not bring him back to you and set
him before you, then let me bear the blame forever." (Gen. 43:8–9)*

*Judah, your brothers shall praise you; your hand shall be on
the neck of your enemies; your father's sons shall bow down
before you. . . . The scepter shall not depart from Judah, nor the
ruler's staff from between his feet, until tribute comes to him;
and to him shall be the obedience of the peoples. (Gen. 49:8, 10)*

WITH ALL ITS TWISTS AND TURNS, everyone enjoys the story of Joseph in Genesis.

Joseph's brothers sell him into slavery. Yet there he prospers and blesses his master.

He says no to a woman's sexual advances and gets jail time. Yet then he is miraculously able to interpret the king's dreams and emerges as second-in-command over Egypt.

He hides his identity from his brothers, and his vengeance seems imminent. Yet then he embraces and blesses them.

Along the way, he saves the land of Egypt and surrounding nations from famine.

It's a remarkable tale, and we're quick to hold Joseph up as a moral example of trusting God. Yet truth be told, Joseph is a little hard to emulate. His story is a little too unique, a little too miraculous, and he's a little too perfect. No doubt, the real-life Joseph sinned, but here Joseph's purpose is to help readers envision an ideal Christlike figure. He descends into the pit yet is resurrected. He resists temptation and then saves his people.

Meanwhile, slinking off to the side in the shadows is another character: Judah. When we're introduced to Judah in Genesis 37 and 38, he's the opposite of Joseph. He doesn't try to save God's people but sells his brother into slavery (see verses above). He doesn't resist temptation but sleeps with his daughter-in-law and then tries to kill her (see verses above).

Judah is the anti-Joseph, and he's more like us. He's an opportunist, and he quickly succumbs to temptation. But maybe that's why his story should offer us hope. We barely notice him at the beginning of the story, since Joseph holds center stage. But keep your eye on him as the story continues. He'll emerge from the shadows to become his own kind of hero.

Something radical changes in Judah's life. He concludes the episode with his daughter-in-law by declaring, "She's more righteous than I" (see verses above). It's as if Judah is converted here, because his every appearance in the story thereafter is positive.

The clearest piece of evidence of Judah's conversion comes several chapters later. Judah offers himself as a sacrificial substitute for his younger brother Benjamin, first to his father (see verses above) and then, when it really counts, to Joseph (Gen. 44:32–33). And right here in this moment, the once-terrible-sinner Judah, this anti-Joseph, begins to point to Christ, who himself was a substitute for his people.

The book of Genesis then concludes by placing Judah more clearly in the spotlight, but now he has become the Joseph figure. His father blesses him and tells him that his brothers will bow down to him (see verses above), even as the brothers had once bowed down to Joseph (see Gen. 37:5–10). His father promises that all rule and authority will belong to him, even as it had belonged to Joseph. Judah is now Joseph, and his line is the one that will lead to Christ.[1]

Bearing the Cost

The goal of this chapter is to meditate on this connection between good authority and bearing the costs of someone else's mistakes or absorbing the consequences of someone else's sins, like Judah does. To be sure, it would have been easier or cleaner to pick Jesus to make this point. Judah's example is messier. He might be standing in for the sins of his brothers, but he's also in the predicament because of his own sin. He is hardly the sinless sacrifice, like Jesus.

Yet that's why Judah is worth meditating on. He's not sinless, just like you and I are not. Picture him for a moment, selling his brother into slavery or trying to kill his daughter-in-law after impregnating her. This man is a first-order scoundrel!

Yet God changed him so that he could point to Christ. God says, "I'm so big and mighty, I can change anyone and teach them to be like my Son. Look at Judah. And my Son's blood is so infinitely precious that it can cover every sin you might commit. Look at Judah."

For that reason, scoundrels like you and I can also learn to rule like Jesus rules, if we repent of our sins, put our trust in Christ, and follow after him. And a vital part of ruling like Jesus rules, then, is being willing to bear the costs of others' mistakes, stepping in to absorb the consequences of their sin, or simply carrying their burdens even when there is no moral dimension. "Have this mind among yourselves," Paul says, while looking at Jesus's sacrifice (Phil. 2:5). Or again, look at Judah offering himself in Benjamin's

---

1   This comparison of Joseph and Judah is drawn from personal conversations with Sam Emadi. See also Emadi's *From Prisoner to Prince: The Joseph Story in Biblical Theology* (Downers Grove, IL: IVP Academic, 2022), 57–64.

place. Or Moses bearing the reproach of his people. Or David stepping before the enemies of God's people and facing Goliath himself.

To be sure, Jesus's work of paying for sin "once for all" was unique and entirely efficacious in the courts of heaven (Heb. 7:27; 9:12, 26; 10:10). When we bear the costs of someone else's mistakes, absorb the consequences of their sin, or carry their difficulties more generally, we're not paying a debt in the heavenly throne room. No eraser gets applied to those ledgers.

Instead, we are, first, offering a picture of what Christ has done, even if it's nothing more than a crayon drawing (see Col. 1:24). And we are, second, learning to love and rule like Christ loves and rules.

In other words, the Bible takes the unique and unrepeatable work of Christ on the cross and draws various moral lessons out of it (see 1 Pet. 2:21). It even connects Christ's work of substitution and how we should sacrifices ourselves for one another—"have this mind among yourselves." And so Judah, fresh into leadership training without realizing it, stood in for Benjamin.

Similarly, a member verbally dresses down the pastor, but the pastor offers a word of affirmation, forswears resentment in his heart, and speaks of the matter no more. He doesn't sulk or complain to his friends, knowing that Christ has been merciful with him.

A teenager's misbehavior costs the parent a work opportunity, but the parent responds like the pastor, thinking on how Christ paid so much more.

A wife neglects or sinfully scolds her husband, but the husband forsakes recrimination and lives with her in an understanding way (1 Pet. 3:7), knowing that Christ forsook recrimination with him.

An employee loses an important file. The manager considers whether this is a pattern that requires addressing, but otherwise doesn't let frustration waylay his overall purpose in that employee's life: to help him or her succeed. So he absorbs the cost, even as Christ absorbed a cost for him.

The police officer receives a sharp elbow to the face when someone resists arrest, but he doesn't lash out in rage. He remains self-controlled and uses the minimum force necessary for subduing and handcuffing the offender, knowing that Christ could have destroyed *him* immediately but instead delayed judgment.

It's true that the opportunity goes both ways in these scenarios. To a varying degree, the member has the opportunity to do the same for the pastor, the teenager for the parent, the wife for the husband, the employee for the boss, even the offender for the police officer. After all, everyone created in God's image should rule like Christ rules. Still, God grants certain individuals a formal office of authority precisely so that they will demonstrate, illustrate, and embody what his rule looks like. Sometimes his rule involves discipline, like we saw in the previous chapter. Yet sometimes it involves bearing the cost.

Indeed, these two chapters are next to each other because both need the other. The solution for responding to people's mistakes is not always discipline. Sometimes it's being patient, forbearing, showing compassion, and bearing the cost. A good authority figure knows how to do both, because both are essential to exercising authority rightly.

Discipline is essential to exercising authority rightly for purposes of correction and training. Yet why is bearing the cost essential to good authority?

To be in authority is to possess more of something—more power or strength, more leverage or clout, more resources or capital. And why do you have more? Not for its own sake. Not for your glory and gain. You have it to spend it. You have more power and moral resources so that you can spend and use them for the good of those who have less. That's the job. Which means, a big part of the job is bearing the costs incurred by those you're over. Indeed, Jesus, who had more of everything, spent it all for our sakes. "The Son of Man came not to be served but to serve, and to give his life as a ransom for many" (Mark 10:45; cf. Phil. 2:6–8).

To be in the position of authority is to know the buck stops with you. So said the famous sign on President Harry Truman's desk: "The buck stops here." The sign was Truman's way of saying he would not absolve himself of responsibility for any mistakes made by his administration. He would accept the blame, even if the mistake occurred in some lower-level administrator's office and he knew nothing about it when it happened.

It's like you're the father of the bride and you're holding the checkbook. The final wedding bill goes to you. You're responsible. You're expected to have the resources, and you're expected to spend them on your daughter's big day. People feel a little sorry for you, but not *that* sorry. That's the job.

So it is with every position of authority you have. You're holding the checkbook. You can complain and push the costs off to others. But then you're failing to see why you have the job: to bear the costs for others.

If you've ever seen the photographs of presidents when they entered the office and then compared them to photographs of when they leave office—with the far grayer or whiter hair, the deeper lines on the face, the haggard and gaunt smile—you've seen what "bearing the buck" does to the physical body.

How the Buck Stopped with Tex

Whether such buck-bearing was common in Truman's day, Peggy Noonan argues in the *Wall Street Journal* that it's unusual in our own day. She remarks that, when the 2008–2009 financial crisis occurred, no mortgage lenders, federal regulators, or congressmen stood up to say, "Our fault!" Instead, everyone blamed everyone else.[2]

Yet Noonan offers this observation to provide a backdrop for her real story: an account of someone who did accept blame, and a two-star general, no less, whose pilot's call sign is Tex.

The story began in the late morning of December 8, 2008. While it was flying off the coast of San Diego, the two engines of a Marine pilot's F/A-18 Hornet went out, one after the other. While the plane was still on one engine, air traffic control directed the pilot to Miramar Base instead of North Island, which led to his crashing into a San Diego neighborhood. The pilot ejected just before crashing and survived. But his craft struck two homes, killing a thirty-six-year-old woman, her fifteen-month- and two-month-old daughters, and her mother-in-law. Her husband was at work.

Directing a wounded jet over a heavily populated area instead of over the ocean toward North Island was in fact the third mistake. Mistake one: mechanics had known about a problem in the jet's fuel-transfer system for months. Mistake two: the pilot failed to perform the safety checklist during the event.

Several months later, Major General Randolph "Tex" Alles, then the assistant wing commander for the Third Aircraft Wing of the US Marines, stood before the press and took full responsibility for the tragedy on behalf

---

2   Peggy Noonan, "A Tragedy of Errors, and an Accounting," *Wall Street Journal*, March 6, 2009.

of the Marine Corps. The crash "was clearly avoidable" and was the result of "a chain of wrong decisions," he told the press. General Alles, or as I know him, Randy, didn't mention that he was in Iraq at the time of the incident.

People were amazed that the Marines spoke so frankly. A neighbor whose house was almost hit remarked, "The Marines aren't trying to hide from it or duck it. They took it on the chin." A naval aviator who flew the same kind of plane said he was amazed with how Alles's remarks contrasted with "the buck-passing" typical of government and Wall Street. "There are still elements within the government that take personal responsibility seriously."

Noonan herself said of Alles's remarks, "This wasn't damage control, it was taking honest responsibility. And as such, in any modern American institution, it was stunning."

My first meaningful conversation with Randy occurred around this time in a coffee shop on Capitol Hill. But this time he was asking the questions. How's your marriage and parenting? What temptations do you struggle with? Why do you want to serve as an elder? Randy was one of the elders who volunteered to meet with me when the board decided to consider me as an elder. I then had the opportunity to serve with this man of God for a number of years. His leadership style is direct, simple, and plain-speaking. He listens at length before speaking, and he speaks only a few sentences. Never once do you get the whiff of ego. Instead he's a man who, together with his wife, will spend long hours pouring themselves out for hurting sheep. While I was serving with him, he became the deputy commissioner for US Customs and Border Protection and then the director of the US Secret Service.

More recently, I asked Randy about the San Diego incident itself. In his plain-speaking way, he made it all sound pretty simple. Folks at the Marine Corps headquarters and in his office wondered what to tell the press. Randy responded to them, "What are we going to tell them? There's nothing to tell them. It's our fault. So we just need to explain how it's our fault. That's it. We will reveal everything that happened and just lay out the facts. And we take our lumps."

So that's what Randy did. He laid it out for me, too:

There was deferred maintenance on the aircraft. There were bad decisions on the part of the commanding officer and duty officer in the ready room of the squadron. They should not have brought the airplane back to Miramar. They should have had it land on North Island because it would have been over water the whole time. Had it crashed, it wouldn't have hurt anybody. And then we explained the actions we took. We fired the squadron commanding officer, the operations officer, the aircraft maintenance officer, and the operations duty officer.

How did the public respond?

The public and the media were, in a sense, disarmed because there wasn't really anything else to do. And they couldn't really accuse us of anything because we had basically laid it all out and said it's our fault totally and completely.

No spin here. Just taking someone else's lumps.

I can imagine someone responding to that story by arguing that the officers who were fired bore the costs more than Randy. It's true, they bore costs, too, and greater ones in this case. Yet Randy became the face and voice of bearing moral responsibility on behalf of the Marine Corps for a terrible mistake that he had nothing to do with. He was in Iraq at the time of the crash, remember?

The Harder Job

Taking someone else's lumps is not what starry-eyed young people consider when aspiring to positions of authority and leadership.

I think of young men in churches—or myself in an earlier decade—who aspire to being a church elder or pastor. They can romanticize being counted among the church's leaders. Yet after spending several years as an elder, they quickly learn that the job is not so glamorous after all. So much of pastoring or eldering involves entering into people's trials and temptations and bearing their pain. It involves being blamed for the misdeeds of others over which you have no control. It means being punched in the chest, figuratively speaking, and saying nothing, when everything in you wants to tell people the real story so that they might understand who really bears the blame. Yet you absorb it. If the opportunity comes for a sabbatical, you grab it greedily. And the other elders smile at you with sympathetic jealousy.

Here's the broader lesson: the person in authority will nearly always have the harder job, at least if he or she is doing it correctly. That's why Andy Crouch is right to argue that good authority makes itself vulnerable.[3]

The temptation in leadership is to use the control we possess to push the costs downward. My eight-year-old daughter and I both sit comfortably in the living room. I ask her to get me a drink from the refrigerator, since I know she's compliant and—at this age—happy to serve me. Yet notice what I'm doing. I'm using my authority to push the very light costs of getting out of a chair downward in the hierarchy to her. You might argue that this serves a good purpose in her life of teaching her to honor her father. Yet whether that's true or not, I know my heart in that moment isn't seeking her good. It's just being lazy. I want to avoid the cost, so I pass it on to her.

And, no doubt, part of being in authority is distributing the costs of labor to different parts of a body or organization. Good leaders will delegate. So the Roman centurion says to Jesus, "For I too am a man under authority, with soldiers under me. And I say to one, 'Go,' and he goes, and to another, 'Come,' and he comes, and to my servant, 'Do this,' and he does it" (Matt. 8:9). Each of those comings and goings has a cost. Think in particular of the cost a commanding officer imposes on his soldiers when he asks them to rush into enemy fire and seize a hill. That's a heavy cost, indeed.

Still, there is a sense in which good leaders seek, as best as they can, to minimize the costs for those beneath them, all the while absorbing what costs they can upward, including the costs for which a person is morally culpable. They want to spare those beneath them those difficulties and hardships. As I said, that's the job. It's what God intends because it reflects him. Every parent looking down into a crib with pity at their sick infant writhing in pain knows this impulse: "If only I could take the sickness for you, I would."

In that sense, being "the boss" often is and should be one of the hardest jobs in any group. How often is the school principal the first to arrive and the last to leave the school building on any given school day? So with the hard-working mother. So with the coach.

---

3   Andy Crouch, *Strong and Weak: Embracing a Life of Love, Risk, and True Flourishing* (Downers Grove, IL: InterVarsity Press, 2016), ch. 2.

In a healthy church, company, or family, it's the leader who bears the heaviest worry when finances run low or a schedule isn't kept. That's why the press understandably sneers when major financial institutions or companies collapse and the CEO floats away with a multimillion-dollar "golden parachute."

Paul modeled something very different. He listed many of the harrowing trials he had endured: far greater labors, far more imprisonments, with countless beatings, and often near death. He was beaten with rods. Once he was stoned. He lived in danger from rivers, danger from robbers, danger from his own people, danger from Gentiles, danger in the city, danger in the wilderness, danger at sea. He lived in toil and hardship, through sleepless nights, in hunger and thirst, in cold and exposure (see 2 Cor. 11:23–27). Then he concluded his list this way: "And, apart from other things, there is the daily pressure on me of my anxiety for all the churches. Who is weak, and I am not weak? Who is made to fall, and I am not indignant?" (vv. 28–29).

Here is an authority figure—an apostle—who absorbed the costs upward. He felt the weaknesses of the churches as his own. He identified with the churches because he loved them. Apparently, Paul remembered what Jesus had said to him before his own conversion: "Saul, Saul, why are you persecuting me?" Jesus, too, identified with the churches. Persecuting them counted as persecuting him. This is what love and good authority working together do.

I think of my friend Michael. He's a pastor, too. During the first year of COVID, some members of his church became angry at the various state requirements, how they impacted the church, and the politics surrounding the whole ordeal. Michael remarked to me, "They're angry. Those on the [political] left are angry. Those on the right are angry. Gratefully, they don't express it to each other. They express it to me. And so I carry their anger. It's not that they're directly mad at me. But they hand it to me. They want me to do something about it, and so in some ways it gets transposed onto me." In one sense, it's unfair for people to transpose their anger onto their pastor. In another sense, that's the job you sign up for when you become a pastor. We're to bear one another's burdens, and pastors lead in such burden-bearing especially. Therefore, I thank God for Michael's—for every pastor's—willingness to carry his church's anger.

Jumping to a different domain, I think of my friend Jeff, who managed a physical therapy office. During COVID, many members of the staff quit or got sick, leaving him to absorb their shifts. So many shifts wore him and his family out. Yet that was the job. I'm grateful for Jeff.

My friend Pat, whom I mentioned in the previous chapter, eventually stepped down as chief astronaut at NASA with his wife's encouragement. The job had prestige, to be sure. He could get on the phone with the heads of space agencies around the world, all of whom would love to send one of their astronauts into space. Yet too many long days add up. So much listening. So much burden-bearing. His wife suggested he stay only if he could find more balance in his life. But Pat knew he couldn't.

Jesus most perfectly embodies the idea of a king who makes himself a substitute and bears the cost. Yet just as the common-grace institution of marriage points to Christ's redemptive love for his bride, so every good common-grace authority has the opportunity to point to Christ's redemptive cost-bearing authority.

Difficult for Our Vanity

Throughout our marriage, I've said to my wife as challenges have arisen, "Let me carry the burden. You don't need to worry about it." It's a lovely offer on my part. The trouble is, I don't always take the necessary actions to make it a reality.

Of the five qualities of good authority mentioned in part III, the idea of absorbing the mistakes or sins or burdens of others is the hardest for me, though I assume it might be the best test of good authority. Will you sacrifice yourself? It's comparatively easy to submit to others; to set my mind on working to strengthen others; to seek wisdom from people around me; and to aspire to administer a measure of discipline. But to absorb the consequences of someone else's errors or sins? To take the blame when I'm not the one who deserves blame? That's hard. It can feel unjust and offend my vanity.

Suppose, for instance, that something goes wrong in my home and my wife blames me. And let's assume this is one of those situations where I did nothing to cause the problem. At that moment, several thoughts flit through my head: "I can defend myself right now by explaining how she or the kids are responsible. Or I can keep my mouth shut and get to work on rectifying the situation." The voice telling me to keep my mouth shut knows that defending myself is less about accomplishing anything meaningful and more about protecting my ego. Meanwhile, the voice calling for a defense is shouting, "Oh, this is an injustice! It's an outrage!"

Ah, vanity!

To absorb the sin or bear the cost requires you to sacrifice yourself. It means forsaking vanity and ego and your personal agenda, whatever it is. It involves a kind of death to self. The only reason to do it is that you really do love the cause, company, or kids you're leading more than yourself. So you'll throw yourself on the grenade for their good.

I once asked an older and godlier man how he dealt with his wife's frustrations toward him. He replied, "Oh, Alice [not her real name] knows she can chew on my arm, and I'll be fine." By this colorful phrase he meant that she might wrongly vent her frustrations toward him from time to time, but he wasn't going to hold it against her or even correct her. He was going to graciously take it. That's not advice for any and all marriages. A characteristically cranky or critical spouse should be corrected. Yet, knowing my friend and his wonderful wife, I was struck by his strength, particularly in comparison to my own frustration at being misrepresented. He is humble and unflappable, and that allows him to be a good sin-absorber and burden-bearer, to live with his wife in an understanding way, and to love her patiently and gently.

Difficult for Discernment

Yet this illustration does raise another reason why this last quality of good authority is difficult to exercise: it requires great wisdom to know when you should bear someone else's cost. As I said, my friend's response is not the right advice for all moments and all marriages.

Sometimes discipline is the better course of action. To borrow from the illustrations above, a wife who makes a habit of wrongly venting her anger may need correction. I'm not encouraging people to adopt messiah complexes, such that they think they should cover every cost.

Sometimes you forbear with your spouse and keep your mouth closed. Sometimes you offer a word. Sometimes you correct an employee's error. Sometimes you fix it yourself. Good authority requires discernment. You might decide that it's best for an employee to bear his own consequences so that he might grow and learn. Or you might decide that, due to a host of circumstances, it's best for you to bear them. There's no easy mathematical formula to tell you precisely when discipline is best or when cost-bearing is best. In any given moment, you have to consider the particular details of the sin or error, the character of the person who committed it, the overall trends of their growth and behavior, how your judgment will impact other people, and so forth. There are always many variables involved, and we must always ask the Lord for wisdom so that we might discern what is best.

What is straightforward is, if you're not seeking to serve yourself or aggrandize your own stature, your eyes will be clearer. You'll be in a better position to judge what's best in any given moment, and whether disciplining someone or bearing their cost will do them the most good.

What gets in the way of such clear-eyed-ness is our vanity and our desire to avoid vulnerability.

Making Yourself Vulnerable and Accommodating Weakness

My friend Amy, whose story I told in chapter 2, once said to me, "Even after everything that's happened to me, I still believe what the Bible says about men serving as elders and being the heads of households. Yet I want pastors to recognize how this teaching can make women vulnerable to harm." Amy's right. This teaching does place women in a position of vulnerability.

So with all authority, whether in the home, workplace, church, or nation. Parental authority makes children vulnerable. Police authority makes citizens vulnerable. And so forth.

One might quickly counter that abandoning all authority makes things worse for children and parents, police and citizens alike. Which is true. Still, those of us who believe in the good of authority need to stare Amy's challenge straight in the face and acknowledge it.

The solution, then, is either to abandon the idea of authority altogether or to better understand and practice it. Assuming we're not going to abandon it, we need to recognize that good authority does everything it can to absorb the vulnerability. A husband puts himself at risk so that his wife doesn't have to, a mother so that her children don't have to, a pastor so that the congregation doesn't have to. Each leader wants people to feel protected and safe. So they make themselves vulnerable.

Good authority figures make themselves vulnerable by taking on the risk of leadership. They risk the buck stopping with them. They risk being blamed for bad decisions they had nothing to do with. They risk being punched for mistakes they didn't make. Then again, they risk actually making bad decisions and living with the regret that follows. They risk the censure of the world and a bad reputation (e.g., 1 Cor. 4:9). They risk public critics and public shame and public failure. They risk exposing their weaknesses and limitations before the watching world, since the challenges of leadership more quickly reveal our limitations and sin. They risk working harder than they ever have. They risk the arrows received when working to shelter others. Most frightening of all, they risk an extra measure of divine judgment (see, e.g., James 3:1; Heb. 13:17).

How many women and men have been trained like Amy to view authority figures with a shudder, when the opposite should be the case because we are taking the vulnerability onto ourselves? How often does the psalmist instead refer to God as a shelter, as in, "For he will hide me in his shelter in the day of trouble; he will conceal me under the cover of his tent; he will lift me high upon a rock" (Ps. 27:5)?

Husbands and fathers, if I may exhort you for a moment, would your wife describe you as a shelter? Would she say that you put yourself in the position of vulnerability? Would your children say that? If not, you will hear about it on judgment day.

Pastors, would your congregation regard you that way? Would they be willing to share the tougher bits of their lives with you, knowing that you will treat them with tender care?

Workplace managers, military officers, company owners, police officers, coaches, are you stepping into the place of vulnerability now? If not, you make yourself vulnerable later, before the judgment seat of God. Perhaps it would be safer for you to quit now and give your position to someone who will accept the requisite vulnerability of the job.

Many times I've pondered how grateful I am for the godly men over me. The word umbrella comes to mind. They've served as an umbrella of protection for me and my family. They absorb the stress, the worry, the care, the challenges. On multiple occasions, I've watched a challenge rise up within or against our ministry or organization and have had the luxury of walking away. "You guys get to worry about that. Have a great weekend! I'm going home."

Part of stepping into vulnerability and absorbing the cost means accommodating frailty and weakness and sin, as I've mentioned previously. Think of Jacob slowing down his own pace in order to accommodate the pace of the herds and his children (Gen. 33:14).

A friend once complained to me about a leader we both knew, and how this leader tolerated the troubles of one of his employees. "Why does he put up with it?" my friend asked. I immediately thought of how this leader habitually shows grace and gives people the benefit of the doubt. "Because he knows how to give opportunities to people with a limp," I answered, "even if those limps never go away."

Or think of a first-grade teacher. She doesn't treat the children like they are in the eighth grade, but like they are in the first grade. She adjusts her expectations and is careful in her demands.

Good leadership is always mindful that one leads finite and fallen sinners. It accommodates frailty. And in that regard it must also always absorb the effects of sin without always giving sin what it deserves. If you feel compelled to always impose an immediate and exacting justice on those you lead, if you can never allow for weakness and error, you will be a tyrannical leader. A few of the people you lead will grow. Many will not. They'll be crushed or will leave.

If it takes ten steps to arrive at maturity or competence, a good leader typically only asks for one or two at a time.

What about You?

Good leaders, in short, account for the sin, weakness, and error of those they lead. They offer corrections and sometimes change course, but they absorb the grievance. They take responsibility for the sin or error, and don't let it control them. That's the job. The buck stops with the leader. The model for this, of course, is Jesus dying for sins, unlike the rulers of this world who lord it over others.

Have you heard of a 360-degree review? It means soliciting feedback from all directions: from your boss or managers, your peers, and those who report directly to you.

If you've never done one, you might try it. Use the content of this chapter and the previous four. Ask those over you, would they regard you as submissive? Do you make their jobs easier or harder? A delight or a challenge?

Ask those under and around you whether they feel invested in and strengthened? Better at their jobs or roles because of you?

Would they regard you as open to their suggestions? Do you solicit their counsel?

Ask those above and below you whether you follow through on your word. And for those below you, do you offer them a predictable set of outcomes based on what they do? Or do they find you whimsical and mercurial?

Finally, do they find your office (whether mother or manager) a place of refuge and rest? Do they trust that you won't ask them to absorb costs merely out of selfishness, but only because it's necessary for the mission or it's for their good in some other way? Do they feel like you have their best interest in mind, or your own?

If you invite such feedback, assure people they will experience no re-crimination for honest answers, and then follow through on that promise!

PART IV

WHAT DOES GOOD AUTHORITY LOOK LIKE IN ACTION?

11

Two Kinds of Authority: Command and Counsel

AUTHORITY, I ARGUED IN CHAPTER 1, is the moral right or license to make decisions or employ power for a particular purpose. It is an authorization to do something. And notice that I said *some*thing, not *any*thing or *every*thing. The scope of that something—that authorized task—helps to establish an authority's boundaries or jurisdiction. We therefore always need to ask the question, "What's the purpose of this authorization or assigned task?" Answering this will help us determine the purposes and limits of an office.

As I also said in chapter 1, I like the word "office" because it works like an X-ray machine. It makes us mindful of the fact that roles like "mother" or "mayor" or "minister" possess an unseen skeleton or institutional structure hiding underneath the skin. To give Jane the title of "mother" with respect to Molly, for instance, is to say that Jane possesses a particular set of responsibilities and powers in Molly's life, at least until Molly reaches a certain age, while also obligating Molly toward Jane in a certain way. In other words, Jane holds the office of mother, and this office gives a moral shape or structure to Jane and Molly's relationship.

People hear "authority" and think immediately of a one-dimensional—higher or lower—hierarchy. That dimension exists. Yet the bigger picture is one of office. God is not as preoccupied with our ranking or status as we are. He assigned all of us inestimable and equal worth by creating us in his image. All human beings possess equal God-imaging value—from the embryo in the womb to the king on the throne. In that sense, Christianity offers a more radical egalitarianism than anything else. Yet then God gives us various jobs to do—some higher, some lower—for the sake of his purposes in our lives, in the church, and in creation.

Furthermore, God doesn't arbitrarily impose these offices. The office of parent makes sense in light of the undeveloped but maturing nature of a child. The office of government makes sense in light of the need for social coordination between human beings. The office of elder makes sense in light of the fact that younger Christians need older Christians to imitate and follow. The office of husband makes sense in light of the distinct physical endowments given to men and women, particularly as it relates to childbearing. In other words, God's office assignments don't work against creation as he's designed it, like happens when you try to mash Lego brand blocks on top of the generic brand, and they don't quite fit. Rather, God's commands and authorizations fit his design patterns. Creation (and with regard to elders, new creation) and morality are suited to each other.

It's worth observing, then, that our first obligation is to love God's creation design. If we don't love the design, we'll resent the offices.

Insofar as we're preoccupied with ourselves and our status, we work at cross-purposes with God's larger purposes. We're like the entitled new hire who demands to be treated as if he's been in the company for twenty years. He has his own agenda in mind rather than the company's, not to mention an exaggerated sense of his own importance. Getting on board with God's agenda means being willing to be last instead of first, lowest instead of highest. It's the person who says, "Lord, I'm happy to be lowest and last," who God grabs and says, "You're just the kind of worker I'm looking for. I'll put you first" (see Matt. 20:16). Yet God wants everyone to adopt this posture, both those who are above and those who are below, the parent and the child, the manager and the worker.

The main question each of us must ask when it comes to God's different offices or job assignments is, what jobs has God assigned me? What are their purposes or goals? And what are their limits?

The purpose of part IV of this book is to explore the Bible's most basic offices: husband, parent, government, manager, church, and elder. With the exception of manager, I tackle them in the order in which they appear in Scripture, which is also the order in which we tend to experience them in life.

Readers might find themselves disagreeing with me on secondary theological matters in this section. For instance, the fact that I believe the Bible teaches elder-led congregationalism will show up in how I characterize the congregation's authority versus an elder's authority. Presbyterians, Anglicans, and others who affirm some form of elder-rule, where the pastors or elders possess the final say within a church, may find themselves disagreeing. Likewise, the fact that I'm a complementarian means that I believe husbands possess a certain kind of authority in the home, and egalitarians will disagree with this. Still, I hope readers with these different convictions will be able to learn something nonetheless.

Feeling for the Biblical Texture

In the following chapters, we'll look at these different job descriptions one by one. In this chapter I want to get a bird's-eye view of all of them together. As I said, we tend to think of authority as one kind of thing: some have it, some don't, period. Yet Scripture doesn't treat authority so simply. It treats each office distinctly, and doing a little side-by-side comparison should be helpful.

To switch metaphors, different kinds of authority have different textures. One feels like cotton, another like silk, another like burlap. Plus, these different materials not only have different feels but different functions—e.g., one to keep snow off, another to hold the tomatoes in a grocery cart.

Compare, for instance, a husband's and a pastor's authority or office. Are they the same thing? Well, church members and wives are both told to "submit," so they share something in common. Yet the Bible instructs elders to "command" what they teach (1 Tim. 4:11), while it never tells husbands to "command" their wives. Instead, it tells them to "love" their wives as their own bodies.

Picture it like this: It's judgment day. In dealing with a pastor, Jesus opens the Bible and says, "Alright, right here in 1 Timothy 4:11, I told you to 'command' what you teach. How do you think you did?" Those are the words on the page to which he'll hold the pastor accountable.

But then Jesus will say, "Now let's talk about your marriage." Then he'll turn the Bible back to Ephesians 5, run his finger down the page, point, and say, "Let's see, right here, I told you to 'love' your wife. Do you think you did a good job?"

Two conversations, two kinds of cloth, each with its own feel.

Or compare the texture of the Bible's descriptions for the government and for the parent. Israel's governance was patriarchal, meaning civil and familial authorities blurred together. At one point David calls King Saul "my father" (1 Sam. 24:11), and Isaiah anticipates a day when "kings shall be your foster fathers" and "queens your nursing mothers" (Isa. 49:23; cf. Num. 11:12). Still, Paul describes a king as "an avenger who carries out God's wrath on the wrongdoer" (Rom. 13:4), while he instructs fathers "do not provoke your children" (Eph. 6:4). In other words, they are not the same office.

The lesson is, we can draw analogies between one office and another, but we should be leery of mapping different offices on top of one another too precisely, as when fathers characterize themselves as kings of their own little castles and then treat their families as a king might. Or, coming at it from the other side, I've not spoken with Chinese Communist Party General Secretary Xi Jinping, but my guess is that he loves it when Chinese citizens refer to him as "Xi Dada."[1] It seductively softens and personalizes this oppressive and tyrannical ruler, as with George Orwell's infamous and totalitarian government which stylizes itself as "Big Brother."[2]

In short, we need to pay close attention to both what the Bible says and what it refrains from saying. Whom does it lay the moral burden on—the one in authority or the one under authority?

Two Kinds of Authority: Command and Counsel

Perhaps the most significant categorical difference we find on the pages of Scripture is whether Scripture grants an authority the power of dis-

---

1   See https://www.nytimes.com/2022/10/28/briefing/xi-jinping-china-authoritarian.html.

2   See Orwell's *1984*. The Westminster Confession, the Cambridge Platform, and many of the Magisterial Reformers generally pointed to Isaiah's prophetic promise just mentioned to justify naming the civil magistrate a "nursing father" and "nursing mother." But is that prophetic promise fulfilled in the nation state today or in the church (see 1 Thess. 2:7)? I'm not convinced these are the best labels to use for the civil government. (Westminster Confession, 23.3; Cambridge Platform, 11.4.)

cipline, which is to say, a mechanism for unilaterally enforcing what is commanded.

In chapter 9, I argued that authority is toothless, even substance-less, without the power of discipline. Take away someone's power of discipline and you effectively take away their authority. Yet now it's time to complicate the story. The Bible presents two kinds of authority—one with the power of discipline and one without. The former we can call the authority of command; the latter we can call the authority of counsel.[3]

As you can see in the table of contents and in the actual titles of chapters 12 through 17, I believe the Bible teaches that the parents of young children, the state, a church, and a workplace manager possess an authority of command. Husbands and elders, on the other hand, possess an authority of counsel. Understanding the difference will help us to exercise our authority rightly.

Both the authority of command and the authority of counsel should be counted as true authority because God has given its holders the moral right to issue directives that bind the conscience. The difference is, someone with an authority of command also has the right to enforce what's commanded through the power of discipline. The authority is unilaterally efficacious. It can enforce or make something happen against the will of those being commanded. With an authority of counsel, on the other hand, the power of discipline is dramatically reduced, if not altogether eliminated. It's not unilaterally efficacious in the same way.

Consider these three different biblical offices, all of which illustrate an authority of command:

- *Parents of children in the home.* Parents can both require obedience and enforce it. "You will go to bed now." The Bible summarizes that power of enforcement in one word: the rod (Prov. 13:24; 22:15).
- *A civil government or the state.* The state, too, can require obedience and enforce it. "You are under arrest." The Bible also describes its enforcement mechanism in a word: the sword.

3   This distinction is adapted with some modifications from Oliver O'Donovan, *Resurrection and Moral Order: An Outline for Evangelical Ethics,* 2nd ed. (Grand Rapids, MI: Eerdmans, 1994), 170–75.

- *Churches or whole congregations.* The whole church or congregation can unilaterally effect its will. "The church voted to remove you from membership as an act of discipline." The single word: the "keys" (Matt. 16:19; cf. 18:18).

Yet now let's turn to husbands and elders. Both possess an authority of counsel, meaning their directives should bind the conscience, but their power of discipline is drastically reduced, if not altogether eliminated:

- *Husbands.* The Bible calls wives to "submit" to their husbands in the same way that the church submits to Christ (Eph. 5:22, 24). Therefore, a wife should treat her husband's instruction as conscience-binding. Before God, she should feel that weight. That said, does the Bible give the husband any God-given mechanism for disciplining his wife? Scan your mind's eye over the entire Bible, Old Testament and New. Can you think of a single verse where we encounter something like the "rod," the "sword," or the "keys" with regard to the husband/wife relationship? The answer is no. In other words, a husband has no right to raise a hand, raise a voice, issue threats, or force his wife to do something against her will. The second he does so, he becomes an abuser. He's gone beyond his authorization. Jesus will have words with an antagonistic wife on the last day. Jesus certainly holds the power of discipline over her. But a husband does not.
- *Elders/pastors.* Pastors have authority. They should "command" what they teach and "exhort and rebuke with all authority" (1 Tim. 4:11; 5:7; Titus 2:15). Members, meanwhile, should "obey" and "submit to" their leaders (Heb. 13:17). The leaders' directives bind consciences. Yet a second question follows: can elders enforce those commands? An elder-ruled church, whether Presbyterian, Anglican, or nondenominational, says yes. As a Baptist or congregationalist, I say no, at least not at the level of formal discipline. The Bible presents congregations and apostles enforcing their decisions through excommunication (see Matt. 18:15–18; Acts 8:20–23; 1 Cor. 5; 1 Tim. 1:20); never once does a

pastor or elder excommunicate or otherwise enforce a command.

An elder or pastor's authority, too, is an authority of counsel.

To be sure, elders will sometimes act in ways that could be construed as discipline. If they discover that an usher is making inappropriate remarks as he greets people at the door, they might remove him from that assignment. And, elders are ordinarily the individuals who will present a case of church discipline to the entire church. Yet in the final analysis, the Bible never authorizes elders or pastors to receive someone into membership or remove someone from membership. They must appeal to the congregation.

In extreme situations, a husband might also act in a way that could be construed as discipline. For instance, he would have the right to take a credit card away if his wife is carelessly putting the family into debt. Yet what makes such an action acceptable is that it prevents harm to the family, and I have a hard time thinking of an example where he could force something on her where the threat of harm is not involved. Besides, wives, too, have the right to act in self-defense or the defense of their children, as discussed in chapter 5. If a husband is gambling away his paycheck, leaving the wife and children without food, does she have no right to take measures to foil his plans for his and the family's good? I believe she does. Think of Abigail, who was married to the "worthless" Nabal. His wickedness threatened "harm" against "all his house." Without telling him, she appealed to another authority, David, which saved herself and her husband (1 Sam. 25). So recall that the Bible says a husband is the "head" of the wife like Christ is the "head" of the church (Eph. 5:23). It would seem perverse indeed if a husband like Nabal grabbed that teaching and held it over his wife in order to argue that his headship means she should endure and absorb all of his sin without protecting herself, but he need not endure and absorb her sin. That's upside down. Christ endured and absorbed all of the church's sin. She didn't endure and absorb his.

To repeat, therefore, an authority of counsel means that an elder or a husband has the moral right from God to insist on a particular direction in a way that binds the conscience, but their power of discipline is drastically reduced, if not altogether eliminated.

Table 11.1: Authority: Command versus Counsel

	Authority of Command	Authority of Counsel
How they're the same	Right to issue directives that bind the conscience	Right to issue directives that bind the conscience
How they're different	Right to enforce through discipline	No right to enforce through discipline
Examples and mechanism of enforcement or discipline	• Parents of young children—the rod • The state—the sword • The church—the keys	• Husbands—none • Elders—none
Theological emphasis	God's transcendence	God's immanence

Someone might ask, is an authority of counsel really authority? Isn't it just counsel? After all, I said earlier that the power of discipline gives authority its substance.

In response, I'd say it's not just counsel, it's an *authority of* counsel, because the wife and the church members are morally bound to submit. And that's because Jesus "said so," and he himself holds the power of discipline. If we wanted, we could call it an authority of "delayed discipline" or "eschatological discipline."

That makes an "authority of counsel" qualitatively different from what people mean when they refer to "moral authority" or "authority of truth."[4] Moral authority refers to the idea of giving a person's words extra weight because of that individual's character or competence. Ironically, there is nothing morally binding about moral authority. It's informal, more like influence. The same is true for what people call epistemic authority or an authority of truth, as when we refer to "medical authorities." We defer to doctors. It's generally wise to do so since they're the experts. But we're not morally obliged to obey their orders, at least not by biblical mandate.

What someone possessing an authority of counsel cannot do is *force* or *enact* an outcome, at least not with the same efficacy as someone possessing an authority of command. When a church excommunicates someone, he

---

4   On moral authority, see J. I. Packer, "The Reconstitution of Authority," in *Readings in Christian Ethics*, vol. 1: *Theory and Method*, ed. David K. Clark and Robert V. Rakestraw (Grand Rapids, MI: Baker, 1994), 93.

or she is excommunicated—unilaterally. When the judge pounds the gavel declaring, "Guilty," the person is rendered guilty in the eyes of the legal system—unilaterally. Husbands and elders cannot unilaterally effect such outcomes, other than in far less consequential programmatic matters, like who gets to serve as an usher, or in tie-breaking situations for a husband (see ch. 12 on this).

Different Theological Lessons

The fact that one has an enforcement mechanism and the other does not means these two types of authority operate differently, and they teach different kinds of lessons. For starters, an authority of command teaches us more about God's transcendence, while an authority of counsel teaches more about his immanence. I'm not saying either type is all transcendence or all immanence. I'm talking about a tendency, or shades of difference.

The government is "sent by [God] to punish those who do evil and to praise those who do good" (1 Pet. 2:14; cf. Rom. 13:3–4). Its lessons lean toward the transcendent. It can announce law by horseback messenger or by evening news. No relationship required. Yet it teaches us that God is a lawgiver and judge.

Whole churches, too, when they act jointly with the keys of the kingdom, lean toward the transcendent. By binding and loosing on earth what is bound and loosed in heaven (Matt. 16:19), they formally represent heaven. Drawing a professing believer into membership teaches us that God saves. Excommunicating a person teaches us that God punishes.

Toward the other end of the spectrum, meanwhile, elders and husbands demonstrate how God exercises his authority immanently. Their authority doesn't depend on the threat of discipline, like a policeman's. It depends on being *with* my wife and *with* my church. Knowing them. Understanding them. Reading their body language. Asking questions. Moderating my counsel according to my sense of how they are doing.

Somewhere in the middle of the spectrum, combining large quantities of both transcendence and immanence, are parents. Fathers on earth are named after the Father in heaven (Eph. 3:15). And, as we'll see two chapters from now, a parent represents the broadest expanse of God's own authority. That said, the older children become, particularly moving into the teen years, the more a parent should lean into immanence or relationship.

That's exactly what we saw with Angela and her father in chapter 1. Parental authority, in other words, begins with greater quantities of transcendence but then aims toward immanence as the children grow. It comes with a discipleship trajectory. Parents always seek to grow their children *up into* themselves, which is why the parent will adopt a different posture toward the three-year-old, the thirteen-year-old, and the twenty-three-year old. Their task is to teach their children to rule like God rules in all of life.

Figure 11.1: Spectrum of Authority: Immanence versus Transcendence

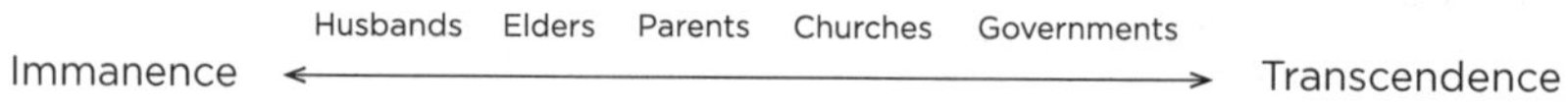

It's also worth noting along these lines that Scripture presents Christ exercising his authority differently in relation to his first and second comings. In his first coming, Christ, the Bible's supreme picture of God's immanence, commands people to follow him. He verbally rebukes people. Yet he doesn't punish or exercise the sword. Instead, he draws near. It's as if he's exercising an authority of counsel. Punishment is delayed until his second coming, when he will come with the sword and an authority of command (e.g., Rev. 6:15–17). It's after his second coming that all people on earth, friend and foe, will bow their knees to him as transcendent Lord (1 Cor. 15:27–28; Phil. 2:10).

It's not surprising, then, that Scripture most closely matches a husband and elder's authority with Christ's as we experienced it in his first coming (e.g., Eph. 5:21–31; 1 Pet. 5:1–4; also 1 Cor. 11:1). A husband's and an elder's authority should *feel* far more immanent and different than a government's or even a parent's, which brings us to the next point.

How to Exercise an Authority of Counsel: Its Manner

Both those possessing an authority of counsel and those possessing an authority of command can require their directives to be followed. Inside the boundaries of their respective jurisdictions, a governor and a husband can both say, "You must," and these words morally bind a citizen or a wife.

But woe to the husband or elder who stops here, giving no more thought to the office than that!

Let's go back to the idea of different textures. The fact that husbands and elders don't possess an enforcement mechanism dramatically changes *how* they should exercise their authority—*its manner*. And they exercise it differently in a number of ways. An authority of counsel . . .

(1) *acts with a much lighter hand.* Suppose you're standing at a fork in the road with someone over whom you possess authority, and you want the person to take one path rather than the other. You can use language that asserts your authority more lightly or more heavily. Most lightly of all, you might say, "May I invite you to take this path?" Or, with growing degrees of heaviness, click by click, you can say, "I would encourage you," or "I recommend that you," or "I urge you," or "I require you," or "I will now force you." Perhaps you have a different feel for the comparative heaviness of these verbs. Pick your own verbs. Yet I trust you see the spectrum of heaviness. Furthermore, this spectrum overlaps, more or less, with the spectrum between immanence and transcendence. God in his transcendence, like a government, can force. God in his immanence, like a husband, invites. "Behold, I stand at the door and knock," says Jesus (Rev. 3:20).

Figure 11.2: Spectrum of the Implementation of Authority

	Husbands	Elders	Parents	Churches	Governments	
Immanence ⟵						⟶ Transcendence
	Invite	Encourage	Recommend	Urge	Require	Force

Husbands and elders, with their authority of counsel, will lean toward language on the lighter side of the spectrum. In fact, they should never make it all the way to "force," and should use the language of "require" or its equivalents like "must" very sparingly unless speaking straight from Scripture, as any Christian might. Meanwhile, churches (acting jointly with the keys) and governments, with their authority of command, will often lean toward language on the heavier side. Parents—God bless them—cover the gamut.

To be sure, friends and peers can use those words on the lighter end of the spectrum, too. Yet when an authoritative office is in play, those words bear an extra measure of psychological and moral weight, since the presence of the office means someone has already been commanded to submit. For instance, the words "I would encourage you to take this path instead of that one" weigh more coming from your pastor than from your friend, even if they're said in the exact same tone of voice.

Speaking of tone of voice, the pastor or husband should generally offer such words in a milder manner precisely because of their authority. I can speak with much more intensity and heat with the three guys I meet with a couple of times a month for accountability than I can with my wife or children: "Dude, you CANNOT do that." With wife and daughters I need to dramatically lower the temperature, lest I discourage or crush them. They know God has called them to submit. Therefore, I can let the office do the work for me, knowing that their business is ultimately with God, not with me. I can speak with resolve, but also with compassion and empathy.

Another way of making this first point about manner is to say that elders (in an interpersonal as opposed to a preaching context) and especially husbands should *appeal* more than they should *command*. Paul sets an example for elders when he says to Philemon, "though I am bold enough in Christ to command you to do what is required, yet for love's sake I prefer to appeal to you"; and moments later, "I preferred to do nothing without your consent in order that your goodness might not be by compulsion but of your own accord" (Philem. 8, 9, 14). After all, a pastor does not relate to a church member like a father relates to his three-year-old. His goal is to see born-again hearts *choosing* obedience to God on their own. That's the point of the new covenant, after all. It serves no purpose to scare people into submission.

This is even more true for a husband. God has given authority to husbands not so much to "command" their wives but to love and lead and invite them toward sharing in the Lord's work of dominion. She should feel the Lord's obligation on her to submit and follow, but not because her husband exercises a heavy hand that insists on compliance.

(2) *operates through trust and relationship*. An authority of command impels compliance, at least in part by the threat of discipline. An authority of counsel, however, impels compliance by earning trust and building a relationship. Church members and wives need to be able to trust the character, competence, and confidence of the men leading them. Trust is

the currency that pastors and husbands have to spend. The gas that makes the car move. Wives and church members will feel more inclined to follow when they trust the personal integrity and self-sacrificing love of the man or men who lead.

After all, Christ never forces the church to obey and follow him. That would reverse the very promise of the new covenant, which includes hearts longing to obey (see Jer. 31:31–34). Rather, the church follows Christ because it trusts him. Its obedience is rooted in faith, hope, and love, which is the only obedience worth anything in Christ's kingdom. Everything else is sin (Rom. 14:23). In the same way, what good is the forced or grudging obedience of a wife? Such obedience might give a husband what he selfishly wants in the moment, but it does not serve the purposes for which he's been given authority—to draw his wife into a shared Christlike rule over creation. A husband should not use his authority to force, but to invite and elicit the same kind of faith-filled and loving obedience from his wife that Christ desires from the church. He wants to see her obedience and support grow of its own accord, like a flower growing up out of the heart.

The same is true of elders. They strive for an obedience that is rooted in "love that issues from a pure heart and a good conscience and a sincere faith" (1 Tim. 1:5). They don't possess authority for the purpose of forcing decisions but of eliciting them.

(3) *is earned*. Related to the last point, insofar as an authority of counsel works by trust and by relationship, elders and husbands should aspire to earn it. It wouldn't be right to say they "need" to earn it, because the Bible calls wives and church members to submit. It places an obligation on them. That's why, earlier in the book, I used the illustration of a person wrongly saying a pastor had to earn his trust, because the call to submission rests in an office given by God. Submitting to a pastor or a husband is not finally submitting to the man but to the Office Giver. Still, a good husband or elder will continually strive to remove all stumbling blocks and will work to make following him as easy as possible. He will, in that sense, work to earn the trust of the people under him. He will do this by working hard, by sacrificing himself in the job, by living in a manner that is above reproach, and by leading with confidence.

How many husbands have discovered that sitting all weekend watching football games while his wife works hard to prepare the house and the children for the upcoming week hardly wins her trust and affection! Does Christ make the man head so that he can rest while his wife works? Hardly. The head should work hardest of all, sacrifice the most, and walk with greatest integrity.

Not only that, Paul's instruction for elders to be "sober-minded" points to the stability and even gravitas that a good pastor and husband possesses. He knows who he is, and is confident in his headship. He's emotionally self-controlled and in control of his passions. He's steadfast. His presence is felt in the room. In fact, good leaders have this, whether they're Christians or not. There's a sense in which his gravity does his work for him, which in turn allows him to be gentle. Weak men feel the need to yell. Strong men stand steady like a flagpole, even as the wind tosses the flag of circumstances all about.

(4) *is patient and plays the long game.* A policeman will command you to slow down your car now. A parent will command a child to go to bed now. But the nature of a husband's or elder's authority forces a man to be patient, long-suffering, tender, consistent. It requires him to live with his wife and church in an understanding way. It's never harsh, but requires him to woo and be winsome. It works for growth over the long run, not forced outcomes and decisions in the short run, which is why Paul tells Timothy to teach "with all patience."

(5) *respects those they lead as their equals.* Elders and husbands must honor and respect those they lead as possessors of equal agency in every decision. While a police officer or the parent of a young child will sometimes override the agency of those they lead for purposes of protection and instruction, a husband or elder should almost never do that. They must ordinarily appeal to a person's own agency, as Paul does with Philemon: "not by compulsion but of your own accord" (v. 14).[5] A husband and elder's

---

5   I believe Paul as an apostle could override a church member's agency, as when he handed Hymenaeus and Alexander over to Satan (i.e., excommunicated them) to be taught not to blaspheme. Nonetheless, I believe the more common pattern with the New Testament epistles was for the apostles to act more like pastors, as if to say, they were more interested in setting an example that pastors or elders could follow than they were in invoking their own apostolic authority. Beyond the example of Philemon, see, for instance, how Paul tells the Corinthians that he had already passed judgment on the adulterous man (1 Cor. 5:3), yet the man was still not effectually removed. He called on the church to exercise their judgment and remove the man (vv. 2, 5, 12). Likewise Peter, in addressing local elders, refers to himself as their fellow shepherd (1 Pet. 5:1).

authority is particularly suited to partnership and collegiality because they don't hold the ability to coerce. Their authority requires collaboration, involvement, and calls for consent. Nineteenth-century Presbyterian commentator W. S. Plumer, pointing to passages like Ephesians 5:22 and 1 Peter 3:1, observed that "the wife owes to her husband reverence and obedience." Yet he continues, "The reverence and obedience required are not those of a servant nor even those of a child but of a companion who is yet the weaker vessel."[6]

The only exception to this principle that I can envision is when the husband and wife find themselves at loggerheads over an important decision— "where should the kids go to school?"; "should we buy this house?"; etc. The challenge here has nothing to do with discipline, of course, but with the fact that someone must make the final call. And Scripture teaches that that should be the husband. That said, husbands and elders . . .

(6) *are quick to forgo their rights.* Husbands and elders should also be quick to forgo their rights, perhaps especially when disagreement continues. Possessing a right does not imply an obligation to exercise it. Paul tells husbands and wives both to give their "conjugal rights" to their spouse (1 Cor. 7:3), while simultaneously modeling a willingness to give up his own rights to physical sustenance: "I have made no use of any of these rights, nor am I writing these things to secure any such provision" (1 Cor. 9:15). To put these two things together, we can say the Lord might command spouses to give, but that doesn't mean he licenses us—husbands especially—to take, or even to demand that something must be given. The larger lesson is that men possessing an authority of counsel, whether in the home or the church, should be the quickest to surrender their rights, because that is the example Christ left for us. He came not to be served, but to serve and to give his life as a ransom (Mark 10:45).

Suppose, then, you find yourself at loggerheads with your wife or congregation. Do you quickly assert your way? More often than not, you should slow down and wait. Pray. Encourage. Maybe teach. Listen again. Remember, the goal for a husband or elder is not to get your way. The goal

---

6   William Swan Plumer, *The Law of God: As Contained in the Ten Commandments Explained and Enforced* (Philadelphia: Presbyterian Board of Publication, 1864), 470.

is to grow and lead people toward Christ, so that you get to wherever you're going together and by happy consent.

An Evangelistic Authority Suited to a Gospel Logic

What an authority of counsel offers, in the final analysis, is a type of authority that follows a gospel logic. Consider: The gospel includes a new heart, and that heart, in its ideal form, wants to obey. An authority of counsel, then, is suited to this ideal. It doesn't use force, but renounces force because doing so displays the beauty of whatever compels those new desires. Instead, an authority of counsel works best by pointing to that beauty. By inviting. By compelling with kindness. Then the hearts "under" it want to follow.

God gives husbands the opportunity to exercise this type of authority with the drawing power of a Song-of-Solomon-like love. This is his common-grace gift for all creation, and part of the underlying logic of the typological connection between husbands and wives and Christ and the church.

God then gives elders the special-grace opportunity to exercise it with compelling lives of righteousness. Their righteousness should prove attractive to a born-again congregation, so that elders can say with Paul, "Be imitators of me, as I am of Christ" (1 Cor. 11:1).

All of this means that an authority of counsel is essentially evangelistic. You invite. You don't force. Sometimes you correct, but mostly you compel with hope. You point to the law, but mostly you announce grace. You speak plainly, but you also speak kindly, because your goal is to win people over— wives toward unity, church members toward righteousness. You're not to be a pushover, any more than Jesus was a pushover, nor to capitulate, any more than Jesus capitulated. Yet like Jesus calling his disciples from their fishing nets, so husbands and elders exercise authority by initiating and pointing in love toward the path forward. They, in turn, possess an obligation to obey, even as the non-Christian hearing the gospel does.

Conclusion

Too often, Christians discuss authority as if it is one kind of thing. Hopefully, the discussion here demonstrates that authority comes in a variety of fabrics with a variety of textures that serve a variety of purposes. This means we, likewise, need to be more textured in our descriptions and practice of it.

The one form of authority I haven't discussed in this chapter is the authority of an employer or manager or boss or commanding officer. The commanding officer appears in Scripture, since his authority operates as an extension of the authority of government, but the authority of employers or managers is not delineated as such. Insofar as the economies of the ancient world largely depended upon apprenticeship and slavery, there's no quick biblical connection to be made to the modern-day manager-employee relationship, which to some extent is usually voluntary. A boss can fire you, but you can also quit at will. We'll consider this more at length in a subsequent chapter.

We turn now to the job descriptions of the various offices of authority that we are considering.

12

The Husband (Counsel)

Covenantal Authorization: Adamic (Common) Covenant

Be fruitful and multiply and fill the earth and subdue it, and have dominion over the fish of the sea and over the birds of the heavens and over every living thing that moves on the earth. (Gen. 1:28)

The LORD God took the man and put him in the garden of Eden to work it and keep it. . . . Then the LORD God said, "It is not good that the man should be alone; I will make him a helper fit for him." (Gen. 2:15, 18)

Then the man said,
"This at last is bone of my bones and flesh of my flesh;
she shall be called Woman, because she was taken out of Man."

Therefore a man shall leave his father and his mother and hold fast to his wife, and they shall become one flesh. (Gen. 2:23–24)

Other Elucidating Biblical Texts

Wisdom has built her house. . . . She has sent out her young women to call from the highest places in the town.

The woman Folly is loud;
she is seductive and knows nothing. (Prov. 9:1, 3, 13)

An excellent wife who can find? . . . The heart of her
husband trusts in her, and he will have no lack of gain.
She does him good, and not harm. (Prov. 31:10–12)

The head of every man is Christ, the head of a wife is her
husband, and the head of Christ is God. (1 Cor. 11:3)

Wives, submit to your own husbands, as to the Lord.
For the husband is the head of the wife even as Christ
is the head of the church, his body, and is himself its
Savior. Now as the church submits to Christ, so also wives
should submit in everything to their husbands.
Husbands, love your wives, as Christ loved the church and gave
himself up for her, that he might sanctify her, having cleansed
her by the washing of water with the word, so that he might
present the church to himself in splendor, without spot or wrinkle
or any such thing, that she might be holy and without blemish.
In the same way husbands should love their wives as their own
bodies. He who loves his wife loves himself. (Eph. 5:22–28)

Likewise, wives, be subject to your own husbands, so that even if
some do not obey the word, they may be won without a word by
the conduct of their wives, when they see your respectful and pure
conduct. . . . let your adorning be the hidden person of the heart with
the imperishable beauty of a gentle and quiet spirit, which in God's
sight is very precious. . . . do not fear anything that is frightening.
Likewise, husbands, live with your wives in an understanding
way, showing honor to the woman as the weaker vessel,
since they are heirs with you of the grace of life, so that
your prayers may not be hindered. (1 Pet. 3:1–2, 4–7)

Job Description

To cultivate oneness by leading and loving his wife in the shared work of earthly dominion, relying on her help, competence, and wisdom.

———

BEFORE GETTING TO THE OFFICE of husband, let me offer a few principles on how to read the Bible institutionally, which will apply to this and
the next five chapters.

1. *Covenants constitutionalize.* You'll notice I begin each chapter by referring to that office's "covenantal authorization." That's because God structures
his relationships with humanity through covenants. To use a word that's a
little more familiar to people today, these covenants "constitutionalize" our
relationship with God. You know what a constitution is. It's the set of rules
for making the rules, and for saying who has what authority. For example,
the US Constitution says the president has *this* authority, congress has *that*
authority, and so forth.

2. *Covenantally specific institutions.* Likewise, one of the things the
Bible's major covenants do is establish various institutions which then help
regulate life within those covenants. God's covenant with Adam includes
the institutions of marriage, the parent-child structure, and, by implied
necessity, the workplace. His covenant with Noah includes the institution of government, at least in its post-fall form. We could talk about the
various institutions that the Abrahamic, Mosaic, and Davidic covenants
established, such as circumcision or the priesthood, but we don't need to
do so for our purposes here. Finally, the new covenant itself didn't directly
establish the institutions of the local, visible church and its elders, but God
established them along the way in order to regulate life within the new
covenant before Christ's return.

3. *Common and special covenants.* Furthermore, God's covenants with
humanity come in two kinds: common and special. The Adamic and Noahic
covenants he made with humanity in common. The Abrahamic, Mosaic,
Davidic, and new covenants he made with his special people. Therefore, the
offices he establishes in the common covenants apply directly to all humanity, as with marriage, family, and government. The offices he establishes for
his special people directly bind those belonging to those particular covenants, as with church and elders. How the common and special covenants
relate to one another, as well as how the various special covenants relate to
one another, we'll get to in the chapter on government.

4. *Further textual elucidation.* Once a covenant has authorized an office,
later biblical texts then help us to better understand the nature and scope of
that office. God established marriage in Genesis 1 and 2, for instance, but

Paul's later teaching on marriage elucidates and fills out our understanding of Genesis 1 and 2. At the beginning of chapters 12 through 17, I've included both the original authorizing texts as well as a few significant elucidating texts.

Turning to the office of husband, then, there is no other place to begin than in the first two chapters of Genesis with God's original covenant with Adam to "Be fruitful and multiply and fill the earth and subdue it."[1] Most immediately, marriage serves the purpose of bringing God's dominion to the earth. God placed Adam in the garden to "work it and keep it." Then he created Eve as a "helper" to do the work with him (Gen. 2:15, 18). It is a partnership and a collaborative endeavor. Neither man nor woman can be fruitful and multiply without the other. Nor can they fill and subdue without the other.

When a single man asks me for advice on dating someone, I'll sometimes tell him to look for opportunities to do a work project or serve other people together. For instance, here's a first date idea: visit older church members in a nursing home.

The point is, marriage isn't just about staring into one another's eyes all day. It's about undertaking life together. Dig the hole, pour the concrete foundation, build the house, decorate the house, fill the house with children, help them with homework, teach them an instrument, till the field, plant the seeds, harvest the crop, study the Bible, pray, sing, show hospitality, share the gospel, wave goodbye to adult children as they go to subdue new territory, and on and on. All of that is where marriage happens, and much of what it's for: husband and wife partnering together in this magnificent endeavor of dominion, all the while representing God's own rule, righteousness, and love as creatures made in his image.

Back to the conversation with the young man about dating: I'll say to him, "If that's where you're going to live out your life with a woman, maybe test that in dating. Sure, you'll enjoy sitting in a coffee shop and staring into her eyes. But is she a hard worker? Is she competent? Does she fixate on herself or on others? Does she understand forgiveness and mercy? Those are questions you want answers to."

---

1   I'm not referring to the "covenant of works," which is a theological construct. Rather, I'm referring to what's called his covenant with creation, which is bound up in the creation mandate. See Peter J. Gentry and Stephen J. Wellum, *Kingdom through Covenant: A Biblical-Theological Understanding of the Covenants*, 2nd ed. (Wheaton, IL: Crossway, 2018), 211–58.

Naturally, I've said the same thing to my teenage daughters, both as they consider what kind of women they want to be and as they consider what kind of man they're looking for. Is he a hard worker? Is he competent? Will he lead you to take dominion and serve others?

Marriage serves dominion.

What Is the Husband's Authority?

Yet marriage doesn't only serve dominion. It also serves a previous and higher purpose: oneness. So, perhaps there *is* a time to sit in the coffee shop and stare into one another's eyes!

You'll notice this is the first thing I highlighted in the "job description" of the husband's office above: *to cultivate oneness* by leading and loving his wife in the shared work of earthly dominion.

In other words, marriage serves dominion, but dominion is bigger than marriage. Dominion belongs to every human, man and woman, married and single. It's a human thing, not just a marriage thing. So when a husband wakes up in the morning and punches the clock to begin his daily dominion activities, his job *as a husband* is to cultivate oneness with his wife in that work. That's what it means to be a husband: as you pursue dominion, you do it by cultivating oneness with your wife. You possess an "evangelistic authority" (see p. 164) for this purpose.

Here's another way to make this point, courtesy of Pastor Michael, who did our pre-marriage counseling. "Marriage is not one slice of the pie of each of your lives," he said, "like, you got your work slice, your parenting slice, your church slice, as well as your marriage slice. Rather, switching metaphors, marriage is more like a lens through which you're now to look at all of life." What Michael called putting on a lens, I'm calling oneness in dominion. Cultivating oneness means approaching all of life in partnership with your spouse. Both husband and wife do this, but the husband should feel the responsibility to initiate it.

Notice the first thing Adam says when he discovers Eve: "This at last is bone of my bones and flesh of my flesh" (Gen. 2:23). It's a Hebrew way of saying, "She's my flesh and blood." Yet why would Adam say that? A wife shouldn't be your flesh and blood. Marriage begins instead with a covenantal choice and commitment.

Yet that's just the point of Adam's remark. That choice and covenantal commitment should prove wider, longer, higher, and deeper than biology (see Eph. 3:18). The marital covenant enacts God's own work. It turns out that God himself unites husband and wife (Mark 10:9), not finally the minister, the vows, the rings, a legal document, or the marriage bed. God joins them together, said Jesus. Call it born-again biology, typologically speaking. It's a kind of new creation.

The passage's narrator, Moses, then shows us a picture of this born-again family taking precedence over the biological family: "Therefore a man shall leave his father and his mother and hold fast to his wife" (Gen. 2:24a). Somehow, he's now closer to her than he is to Mom and Dad. This cove-nantal and finally supernatural reality is then officially confirmed, pictured, and practiced through a marital seal that graphically demonstrates their oneness: "and they shall become one flesh" (v. 24b).

So the marital partnership serves the purposes of dominion. They work together to fill and subdue the earth. Yet the husband's particular job as a husband is to lead his wife to subdue the earth *with* him as his helper. He takes his eyes off the landscape, turns his face toward her, takes her hand in his, and says, "I want to do this with you." Dominion-work provides the landscape—the *where* and *how*—for cultivating marital oneness.

This central emphasis of oneness is something that distinguishes a husband's authority from every other form of authority we'll discuss in the chapters that follow. Yes, parents, governments, managers, churches, and elders work for a unity of heads, hearts, and hands, too. Yet the Bible features oneness in the marital relationship especially.

It is tragic, then, how often pastors hear from wives who feel neglected by their husbands, either because they spend long hours at work or be-cause they're emotionally absent when home. Such husbands have aban-doned their first duty: seeking oneness with their wives. They're negligent. They've failed. They're losers. And while such a husband will probably be only too happy to practice the oneness of the marriage bed, the more important work, it turns out, is living with his wife in an understanding way (1 Pet. 3:7). It's knowing and understanding her—her frame, her gifts, her vulnerabilities, her hurts, her joys, and her opportunities to grow and flourish.

This brings us to the precise nature of that oneness. The oneness which Scripture describes between husband and wife is not undifferentiated, like two pieces of gray clay that merge to form a bigger ball of gray clay. Rather, Scripture points to the oneness shared by a head and a body. Knowing and understanding one's wife—her frame, her gifts, her vulnerabilities—then, should be pursued with the same care one gives to one's own body. After describing the husband as "the head of the wife," Paul continues, "husbands should love their wives as their own bodies. He who loves his wife loves himself" (Eph. 5:23, 28). You love her as yourself (oneness), but specifically as a head loves the body (differentiation). Paul goes on to say, "For no one ever hated his own flesh, but nourishes and cherishes it" (Eph. 5:29).

Every husband is his wife's head. And what's crucial to recognize is, this is inevitable. Once married, a man doesn't need to make himself the head. He simply is. He can be a life-giving head or a life-stealing head, a present head or an absent head. But he is the head. It is rooted in creation design itself.

The world today can scream and deny all this until it's blue in the face. Yet watch just about any romantic movie you want, and these dynamics will sneak themselves in, no matter how distorted everything else in the relationships they portray may be. Pay close attention, and you'll probably see that the man possesses a kind of inevitability of initiative. Or, even if the woman initiates and controls every scene, he still, somehow, sets the terms of the relationship. So woven into the fabric of reality is the man's headship that, even when authors deliberately set out to squelch that narrative, they end up writing it in. They can't help it. It's natural. Or normal. And no love story between a man and a woman makes intuitive sense without it. Ironically, the very rise of the feminist movement testifies to the inevitability of a husband's headship. Why else would male authority in the home be nearly universal, and the enemy to be contested?[2]

The only matter up for grabs is what kind of head a man is—a faithful one or an unfaithful one? Does his presence lead or does his absence lead?

---

2 Notice, also, what happens when a culture decides to formally remove authority from the marital relationship in the name of "equality" (and see the discussion of equality in the conclusion). That culture will soon find little reason to distinguish between men and women at all, other than to acknowledge that those gray lumps of clay have a couple of different bumps and holes, which surgery can change anyway. If men and women are basically interchangeable, there really is no answer to the question "What is a man?" or "What is a woman?" In other words, God's good gift of authority to marriage helps to preserve the distinctness of the sexes in people's understanding. Lose the first and you'll soon lose the second, as recent decades have shown.

Does he "nourish" and "cherish" his wife, to use Paul's words for how a man treats his body? Or does he use or abuse her? The inevitability of headship is one reason why a husband's abuse can damage a woman so profoundly. To be sure, abusive wives undermine their husbands, too, leading to anxiety, depression, withdrawal, and other such problems in men. Men and women are equally capable of sinning against each other, and a foolish woman can tear down her house, says Proverbs (14:1). Still, an abusive head, even more, can undermine, shrivel up, crush, or destroy a person's spirit.

That said, few things on this earth can strengthen, embolden, empower, encourage, enliven, or build up a woman like a head who is devoted to her good. This is not to deny God's all-sufficient provision for the woman who never marries. It is to affirm the wonderful gift that God gives to many. Something my pastor friends and I have observed is that married women who are loved well by their husbands often seem to grow more attractive as they age, even as their bodies decline. There's something effervescent about an older woman with a strong and giving husband, something in them that shines. There's a confidence and peace, contentedness and strength, in their eyes and their smile.

What Kind of Authority Does a Husband Possess?

The inevitability of headship, I think, helps to explains why the New Testament doesn't tell a man to assert his authority. You won't find a passage that says, "Rule her" or "Command your wife" or "Lead her with all authority," as it says with church elders. The primary imperatives given to the husband are love (Eph. 5:28; Col. 3:19); do not be harsh (Col. 3:19); live with in an understanding way (1 Pet. 3:7); show honor (1 Pet. 3:7); and (as an indicative) provide (1 Tim. 5:8).

This is not to say a husband should never remind his wife of her obligations to follow his leadership as a part of her faithfulness to the Lord. Several times the apostles command the wife to submit (Eph. 5:22, 24; Col. 3:18; 1 Pet. 3:1). Yet it *is* to say that such reminders may in fact be pretty rare. He doesn't need to work hard at asserting what he already possesses. If he's a good leader, he has confidence in his position. That's not self-confidence so much as it is trust in the Lord and his assignments. This confidence frees up a man to engage his wife calmly and deliberately. He exudes sobriety (see 1 Tim. 3:2). He doesn't feel the need to compete with her. And he doesn't need to raise his voice. Indeed, few things reveal weakness and desperation like a husband who screams.

Instead, he cherishes her. He provides for and protects her. He points her toward the Lord and the Lord's word (see Eph. 5:26). He also points out to the horizon, the landscape, where he hopes they will go in their shared work of dominion. Yet throughout all of this he focuses on loving her, living with her in an understanding way, and honoring her.

His authority is broad since it is geared to dominion, which is to say, to all of life. Therefore, Paul commands wives to submit to their husbands "in everything" (Eph. 5:24). I take this to mean "across every domain of life." Yet as I argued in the previous chapter, it's an evangelistic authority of counsel. He must not seek to rule through fear, but through invitation, presence, earning trust, playing the long game, and a comparatively light hand.

I think of my friend Eric (not his real name), who had been invited to be a candidate for a pastorate. He spent a weekend visiting the church, preaching and interviewing without his wife. He concluded his trip convinced in his mind that the Lord was calling him to pastor this church. Yet when he returned home, he didn't share that conclusion with his wife, nor did he share any positives from the church. He told her only the negatives, but encouraged her to visit the church for herself. Why this tactic? Because he knew this road would be harder than the one they had been planning on taking. Therefore, he wanted her to own the decision for herself. He showed leadership not by working for the quick and compliant words, "Okay, I'll follow you," but by helping her whole person go before the Lord so that God himself would or would not lead her to the same conclusion. That's how an authority of counsel works.

When she returned from visiting the church, she said, "I think God is calling us there." Only then did Eric finally say, "I think so too."

My point is not that every decision works this way: the man hides what he thinks and reveals his feelings only after she arrives at his conclusions. It suited him and his wife at that moment. Rather, I'm pointing to the deeper principle at work in Eric's leadership here. He considered her person and how God had uniquely created his wife. Then, with that in mind, he didn't seek to manipulate her toward quickly giving the answer he wanted. Instead, he sought to honor her as his equal by attending to her whole person. Had his wife abhorred the idea, I assume he would not have forced the matter but would have regarded her reaction as the Lord's leading them elsewhere.

Sometimes, people refer to a husband's authority as the ability to "cast the tie-breaking vote" when husband and wife disagree. In some sense that's true, and I'm willing to use that language. In rare instances a husband might reasonably override his wife's objections on family decisions, such as how to use a vacation or whether to pull a kid out of a certain school (he must never, ever use his authority to force or manipulate his way to physical intimacy). But narrowing down his authority to this tie-breaking illustration misses the bigger picture. The bigger picture is that a man should not be concerned about getting his way, but about knowing his wife and helping her grow in grace and godliness and in their dominion together as one. The husband's possession of authority is less about making the big decisions and more about taking the initiative to love his wife and to bear final responsibility for their livelihood together every single minute of every day of his life. To lead her rightly, he must die to his desires completely, other than in the singular desire of helping her follow the Lord together with him. Which means, he should work to avoid such tie-breaking decisions, whether through prayer, patience, or seeking to persuade, but not in a heavy-handed, manipulative way.

Plus, when a married couple needs to make a decision together, a husband is utterly reliant on his wife to make good ones. God designed him to rely on her help, competence, and wisdom, as I mentioned in the definition above. Why did Adam need a helper? Perhaps because no man is competent in everything, even an unfallen man. Perhaps because he could only do so much work alone. Perhaps because there was no way to multiply without her. Yet no matter the explanation, Adam needed her help. Furthermore, if you've ever hired someone to help you, you know you want the most skilled and competent person possible. Likewise, Adam needed Eve's competence, skill, and strength. So does every husband.

Every woman has a resumé of experiences and talents. Marital oneness happens as the man studies his wife's resumé of gifts and works to make the most of every item on that resumé. He needs to be a good steward of the wife God has given him, and to encourage her to be a good steward of her gifts, all for the sake of getting more dominion work done and bringing glory to God. A good husband should want to see his wife grow and maximize her strengths. If she's good at organizing or writing or handling money or starting a business that sells linen sashes, like the wife in Proverbs 31 (see vv. 18, 24), he should look for ways to help her make the most of those gifts for the benefit of the home, the marriage, Christ's kingdom, and their shared work of dominion.

Husbands should especially seek the wisdom of their wives. I think this is one lesson we can draw from Proverbs. Chapter 7 of Proverbs describes the woman that a man should avoid: the adulteress. Chapter 8 follows up with the call to heed wisdom, and wisdom is personified as a woman who beckons us to hear her. Chapter 9 continues in the same vein, only now two women call to us: both Lady Wisdom and Lady Folly. We will heed one or the other. Multiple times, Proverbs warns against the "quarrelsome wife" (19:13; 21:9; 25:24; 27:15), yet a "prudent wife" is a gift from the Lord (19:14). The entire book of Proverbs then concludes with a picture of another Lady Wisdom, only now she's not a literary device but an actual woman—the excellent wife who fears the Lord (31:10–31). Not all women are wise, but a prudent man seeks a wise wife and then listens to her, knowing that spurning her wisdom makes him the fool who chooses ruin.

In a fallen world, the fallen tendency is for husbands and wives to compete, like two chess players looking to leverage every piece they have against the other. Yet Scripture calls both to renounce using whatever gifts, strengths, or advantages they have to serve themselves and to embrace serving the other. Yet they both do so from their respective positions. One aspect of the man's position might then be likened to Captain Jean-Luc Picard on the Starship Enterprise. The crew would spend an engaging minute discussing which planet to visit next. Then a consensus would be reached, and he would pronounce, "Make it so." This means the buck stops with the man. He bears the greater burden and must pay the greater cost for every sin or error. Again and again the Bible stresses that the authority figure bears the heavier judgment (James 3:1; Heb. 13:17), and God warns the husband that he will turn his back on him if he does not live with his wife "in an understanding way" (1 Pet. 3:7).

That means, when I survey the messes left behind in my house by my children, my spouse, and myself—the dirty dishes in the sink, the hurt feelings at the dinner table, the broken relationship upstairs, the unaddressed sin in the basement—I have to acknowledge that the first person in my family whom God will address on the day of judgment is me. "Why did you ignore this problem with your wife? Why didn't you set better patterns by opening my word around the dinner table? Why didn't you give up that stupid show and spend more time with the struggling teenager? I left you in charge! This is on you, son." Then he will turn to my wife and my daughters and say, "Yes, you, too, are culpable for your part. You knew my commandments and neglected them. You're not unthinking robots, but image-bearers with your own agency. Yet I recognize your leader helped lead you into such-and-such sin. He made it harder. Your culpability is therefore lessened." God, in other words, will include every factor and variable on his scales of justice, and one very heavy object is the husband and father's greater responsibility.

Why Does God Give Authority to Husbands?

Throughout this chapter I have hid the ultimate purpose of marriage and a husband's authority behind a curtain, like the Old Testament does, but hoping that its shape would poke through: the previous and higher purpose of marriage and a husband's authority is to teach a theology lesson about Christ and the church.

I say "previous" because God didn't design marriage and then, after that, design to send Christ to save a people, and then realize he could use the first to teach us about the second. Rather, God decided to send his Son into the world to save a people. Then he designed marriage to picture this previous and higher truth. He wanted a common-grace sign embedded in the DNA of creation itself so that people from every tribe, tongue, and nation could see it.

How do we unpack this idea of a husband's headship? We look to Christ and the church: "The head of every man is Christ, the head of a wife is her husband, and the head of Christ is God" (1 Cor. 11:3). How should a man exercise his headship? By following the example of Christ and the church:

> Husbands, love your wives, as Christ loved the church and gave himself up for her, that he might sanctify her, having cleansed her by the washing of water with the word, so that he might present the church to himself in splendor, without spot or wrinkle or any such thing, that she might be holy and without blemish. (Eph. 5:25–27)

Notice, there's something pastoral in a husband's role, as he should continually point his wife to the word and the gospel of God. God didn't give husbands authority in order to insist on their own desires, but to point toward Christ's desires, as revealed in the Bible.

To be sure, husbands have often cloaked their selfishness by pointing to a Bible passage which seems to give them what they want. But the misuse of Scripture doesn't negate its proper use. As I said in chapter 2, Satan can use the Bible, too. A wise woman, therefore, has no choice but to learn how to read the Bible on her own and through the instruction of godly elders in a healthy church. Otherwise, how else will she challenge her husband's misuses of Scripture? Finally, of course, a woman should only follow her husband because she follows Christ.

Yet a man who loves his wife as he should prepares her, in a sense, for the coming of Christ, her perfect and all-sufficient Savior. A wife should be able to watch her husband in order to learn what Jesus's love and authority are like. It's as if, when Jesus shows up, she'll more easily recognize him because she's been watching her husband imitate Christ's patterns for years.

Husbands exist, in short, to show the world that Jesus Christ loves his people, the church, with a perfect, all-affectionate, and self-sacrificing love. The office of husband doesn't exist for its own sake but to point toward a higher, more ultimate reality—Christ's love for the church. Christ's love for the church is *not* the symbol that points to the reality of being a husband. Being a husband is the symbol that points to the reality of Christ.

What Are the Limits of a Husband's Authority?

Several nights before I got married, I asked my pastor for any final words of advice before I got married. He stopped, looked at me straight on, and said soberly, "Jonathan, you will be God's number one picture of his authority in her life. Never use your authority to harm her, but only to be a blessing."

The easiest way to summarize the limit on a husband's authority is the word sin. He cannot ask his wife to sin, nor should he sin against her, whether in the things he does or the things he leaves undone. He can sin in his heart with its desires. He can sin with his words and his hands. He sins anytime he uses his body or words to hurt or to threaten. He can sin in what he asks her to do or not do. He can sin in how he loves or fails to love her. He can sin by failing to protect or provide for her. He sins anytime he glances outside the marital covenant for selfish pleasure, but also when he seeks to use his wife's body for selfish pleasure—to serve "me" instead of "her" and "us." He sins whenever he puts his own interests before hers and whenever he fails to give himself up for her: "Husbands, love your wives, as Christ loved the church and gave himself up for her" (Eph. 5:25). For all these things and more, a man will be judged.

A husband's authority is a jurisdictionally broad authority because it pertains to the couple's shared dominion. Yet it should be an authority that rests very lightly on her. As I've said already, she should feel its weight from her engaging with the Lord more than from him.

I remember a professor of counseling in seminary teaching our class that the more common sin among husbands was passivity or absence or abdication. Then, when he's been passive for a long time, and something his wife does frustrates him, he blows up and errs in the direction of violence. Abusive men, he said, often combine long seasons of passivity and neglect with brief episodes of rage and violence. They console themselves by thinking they're better than they are because of the long seasons of "peace." But it's not really peace. It's selfish neglect. Living with such a man, I heard someone else say, is like living on the side of a volcano. It does not erupt very often, but you live in perpetual fear that it might. You never really rest.

The solution to abusive authority, in a broad sense, is partly a matter of teaching husbands their limits. It is to say, you have authority of counsel, not command, meaning you have no place to discipline or act punitively. Yet the other part is to teach husbands what their authority is for: to bless, strengthen, and cause a wife to flourish, as I've labored to explain throughout this book, especially in chapters 1, 3, and 6 to 10.

On the flip side, I've known men who let their wives dominate them. They feared their wives more than they feared God. They let themselves be emasculated. Eventually, their wives stopped respecting them and divorced them. Looking back, we can say that such women received what they wanted: control. But they tore down their houses in the process (Prov. 14:1). They undermined the very gift God had given them to do them good. In the end, these women are hardly happy. Nor do they grow in beauty. God will have words of judgment for them. But he will also share such words with their husbands.

How a Husband Gets to Work

Let me conclude with a word of exhortation to husbands. Husbands, think one more time of Paul's command to love your wife

> as Christ loved the church and gave himself up for her, that he might sanctify her, having cleansed her by the washing of water with the word, so that he might present the church to himself in splendor, without spot or wrinkle or any such thing, that she might be holy and without blemish. (Eph. 5:25–27)

Brother husband, you're not your wife's sinless, all-wise redeemer. She has one: Christ. Yet Christ died to save the church and to make the church holy before the Father. That was his aim and ambition. Likewise, helping your wife to become holy and one with you must be your uppermost aim and ambition in marriage.

In other words, brother, when you wake up in a funk, or get to the end of a long day and you're exhausted, or sit and watch her do that thing that annoys you, or she fails to meet your expectations about something, or she spends too much money, or when the well of romantic feelings seems to run a little dry, or even when she fails you in more dramatic ways, you do not sit back and sulk and say, "I'm not satisfied. I'm not happy. I'm not fulfilled." No, these things are what you expect because God intends you to be the one who loves *right there* in her sin and folly and (at times) spiritual ugliness in order to love her toward the working out of her redemption. That's your job. That's your purpose in her life. When you said, "I do," you said "I do" to actively preparing her for her coming Redeemer by showing her what he will look like. Put everything else—all the youthful stuff—out of your head. That's what you signed up for.

How can you do this? Primarily by remembering the redemptive love with which Christ has loved you. Think of how sinful, foolish, and spiritually ugly you were before God saved you. But "while we were still sinners, Christ died for us" (Rom. 5:8). While we were opposing him to his face, he went to the cross and paid the penalty for all those who would ever repent and believe. And he reconciled you to the Father when you repented of your sins and believed. Now you are justified! You are no longer enslaved with proving yourself in front of your wife. You don't have to compete. No!

You are done with the old you. The born-again you is now free to love God and your wife entirely. That means . . .

- You take the initiative in ending arguments by choosing gracious (if need be, apologetic) words. You have nothing left to prove. You are done with self-justification because you are justified in Christ!
- You take the initiative in spiritual leadership in the home by "having cleansed her by the washing of water with the word" (Eph. 5:26).
- You don't have to require perfection of her today. You're playing the long game. The question is not, can you get her to be a perfect wife today. The question is, can you help her to look more like Jesus over the next fifty years by acting like Jesus yourself.
- Even when she is behaving toward you in some way that is frustrating, and perhaps sinful, you take the initiative in exemplifying the patience and forgiveness of Christ. That is how Christ has loved you.
- She is your number one priority, more than friends, work, parents, career aspirations, hobbies. Christ didn't lay his life down for anyone else—only the church.
- You can never, ever use your authority in any way to hurt or abuse her. For Christ has never abused you.

Love her more than your professional ambitions, your cherished dreams, your adolescent expectations of marriage, your strongly held convictions about who should do what with the toilet seat or how an onion should be cut or who wronged whom first in that last argument. Don't be a child who says, "She just needs to understand that I'm this way," or, "If she loves me, she'll respect how important this is to me." No, love her as your own body, says Paul. She is bone of your bone and flesh of your flesh, says Adam. You're taking her and who God made her to be into your own identity. (For what it's worth, that's why I like the tradition of the woman taking the man's last name.)

Brother, you are to lead in your home, and you lead by being the first to die to your own desires, not simply so that your wife's desires might therefore lead, but so that God's desires would.

13

The Parent (Command)

Covenantal Authorization: Adamic (Common) Covenant

*Be fruitful and multiply and fill the earth and subdue it, and have
dominion over the fish of the sea and over the birds of the heavens
and over every living thing that moves on the earth. (Gen. 1:28)*

Other Elucidating Biblical Texts

*When God created man, he made him in the
likeness of God. . . . When Adam had lived 130
years, he fathered a son in his own likeness, after
his image, and named him Seth. (Gen. 5:1b, 3)*

*You shall love the Lord your God with all your
heart and with all your soul and with all your might.
. . . You shall teach [these words] to your children,
talking of them when you are sitting in your house,
and when you are walking by the way, and when you
lie down, and when you rise. (see Deut. 6:5, 7)*

*. . . he commanded our fathers to teach to their children,
that the next generation might know them, the children yet
unborn, and arise and tell them to their children, so that
they should set their hope in God and not forget the works
of God, but keep his commandments. (Ps. 78:5–7)*

*Hear, my son, your father's instruction, and forsake
not your mother's teaching. (Prov. 1:8)*

*For this reason I bow my knees before the Father, from whom
every family in heaven and on earth is named. (Eph. 3:14–15)*

Children, obey your parents in the Lord. . . . "that it may go
well with you and that you may live long in the land." Fathers,
do not provoke your children to anger, but bring them up in
the discipline and instruction of the Lord. (Eph. 6:1, 3–4)

Do not rebuke an older man but encourage him as you would
a father, younger men as brothers, older women as mothers,
younger women as sisters, in all purity. (1 Tim. 5:1–2)

Job Description

To train a child in wisdom (fear of the Lord and skill for living) for fulfilling the dominion mandate and walking in God's ways.

———

WHEN SHE WAS EIGHT YEARS OLD, I killed my youngest daughter's
beloved bunny.

My wife and I were actually out of the country when the bunny, named
"Frodo," died. We learned about Frodo's untimely passing from my mother,
who texted us the news. My daughter, who would cuddle with Frodo for
hours and feed him baby carrots so that the hair around his mouth turned
orange; who carried him with one arm around the house, his bottom feet
dangling down like a rag doll; who diligently cleaned his hutch every other
day and brought him out every time a friend came to the house; she, this
sweet, tender little girl, found the one-and-a-half-year-old Holland Lop
bunny stiff in his cage early that Sunday morning.

Obviously, I didn't mean to kill Frodo. But his hutch was in our basement,
and so the room often smelled like rabbit waste. Therefore, that Saturday
morning, before boarding a plane, I moved the bunny's hutch outside. My
wife warned me to wait until the weather was warmer. The woman who
helped us buy Frodo said that dramatic temperature transitions could be
fatal. My daughter cried when I ignored my wife. She said she was afraid I
was going to kill the bunny. But I reasoned that it was only a twenty-degree
temperature change, and that Frodo would be fine, and that everyone was
being paranoid. As if I knew anything about bunnies.

There's really no point to this story other than it seems honest to tell you
about an abysmal parenting "fail" before sharing all my wisdom on parental

authority. I felt terrible, of course. Still do, a little bit. My daughter quickly forgave me. In fact, she felt bad that I felt bad, which made me feel worse.

Or maybe the point is this: A child's vulnerability to us as parents is profound. I made a flippant, arrogant, and thoughtless choice about my daughter's bunny, even spurning her tears, and she was helpless to do anything about it.

It's a tiny illustration, but the bigger picture is, we can do our children great good or great harm, perhaps more than anyone. We can even destroy them, whether in the womb or in infancy, and they will register no objection, at least not very loudly.

Indeed, when you consider the dramatic power differential between parent and infant or unborn child, it's hard to imagine a more terrible abuse of power than abortion or infanticide. One of our contemporary world's most terrible ironies is that the feminists who claim to represent the oppressed also scream the loudest for the destruction of the weakest.

Of all the authorities we might possess over another human being, parental authority might be the most powerful, both in our ability to shape a person for good and in our ability to destroy them. On the dark side, I believe psychologist Diane Langberg was correct to say, "Contrary to popular belief, children are not resilient, a word which simply means they can return to their original state. They do not 'bounce back' from abuse."[1] God's grace can surely override abuse, but the imprint of child abuse is real.

On the positive side, good parental authority is the very thing God uses to raise up flourishing, dominion-taking, life-creating human beings who display his own image. And it points to the heavenly Father above.

What Is a Parent's Authority?

The first form of authority most humans encounter personally is parental. On the pages of the Bible it is implicit within the dominion mandate: "Be fruitful and multiply and fill the earth and subdue it, and have dominion." Fulfilling this command, clearly, involves bearing children, raising them, and teaching them to go and do the same. The heart of parental authority, then, is training a child to fulfill God's dominion mandate.

---

1 https://twitter.com/DianeLangberg/status/1580951887083614208?s=20&t=C0A9l_jLO_ZB8zI 5lOjYXg.

Parental authority is the most godlike of all forms of authority. It's the creation activity in which we image him most precisely and fully. It's godlike *in its structure*: Seth was in Adam's image and likeness, even as Adam was in God's image and likeness (see Gen. 5, above).

Parental authority is godlike *in what it does*: it authors life where none existed. Through their conjugal union, the couple essentially creates something out of nothing. Then the early years and especially months of a child's life require a parent to do little more than give and give and give. The newborn contributes nothing to her own survival. The parents must do it all, reminiscent of the Lord who himself is not served by human hands, as if he needed anything, but gives us life and breath and everything (see Acts 17:25).

Parental authority is godlike *in its reach*, touching on the whole range of human existence: from teaching a child to speak, wipe himself, and memorize math facts to helping him love, think, argue, marry, and worship. It also covers the gamut from provision and protection to instruction and correction.

Parental authority is godlike *in its objective*: to teach children to hope in the Lord and obey his commandments (see Ps. 78:5–7 above).

Parental authority works by training, instructing, modeling, correcting, discipling, encouraging. It takes a rough rock and chisels and shapes it until a fully formed human being emerges. It raises a child up into mature adulthood. And in all of that, parental authority enables civilization to continue.

Hannah Arendt, in an essay on authority, observed that it's in parenting "where authority in the widest sense has always been accepted as a natural necessity, obviously required as much by natural needs, the helplessness of a child, as by political necessity, the continuity of an established civilization which can be assured only if those who are newcomers by birth are guided through a pre-established world into which they are born as strangers."[2]

One sign of a civilization in decline is that it diminishes, even despises, the significance of childmaking and rearing. People delay having children or don't have them at all. Nations drop below their "replacement rate"—the rate necessary for maintaining their population. The young woman who says

2   Hannah Arendt, "What Is Authority?", in *The Portable Hannah Arendt* (New York: Penguin Classics, 2003), 463.

she wants to get married and have children is regarded as odd, certainly if it would interfere with career plans.

I remember my mother once saying to me as a high schooler, "I may never have built a company, or managed a stock portfolio, or worked in a law firm. But I did help to create and then shape four amazing human beings." There's no rational basis for saying that any of these other endeavors should be counted as better, freer, or more "realized" than shaping a human being. Yet that's the going assumption. Might we be "darkened" in our understanding (Eph. 4:18)?

A second and related sign of a civilization in decline is that parents don't know how to exercise authority in their children's lives. They don't require obedience in a clear, firm, and life-giving fashion. Either those parents have been taught that all authority is bad and that they should honor and respect their children's desires, impulses, and "true selves." Or they've never been trained to use authority well, because their own parents didn't model it well. As such, for one reason or another, these parents veer back and forth between abdication and anger, passivity and abuse. The children, meanwhile, learn how to work the angles for getting what they want. They never learn how to submit to others or to the group. They don't develop the character muscles. Instead, they become entitled individualists who know how to manipulate the system or, failing that, to take what they want by force. And a nation of such individuals is no happy place.

You might think back to the illustration I used in the introduction of this book of the couple in the Washington, DC, coffee shop with the unruly toddler. They didn't know how to discipline or require obedience. Instead, these parents knew only how to affirm and negotiate. Over years, this kind of uncritical affirmation and negotiation weakens children. It undermines their ability to control themselves and be good neighbors. To affirm a piece of unchiseled rock is to leave it unchiseled. The beautiful statue never emerges.

Not only that, children who learn to obey are happier. If you've ever served in the three-to-five-year-olds class at church, you can probably identify with John Piper's warning:

> Laissez-faire parenting does not produce gracious, humble children. It produces brats. They are neither fun to be around, nor happy themselves. They are demanding and insolent. Their "freedom" is not a blessing to

them or others. They are free the way a boat without a rudder is free. They are the victims of their whims. Sooner or later, these whims will be crossed. That spells misery.[3]

In fact, Piper's word "brats" is probably not strong enough. Failing to discipline and draw boundaries for children creates narcissists—kids centered on themselves and ruled by their feelings. Boundaries teach a child, "You're not the center of the universe. You must relinquish some of your desires, conform yourself to the wisdom and structures of the world around you, and consider other people." Not only that, undisciplined children never learn the humility of accepting fences and disappointments. When college and adulthood then impose those boundaries—a failing grade, an employer's reprimand, even encountering people with different political perspectives—they claim to be "triggered" and regard themselves as victims. Sociologists in turn write books criticizing the theories that contribute to a victim mentality. Yet the larger problem is the previous generation's failure to draw boundaries and discipline their children.

God did not design children to rule, but to learn how to rule through discipline and discipleship. When well-meaning but naïve parents grant their children such rule too early, those children fail to reach their fullest potential and are ultimately miserable.

What Kind of Authority?

Other forms of authority take elements of parental authority and continue it. A civil government continues the work of correction when necessary. Managerial authority continues the work of apprenticeship and employment. Churches and elders, too, undertake the work of instruction and discipling toward maturity, albeit now on the landscape of new creation.

Given the breadth and depth of parental authority, then, it's difficult to think of some type of authority that parents don't exercise at one point or another. Sometimes counsel, sometimes command. Sometimes coercive, sometimes declarative. A parent needs every tool a toolbelt might hold.

---

3 John Piper, "Parents, Require Obedience of Your Children," October 29, 2013. Accessed February 14, 2023: https://www.desiringgod.org/articles/parents-require-obedience-of-your-children.

"The rod and reproof give wisdom, but a child left to himself brings shame to his mother" (Prov. 29:15).

Yet if a husband's authority centers on cultivating oneness, and a government's authority centers on cultivating justice (next chapter), a parent's authority centers on wisdom, both exercising it and teaching it.

What is wisdom? It is a posture and a skill. First, it is the posture of fearing the Lord. He's the game-designer, rule-maker, and referee in the game of life. Second, it's the skill of knowing how to play that game. That is, wisdom is the skill of living in God's created but fallen world in a way that yields justice, peace, and flourishing. Wisdom studies creation, in both its glory and its brokenness, and knows how things work, especially people. We could also include mathematics, science, engineering, facility in language, grammar, and all the topics of school under its umbrella. Solomon's possession of wisdom, it would seem, included such knowledge. Yet wisdom then puts this knowledge to work in the fear of God. It counts all these classroom topics as belonging to God and as ways of characterizing his handiwork. It pays especial attention, furthermore, to people and how they work, both in their created beauty and in their fallen propensities.

Wisdom is learned in Sunday school class but also on Mom's piano bench and in Dad's workshop. It's learned by being apprenticed in all the skills of life that are necessary for fulfilling the call to God-imaging dominion—both the theological and the practical, so that one might feed on both the bread of heaven and the bread of earth.

The Bible's book dedicated to parenting, of course, is also its book dedicated to wisdom: "Hear, my son, your father's instruction, and forsake not your mother's teaching," begins Proverbs (Prov. 1:8). Wisdom's words are life, the father says over and over. And rejecting them is death. And so, over and over, Proverbs exhorts the son to hear his father and mother's words of wisdom, which are more precious than gold or jewels.

Interestingly, Proverbs also alludes to a parent's need for wisdom in parenting, since "A foolish son is a grief to his father and bitterness to her who bore him" (17:25). Sometimes a parent should not answer a fool in his folly, lest the parent become like him (26:4). Sometimes a parent *should* answer, lest the fool be wise in his own eyes (26:5). As any parent will tell you, knowing when to correct and discipline and when to stay silent requires tremendous wisdom. After all, "A rebuke goes deeper into a man of understanding than a hundred blows into a fool" (17:10).

One of the more helpful pieces of parenting counsel I've ever received came from my good friend Matt, who has five children. "When children are little," he said, "You're out in front of them." He held out his hands, palms down, and extended one hand out in front of the other. "When they move into their teenage years, you slowly pull back alongside them." Here he pulled that hand that was out front to be side by side with the other hand. "You're not lecturing them as much as you're asking them questions and helping them to think. You're asking them to consider the end of their actions." Then he concluded: "Finally, when you launch them into the world, you pull back behind them and root them on." He moved the hand that was out front now to the back.

That's the transition I described in the previous chapter, where a parent moves from an authority of command, which disciplines, to an authority of counsel, which does less and less. That transition signifies the person growing up, maturing, becoming an independent person. All this, no doubt, takes much wisdom.

Why Does God Give Parents Authority?

As with a husband's authority, parental authority serves an immediate purpose as well as an ultimate purpose.

Immediately, a husband's authority serves to cultivate oneness. Ultimately, his authority points to Christ's love for the church.

Immediately, parental authority serves the purpose of training up a child in the way he should go. Ultimately, it points to the Father in heaven as well as the fellowship of the church. Notice first the Ephesians 3 text above. It tells us our earthly fathers are named after the heavenly Father. They should teach us what he's like.

By God's grace, my own father did that in so many ways. Mostly, I think of my earthly father's forgiving, merciful, and contra-conditional love (contrary to what I deserved). I always felt it as a child and never doubted it. To this day, I never struggle with viewing God as forgiving and contra-conditionally loving toward me. I know friends who struggle to believe this about God. I don't, and I ascribe that particular confidence to God's work through my father.

Our earthly families and parents also point us to the fellowship of the church. Notice the 1 Timothy 5 passage above. God has embedded in creation these types or patterns that teach what he intends for our new-creation fellowship in the church. The apostle Paul is saying to you, "Do you know the reverence that you show toward your father, and the honor you show toward your mother? Good, now treat old men and women in the church like that. Also, do you know how you identify as a family member, and you're always loyal to them, even when you're mad? Good, now do that with the church, but even more so, because these relationships will last for eternity."

The typological connection between earthly fathers and the heavenly Father, as well as between our biological families and our church family, means that churches should care about earthly fathers and earthly families. Since bad fathers and families can make it harder for people to believe in God, we want to help fathers and families to be healthy. Also, people who have learned to enjoy their mothers and fathers, sisters and brothers at home, just might have an easier time loving people at church.

No doubt, God shows special compassion for the orphan, the abandoned, and the child whose brothers despise him. Think of Joseph, thrown into the pit. If your home is broken, despair not! God delights to show his power precisely in such circumstances. Still, in the ordinary course of business, healthy families teach the good lessons we all need in order to know what a healthy church might look like.

What Are the Limits of a Parent's Authority?

As suggested above, the limits of a parent's authority adjust with the child's age. The nature of discipline and correction moves from heavy with the three-year-old to lighter with a thirteen-year-old. But, generally speaking, we can think of two limits. One, a parent should always remember that he or she is not God. Two, a parent should remember that he or she is not the child, and the child's life is finally his or her own.

Both limits are implicit in Paul's instruction, "Fathers, do not provoke your children to anger, but bring them up in the discipline and instruction of the Lord" (Eph. 6:4). First, the child belongs to the Lord, not ultimately to the parent. It's the Lord's instruction that the child needs. My wife and I, therefore, must continually remember that we will give an account to the

Lord for how we love, lead, and discipline our daughters. Our authority is under his authority and represents it.

Second, each daughter (or son) finally belongs to herself and to God, not to us. It's strangely easy to overlook this when they're little. They're so dependent on you. But as they get older you discover—as awkward as it is to say—they're their own persons. You must learn to honor them as their own persons. They possess independent integrity as God-imagers. They're answerable to *his* calling and purposes for their lives, not *yours*. Your task is to teach them to fear God and to walk in his ways by imparting whatever wisdom and skill they are willing to receive. Yet finally they must decide whether to receive it or not.

I can think of one word that helps us to understand parenting and its limits: decrescendo. If you can read music, you're familiar with that term. An elongated greater to lesser sign (>) across a measure of music tells you to decrease the volume as you play. So it is in parenting, as you move from age zero to eighteen or so. You start with high control and heavy input, but the amount of control you assert gradually decreases over the years. Sometimes it gets louder again, like at puberty. But overall the trajectory moves toward silence and loss of control. If you've done it well, and if the child has wisely absorbed your instruction, she internalizes your control, which is to say, your instruction. The discipline belongs to her and her nature now. You've passed it along. And you leave her to herself and her Lord.

How a Parent Gets to Work

Step one of exercising authority in your children's lives is to fear the Lord and get wisdom yourself. God wants you to use your authority, to be a parent, to teach and administer discipline. Yet he wants you to use it compassionately and studiously, always calibrating your corrections and instructions for their weaker frames.

Step two is to use that authority for their good, never for your own selfish convenience or gain. You are the trimmer of roses so that the rose might grow, the braces on the teeth so the teeth might be straight, the regimen of exercise so the athlete runs fast, the word of love so the child might smile. That means you draw lines. You say no. You demonstrate resolve. You administer discipline. You let them feel the consequences and the loss of things they want. Yet you also look for ways to say yes. To bless. To help them experience wonder. You pack their brains with good things. You encourage. You give and give and give, as I've said God does with us.

All this is hard work and often means depriving yourself of what you want—an evening off, a restful Saturday morning, the momentary gratification of expressing your impatience, the joy of giving them what they're asking for but no longer deserve because of a temper tantrum. Yet you keep your eyes fixed on the thirty-year time horizon, not the thirty-minute one, which is where their eyes go.

In the first few years of my girls' lives, I realized that parenting caused me to feel more incompetent than anything else I had ever done. I did well at school, do well at work, receive encouragement at church, perhaps less so on most athletic fields, find that friendships are encouraging. But parenting? I discovered quickly that that made me feel like a failure almost daily. Of the top three regrets I have in life, two of them involve my parenting.

I assume God intends for us to discover our weakness and lack of control through parenting. Really, that's what the decrescendo teaches. It's not just that you deliberately pull back on how much authority you assert; it's pulled back *for* you. My mother always said she did her best parenting flat on her face in prayer. And there's no doubt in my mind that any good in me today is the result less of what my mother said to me and more what she said to her Lord.

Since I've already emphasized the biblically central role of imparting wisdom in parenting, let me conclude with a brief word on parental love and its significance. On the one hand, I may not need to say anything about love because it's the one thing that most parents naturally possess for their children. God hardwires it into us, I believe, so that we might learn something about his love for us. Therefore, telling you to love your children is easy to do, because I believe you want to—really, really want to. Praise God. Still, as parents we don't always do a good job of cultivating that love, or of making sure our children feel loved. And I do think that loving our children might be the most important thing of all in our parenting, even more than helping them to understand all mysteries and knowledge and faith (see 1 Cor. 13:1–3).

Two passages come to mind. First, think of God beholding all that he had just created and saying, "It is very good" (see Gen. 1:31). This is God in creation. He loved creation. Second, I think of the divine Father at Jesus's baptism, saying, "This is my beloved Son" (Matt. 3:17). The Father loved the Son, and later Jesus refers to the love that the Father had for him before the world began (John 17:24).

Likewise, I think one of our most important jobs as our children's authority is to love and affirm them as God made them. They don't need to be smarter than they are, or prettier than they are, or faster than they are. They need to be what they are, because what God made is good, very good, and we love it. And we should let them know every day that we love it. I've emphasized the importance of boundaries and correction in this chapter. Yet too much correction can undermine a child. Too much correction or the wrong manner of correction, I heard someone say, won't cause your children to love you less, but to despise themselves more. I've seen this happen.

It's not enough to spend time with our children. We need to *enjoy* spending time with them, and to let them see that we enjoy it. Kids know the difference. We enjoy the things we love. They do, too. So, do you love them? Then you'll enjoy them. And if you don't, pray about it, confess it, and ask God to grow your heart.

Now, none of us does this all the time. Sometimes your children bore you. Maybe they annoy you. Maybe they drive you crazy. And you have other things to do. You don't love them by making them the center of your permanent attention and interest. These natural little narcissists need to learn that the universe doesn't center around them either. In other words, I'm not talking about any one day or moment. I'm talking about your general posture toward them. If I asked them, would they say, "My dad, my mom, enjoy being with me." I don't want there to be any doubt about this in their minds, because what God created is good.

Yet we also love them most by pointing them to the Beloved Son. In fact, we don't love them at all unless we love them with respect to Christ. Our love is no match for his, and they need his love more than ours. The trouble, as you know, is that from birth they have opposed him. We could talk all day about how what God created is good, but if we don't also acknowledge their hearts of rebellion, our talk is sentimentalism. They are under God's good and just wrath, and we love them by telling them so. It's not love to downplay, dismiss, or deny the justice of God. It's not love to recreate the universe in our own image, saying things like, "I just can't imagine that a loving God would ever . . ." Let God define love for himself, and let his word tells us that his love is holy and just. Over and over, Jesus tells us not to claim that we love God if we don't keep his commandments (John 14:15, 21; 15:10).

The good news is that the Beloved Son has made a way of pardon, so that your children can be reconciled to God. That means, they can be loved by God with the same love that God loves the Beloved Son (John 17:26). Yet they must repent and believe and follow after Christ.

Remind your children of these things every day. Remind them when you discipline them. Remind them when you surprise them with grace and mercy. Remind them when you're proud of them and when they break your heart. There's nothing greater, nothing better, than the love of Christ. Reminding your children of this is your number one job, because the fear of the Lord is the beginning of wisdom, and the fear of the Lord begins with repentance and faith. Indeed, pointing your children to Christ in word and deed, finally, is how you will love your children best.

14

The Government (Command)

Covenantal Authorization: Noahic (Common) Covenant

*Be fruitful and multiply and fill the earth. . . . And for your
lifeblood I will require a reckoning: from every beast I will
require it and from man. From his fellow man I will require
a reckoning for the life of man. Whoever sheds the blood
of man, by man shall his blood be shed, for God made man
in his own image. . . . be fruitful and multiply, increase
greatly on the earth and multiply in it. (Gen. 9:1, 5–6, 7)*

Other Elucidating Biblical Texts

*And all Israel heard of the judgment that the king had rendered,
and they stood in awe of the king, because they perceived that
the wisdom of God was in him to do justice. (1 Kings 3:28)*

*By [wisdom] kings reign, and rulers decree what is just; by [wisdom]
princes rule, and nobles, all who govern justly. (Prov. 8:15–16)*

*By justice a king builds up the land, but he who
exacts gifts tears it down. (Prov. 29:4)*

*Open your mouth for the mute, for the rights of all who
are destitute. Open your mouth, judge righteously, defend
the rights of the poor and needy. (Prov. 31:8–9)*

*And he made from one man every nation of mankind
to live on all the face of the earth, having determined
allotted periods and the boundaries of their dwelling
place, that they should seek God, and perhaps feel their
way toward him and find him. (Acts 17:26–27)*

For rulers are not a terror to good conduct, but to bad.
Would you have no fear of the one who is in authority?
Then do what is good, and you will receive his approval, for
he is God's servant for your good. But if you do wrong, be
afraid, for he does not bear the sword in vain. For he is the
servant of God, an avenger who carries out God's wrath on
the wrongdoer. (Rom. 13:3–4; see also 1 Pet. 2:13–17)

I urge that supplications, prayers, intercessions, and thanksgivings
be made for all people, for kings and all who are in high
positions, that we may lead a peaceful and quiet life, godly
and dignified in every way. This is good, and it is pleasing in
the sight of God our Savior, who desires all people to be saved
and to come to the knowledge of the truth. (1 Tim. 2:1–4)

Job Description

To administer the justice requisite for protecting human life, secure the conditions necessary for fulfilling the dominion mandate, and provide a platform for God's people to declare God's perfect judgment and salvation.

———

SOME GOVERNMENTS ARE BETTER, and some are worse. So says the Bible. The Pharaoh of Joseph's day was better; the Pharaoh of Moses's day was worse.

Governments are God's servants, one passage tells us (Rom. 13:1–7). Yet they're also imposters, says another, because they rage and take their stands against God and his messiah (Ps. 2:1–3).

So, what makes a good government good? A good government provides a basic protective justice for all its citizens, including God's people, whether it recognizes them as God's people or not. (Think of Cyrus sending the Jews back from exile.) That means Christians should care about good government both for their neighbor's sake and for the church's sake.

With the other offices we're discussing in part IV, the focus is on your individual authority—as with a husband, a parent, a manager, or an elder. Yet government and church are a little different, because we're thinking about exercising authority in a group where we may or may not have much influence and where our individual voice may or may not reflect the group voice. This is especially true of the government. The "government" might be one person—the king. Or it might entail "We the people" of the nation. Government is even more difficult because we must deal with the church-world relationship, and Christians disagree about the nature of that relationship. Consider three models. Someone could say that Christians . . .

(1) should seek to enforce Christianity through the government;
(2) should seek to enforce aspects of Christianity through the government, namely, a number of its moral standards;
(3) should not seek to enforce Christianity through the government at all, but should express their faith entirely in the private sphere.

I assume that options (1) and (3), as stated here, don't sit quite right with any reader. Yet people do lean toward one or the other. The (1)-leaning people feel the weight of God's lordship and judgment over all things, and they point to the Ten Commandments. The (3)-leaning recognize that we cannot force our faith on people, and they point to Jesus's instructions about rendering to Caesar what's Caesar's and to God what's God's (Matt. 22:21). Still, most of us, including myself, don't feel like we can move all the way to position (1) or position (3), but put ourselves somewhere in the middle.

Through the centuries, Christians in this middle lane have tried different ways to explain why we can open our Bibles and seek to impose with the sword a verse like "You shall not murder" on unbelievers, but not one like "Jesus is Lord." That's when they start talking about things like Augustine's two cities, or some version of Martin Luther's two kingdoms, or Reformed views on the spirituality of the church, or Baptist views on religious freedom, or even John Locke's distinction between the inner and outer person in his *Letter concerning Toleration*. Whether or not you're familiar with any of these specific viewpoints, where would you place yourself on the spectrum between (1) and (3)?

My goal in this chapter is to answer the questions about authority that we've been considering in part IV, in a way that leads to position (2) as related to governmental authority. This means that, contrary to position (1), I believe we should affirm the separation of church and state, or at least a version of it. Yet contrary to position (3), I don't believe we should affirm the separation of religion and politics. That prospect, I'll argue, is impossible. Yet all these additional complexities make this the longest and most dense chapter in the book. Buyer beware!

What Is the Civil Government's Authority?

In the first instance, governmental authority (this chapter) and managerial authority (next chapter) are necessary entailments of the dominion mandate that God gave to Adam and Eve ("be fruitful and multiply, fill the earth and subdue it"). They're a condition of expanding our presence on the planet with other people, so that we might live together in an orderly, predictable, and cooperative fashion. Even in an unfallen world, someone needs to decide whether we drive on the right side of the road or the left, and to supervise the construction of a skyscraper.

Yet governmental authority and managerial authority after the fall must also deal with sinful agents and the scarcity of resources. That means governmental authority, the focus of this chapter, must recognize that God does indeed command all human beings to fill the earth and subdue it, but also that these humans are now murdering each other (Gen. 4:8), stealing one another's provisions (Gen. 14:11), lying to their husbands and fathers (Gen. 27:13, 19), raping one another's daughters, and slaughtering entire cities in retaliation (Gen. 34).

For this reason, God introduces the authority to use coercive force. Nothing in the original dominion mandate says that one human being has the right to arbitrarily use force over another human being. The natural law doesn't say that either (I don't believe). After all, every human shares equally in creation in our God-assigned authority. Therefore, God must specially authorize the use of coercive force, which brings us to what we might call the "Great Commission" text for governmental authority on this side of the fall: Genesis 9:5–6. Just like Matthew 28 does for churches, Genesis 9:5–6 doesn't spell out everything a government will need to do, but it lays down a few basic constitutional principles.

Let's start with this phrase: "Whoever sheds the blood of man, by man shall his blood be shed, for God made man in his own image." You may not have spent a lot of time meditating on that verse, but it's worth pulling up a chair and staring at it for a moment. It packs quite a punch. First, it authorizes the use of coercive force in order to prosecute the taking of life. By implication it also authorizes a government to prevent the unjust taking of life. For instance, I'd say it gives a government moral permission to say, "Here's the speed limit," or "Commercial aircraft must meet these safety codes" (see Deut. 22:8), or even "Pay taxes so that we can build an army for our nation's protection" (see Luke 3:13; Rom. 13:7).

Second, this verse establishes a principle of due process: parity. The punishment must fit the crime. It's life for life, not life for stealing a horse, like the fifty-one recorded instances of people being hanged for horse stealing in early America, the last one in 1851.[1] The punishment should always fit the crime—"eye for eye, tooth for tooth," as a later passage puts it (Ex. 21:24). People are sometimes scandalized by this principle (called *lex talionis*), but keep in mind that, in the ancient world, this principle typically served to limit the otherwise unconstrained demands for vengeance. Think again of Jacob's sons massacring a city in retaliation for the rape of their sister Dinah (Gen. 34).

Not only that; under-punishing a crime risks devaluing the worth of the victim. It says the life that was murdered or the goods that were stolen weren't worth much, like offering you a stick of gum to compensate for your stolen diamond ring.

The affirmation of parity also implies that every governmental action requires a just measurement. "A just balance and scales are the Lord's; all the weights in the bag are his work. It is an abomination to kings to do evil, for the throne is established by righteousness" (Prov. 16:11–12). Practically, for instance, a government must not bribe or overtax its citizens for selfish gain (see Prov. 29:4 ESV mg.). Any tax requires a clear and just gauge that accords with government's basic life-protecting purposes.

Third, Genesis 9:6 affirms the value of every human life as made in God's image and therefore equally valuable. People of every color and creed, men and women, deserve to be treated as God-imagers and possessors of a basic political equality. Jim Crow laws that read "separate, but equal," pushing blacks to different drinking fountains, were unjust.

---

1 Matthew T. Martens, *Reforming Criminal Justice: A Christian Proposal* (Wheaton, IL: Crossway, 2023), 325.

Fourth, the verse subjects every human to its requirements, including governments themselves. Look again at the first word of verse 6: "whoever" wrongly sheds blood. The verse becomes a boomerang whenever governments use their authority unjustly. It indicts the murderous dictator and the racist town sheriff alike. No government can claim to be "above" its reach. It keeps governments and citizens alike accountable.

Fifth, this verse possesses a theological basis—"for God made man in his own image"—but it doesn't authorize us to enforce that basis. The trigger for action is harm to humans—"blood"—not harm to God. After all, how do you measure or establish parity for an offense against God, to say nothing of the fact that we cannot harm him? As such, the verse doesn't authorize us to prosecute crimes against God, like blasphemy or idolatry, if there is no quantifiable harm done to a human person. It leaves open a space for religious freedom, and that space is anything outside of the government's jurisdiction. On the flip side, however, the verse doesn't allow someone to claim "freedom of religion!" if their religion causes actual harm, like a Christian Scientist who wants to deny medical care to a child whose life is medically threatened.

As I said, there's a lot of punch packed into this one little passage which applies to all humanity, every son and daughter of Noah, and not just to God's special people. As you can see with several of the citations above, I'm reading this passage with later biblical texts in mind. And I'll cite more throughout this chapter.

There is one more thing to notice about verses 5 and 6 of Genesis 9: they are set inside a paragraph bookended with the command to "Be fruitful and multiply" (vv. 1, 7). What does that tell us? The authority to use coercive force facilitates the larger goal of enabling people to fulfill the dominion mandate.

Governments exist, then, to help secure the basic conditions necessary for fulfilling the dominion mandate. For starters, that means governments should protect the basic structures of marriage and the family, so that people can indeed "be fruitful and multiply." Governments should not redefine marriage to include homosexuals, because (i) governments don't have the authority to do so; (ii) they weaken real marriage by defining marriage around the feelings of the couple rather than their potential for fruitfulness; (iii) and the redefinition denies children the right to a mother or father. In a sense, they steal a mother or father away from a child. The children are victims.

One might envision many other factors that hinder the work of fruitfulness, dominion, and the basic God-imaging political equality required for fruitfulness and dominion. The oppression of ethnic minorities hinders it. So do entrenched cycles of poverty. That doesn't mean the government must ensure that every citizen possesses the same economic starting point. But I can imagine a Christian arguing that a basic economic safety net—enough to wake up with a roof over your head, eat, and get to work in the morning—serves the purposes of dominion. As King Lemuel's mother says to him, "Open your mouth for the mute, for the rights of all who are destitute. Open your mouth, judge righteously, defend the rights of the poor and needy" (Prov. 31:8–9; also, 29:14).

A Christian might also argue that facilitating the dominion mandate includes a good monetary policy. Such a policy provides both a stable currency and standardized interest rates. A stable currency protects everyone's wealth and livelihood, and standardized interest rates prevent usury and the exploitation of the poor (see Ex. 22:25; Prov. 22:7; 28:8; Matt. 25:27). Jesus himself affirmed that a coin printed with Caesar's image legitimately fell within Caesar's jurisdiction: "Render to Caesar what belongs to Caesar" (see Matt. 22:21).

Yet whether or not monetary policy or a welfare policy or any other policies we might think of are reasonable deductions to draw out of the relationship between Genesis 9:6 and the bookended verses 1 and 7 ("Be fruitful and multiply"), the Scriptural baseline is that God grants human beings the authority to form governments that protect our lives and promote the conditions necessary for fulfilling the dominion mandate. That's why Paul tells us to pray "for kings and all who are in high positions, that we may lead a peaceful and quiet life, godly and dignified in every way" (1 Tim. 2:2).

What Kind of Authority Is Governmental Authority?

Clearly, governmental authority is a coercive authority, and it's an authority of command, as defined in chapter 11. But it is also a divinely ordained means of justice. All people are made in God's image and therefore deserve righteous treatment. Government serves the ends of justice by protecting these God-imagers.

"By justice a king builds up the land," says Proverbs (29:4). King David's throne, therefore, existed for the sake of upholding justice: "So David reigned over all Israel. And David administered justice and equity [righteousness] to all his people" (2 Sam. 8:15).

What is justice in the Bible? People often define justice as giving people their due. That's not a bad definition. It gets us part of the way there. Yet I think we do slightly better by putting God's law front and center in our definition as well as by observing that the Hebrew word for "justice" is the noun form of the verb "to judge." Biblical justice, I'd say, is making judgments in accordance with God's standards of righteousness.

Think of Solomon standing in front of two prostitutes, both of whom claimed a baby was hers. Solomon's task in that moment was to render a righteous judgment—and so do justice. Gratefully, he did: "And all Israel heard of the judgment that the king had rendered, and they stood in awe of the king, because they perceived that the wisdom of God was in him to do justice" (1 Kings 3:28). Justice depends on a judgment, but that judgment needs a standard, a ruler or scale by which to measure the judgment. The right standard is the law of God's righteousness. Not surprisingly, the Bible says of God's own government, "Righteousness and justice are the foundation of your throne" (Ps. 89:14).

To translate this into an American setting, we can say that all three branches of government should do justice—render righteous judgments— each in its own way. The legislator should pass just laws. The executive branch should enforce just laws in a just way. And judges should uphold just laws and overturn unjust ones. In each case, their work of justice should not be defined by some other god's version of righteousness, but by God's definition of righteousness.

Many Westerners assume otherwise. Our nations are pluralistic, we reason. People believe in many different gods, from the big-G Gods of Christianity, Judaism, Islam, or Mormonism, to the little-g neo-pagan gods of sex, body worship, consumption, and identity politics. Therefore, Christians who lean toward position (3) at the beginning of this chapter say we need to create a public square and establish rules of justice that are neutral between people's competing gods. And we can do that by defining justice as "protecting people's rights."

That solution to societal pluralism is not entirely wrong. But it's like picking the fruit without attending to the root. Justice does include protecting people's rights. The trouble is, it's a society's reigning gods that will define which rights are right. Shall we affirm the right to an abortion, the right to same-sex marriage, the right to define our own gender as children apart from parental intervention?

It's true that justice entails protecting people's rights. I'd agree with those who argue that the fact that we are created in God's image is the foundation for human rights.[2] Returning to our meditation on Genesis 9:5–6, we might say that it grants us the right to life, the right to be treated by our government with equal dignity, the right to worship God free from coercion, the right to insist on a fair trial and due process, even the right to all the liberties requisite for fulfilling the dominion mandate. Still, we possess these rights not because they are inherent in us apart from God, but because God says they are right. Rights are right only when and where God says they're right. Right is the root of justice, rights are the fruit. Pay attention to the "s." And the government's job begins with what's right (see Rom. 13:3–4; 1 Pet. 2:14).

Group (3) and others will quickly reply, "But whose definition of 'right' shall we legislate? Which God or god's?" They ask the question as if anyone has ever abandoned his god when stepping into the public square. In fact, no one ever does or can. We all argue on behalf of our God or gods in the public square and try to win a majority of the votes. Everyone. It's impossible to do otherwise. In the ballot box or on the Senate floor, you fight for what you most value and worship. Inevitably. The real question is, who, whether by hook or by crook, wins any given debate, election, or war?

Why Government Authority?

Why does God give authority to the government? We've already considered the first two reasons the Bible provides: to protect life and to secure the conditions of the dominion mandate and human flourishing. A government does these two things by administering justice. Call all this the proximate or immediate purposes of government. These purposes are concerned with temporal things.

Yet the government's temporal concerns ultimately serve an eternal purpose: setting the stage for God's work of redemption. You might think of guardrails on a mountain road. Their proximate or immediate purpose is to keep cars on the road. Their ultimate purpose is to help cars get from City A to City B.

---

2   See, e.g., Nicholas Wolterstorff, *Justice: Rights and Wrongs* (Princeton, NJ: Princeton University Press, 2008), ch. 16.

This is the real story behind the story of governments in the Bible. The spiritual forces of hell fight to use governments to devour God's people—from Moses's Pharaoh, to the Assyrian Sennacherib, to the Roman Pilate, to the raging nations of Psalm 2, to the beasts in Revelation 13, depending on how you read Revelation. Meanwhile, God raises up particular leaders to protect and shelter his people—from Joseph's Pharaoh, to the Babylonian Nebuchadnezzar after his humbling, to the Persian Cyrus, to the Roman Festus. God's ultimate purpose for government is not merely to keep people alive but to keep them alive so that they might know God. Genesis 9 comes before Genesis 12 and the call of Abraham for a reason. Government provides a platform on which God's redemptive drama can play out. Common grace sets the stage for special grace, like teaching people to read so that they can read the Bible.

Two New Testament texts make this connection crystal clear. First, look at the quote from Acts 17 at the beginning of this chapter. It says that God determines the borders of nations and the dates of their duration *so that* people might seek him (Acts 17:26–27). Our nations and governments help to keep us alive. Why? "So that," Paul says, people can find their way to God. Governments don't bring us to God, but they free us up to seek him.

Now look at 1 Timothy 2. Paul urges us to pray for kings and all in high positions so that we may lead "peaceful and quiet lives, godly and dignified in every way" (v. 2). Fair enough. We want governments that clear the ground for us to live such lives, lives where we can live out the full range of godliness that God intends. Yet is that all there is to say? No. Paul then tell us why we should pray for governments to do this: "This is good, and it is pleasing in the sight of God our Savior, who desires all people to be saved and to come to the knowledge of the truth" (1 Tim. 2:3–4). The two steps in these verses are interesting. Step one: don't pray that governments would work to make disciples but that they would work for peace and safety. Step two: realize that this is important because God wants people to be saved, which apparently is work that belongs to the institution that the rest of 1 Timothy is about: the church. The government's job is to clear the path, smooth the road, set the stage, build a platform. A clear path and smooth road pleases God and should please us—for salvation's sake.

In short, we don't want a government that thinks it can offer redemption, but one that views its works as setting the stage for redemption. It builds the streets so that you can drive to church; protects the womb so that you can live and hear the gospel; protects the currency so that you can make an honest living and give to missions; insists on fair-lending and housing practices so that you can own a home and offer hospitality to non-Christians; protects marriage and the family by not redefining marriage and by kicking strip clubs out of the city so that husbands and wives can better model Christ's love for the church.

Whom should you vote for in the next election? Vote for the party or candidate that seeks to do all that.

What Are the Limits of the Government's Authority?

If a government's job is not to make disciples but to set the stage for disciple making, we need to think about its limits, as well as whether models (1), (2), or (3) from the beginning of this chapter are best. What are the limits of a civil government's authority?

The first and most crucial limit is, no government should regard itself as God. When the individual officers comprising the government don't acknowledge God, they will either worship another god or regard themselves as God. Members of group (3), insofar as they are tempted to believe governments can remain neutral between the gods, may need to be reminded of this point. Every prince and member of parliament, voter and judge, should acknowledge God and recognize that he or she is under God:

> Now therefore, O kings, be wise;
>   be warned, O rulers of the earth.
> Serve the LORD with fear,
>   and rejoice with trembling.
> Kiss the Son,
>   lest he be angry, and you perish in the way,
>   for his wrath is quickly kindled. (Ps. 2:10–12; see also Ps. 82:7)

I'm not saying a person has the right to use the power of government to require another human being to acknowledge God. A moral "is" does not make for a sword-wielding "ought."[3] I'm simply saying that, before God himself, everyone working in government should acknowledge and submit to God—"lest *he* be angry." Remember the principle from chapter 6: good authority is not unaccountable, but submits to a higher authority. That applies to governments, too.

A government of people who refuse to acknowledge the true God of the Bible is a government that has supplanted him. Such governments may, by God's common grace, do justice for a season. But eventually they will turn beastly. As examples, think of Moses's Pharaoh: "Who is the LORD, that I should obey his voice?" (Ex. 5:2). Or the Assyrian Sennacherib's lieutenant: "Do not let Hezekiah make you trust in the LORD by saying, 'The LORD will surely deliver us'" (Isa. 36:15). So with the communist and fascist regimes of the twentieth and twenty-first centuries. Or the Mongol empire of the fourteenth-century Muslim Tamerlane. Or the many indigenous civilizations, like the Aztecs, who sacrificed countless people to their gods.[4] Or so many more.

That said, members of governments might acknowledge God with their lips (see Isa. 29:13), explicitly calling themselves "Christian," yet still perpetrate grave injustices by failing to acknowledge the image of God in their subjects. Throughout the Middle Ages the Christian monarchs of Europe were violently and grotesquely anti-Semitic. Those same governments, as well as the governments of the New World, supported racial slavery, even when their founding documents acknowledged God. The Dutch Reformed

---

3   In other words, it's easy to affirm, "The government should acknowledge God," if the government consists of one person—the king. This is merely a moral claim about what the king should do. Yet when we make that same claim when talking about a form of government that involves a people, as with a democratic republic, things get complicated. If I'm a US senator representing my home state of Maryland, it's true that I should acknowledge God and do so in my job. It's also true that the other 99 senators and everyone who voted me in should acknowledge God. But if they don't, would God have me draft official documents acknowledging him *as if they spoke for the other 99 and all my voters*, even though they disavowed Christianity? To use a real example, should the British government require a Hindu prime minister to take his oath of office by placing his hand on a Bible he disavows? Wouldn't doing so turn his oath into a lie? My goal here is only to make the moral claim regarding individual officers of government: each one should acknowledge God. I'm not saying we should require others to say what they don't believe.

4   See "Feeding the Gods: Hundreds of Skulls Reveal Massive Scale of Human Sacrifice in Aztec Capital" (June 21, 2018), accessed December 3, 2022, https://www.science.org/content/article /feeding-gods-hundreds-skulls-reveal-massive-scale-human-sacrifice-aztec-capital.

government of South Africa, also, devised the doctrine and practice of apartheid. So-called "Christian" governments can turn beastly, too.

In short, creatures who deny the Creator revealed in the Bible, or his image in every individual, will eventually use governments to kill and exploit. It's easy math: creature – creator + government = terrible injustices. I believe this is why God determines not merely the boundaries of nations, but their "allotted periods" or duration (Acts 17:26). By his common grace he employs a nation and its government for a season to do their work, yet eventually their denial of him leads to injustices that require their removal. This is the biblical story of nation after nation (e.g., Gen. 15:16; Isa. 10:5ff.; Hab. 2:2–20).

In speaking of acknowledgment, I'm not arguing that we need to put Jesus's name into our constitutions, just like I wouldn't argue that we need to put his name into home mortgage or auto loan contracts. I'm not going to insist that the non-Christian officers at a bank, in giving me a loan, put words into the contract that they personally disavow. My simple point for now is, the heart of every voter and president on earth, like the heart of every lender and borrower signing loan papers, should acknowledge and submit to God. "By me kings reign," says Lady Wisdom, "and rulers decree what is just" (Prov. 8:15). And where does wisdom begin but with the fear of the Lord?

The government's second limit concerns the threat of its infringing unjustly into the parental sphere. This is a complicated topic, because God surely intends for governments to protect abused or abandoned children. We considered this in chapter 5. Foster and child protective services I regard as a hypothetically good thing. Not only that, but the government also seems to have a legitimate interest in ensuring that its citizens are literate in math, reading, science, and more. Nations with high literacy rates flourish more than those with low literacy.

Yet if education policy *inferentially* falls within the government's domain, biblically speaking, it *explicitly* falls within the parents' domain, as we considered in the previous chapter (see Proverbs). A good government, therefore, will respect the authority of good parents to educate their children. It may educate children or offer standards for education where necessary. And it will protect children against negligent or incompetent parents. Balancing these different objectives, no doubt, requires the wisdom of Solomon.

Meanwhile, a bad government forsakes wisdom and will eventually usurp the authority of good and bad parents alike.

It's worth observing, therefore, that so many of the church versus state controversies of the last hundred years have occurred in a domain that fundamentally should belong to parents—education. Think, for instance, of the controversies surrounding prayer in public schools, whether tax dollars can assist parochial schools, or what's taught about evolution or sexuality in the classroom. Christians treat these as church/state or religious freedom issues, when really the trouble began upstream when parents let themselves become dependent on the state, ceding sovereignty to it, to educate their children. To be sure, we would need to radically reimagine the last two centuries of economic, industrial, and civic development in society as a whole in order to envision a nation where parents take responsibility for educating their kids, perhaps with government facilitating, not owning, that education. My point is not to say there are easy solutions here. It's merely to describe the landscape: the Bible gives primary responsibility to educate the child to parents, and when we hand that off to the state, we can expect further jurisdictional problems to occur, like fights over religion.

The government's third limit, which we will think about at considerably greater length, concerns the church and religion. These comments are offered for anyone leaning toward group (1) (government should enforce Christianity), but hopefully they will help all of us better grasp what the separation of church and state means and doesn't mean. Does the New Testament leave room for the government to criminalize false religions? Or to incentivize and sanction true religion? Does it leave room for officially established churches, or for calling a nation "Christian"?[5] No doubt, doing either curtails religious liberty.

The key word, once again, is jurisdiction, and the key jurisdictional division worth paying attention to is temporal versus eternal, as well as protection versus perfection.

Ever since the days of Noah, we have seen, God has assigned the governments of the nations the task of working for justice in *temporal matters*.

---

5 An "established" church is one that enjoys the patronage of the state. Its doctrine and practices receive the endorsement of the state. Its clergy and members receive certain advantages from the state, if in no other way than financially. And, any changes to the doctrine and practice of the religion require the consent of the state.

Their judgments, ideally, possess an *eternal purpose*—they enable and don't hinder the work of the church. And those judgments possess an *eternal theological basis*—that humans are created in God's image. Still, their judgments offer merely a *temporal reach*—for this life only. A government can protect lives and work to ensure that the basic conditions are in place for people to fulfill the dominion mandate. But a government's work does not go beyond death. Its sword cannot reach into eternity (Matt. 10:28; Rom. 8:35). Its impact is temporary, which is one reason Christians never need to fear unjust governments.

The government's jurisdiction, therefore, must be limited to its actual reach.

That means we should ask our governments to work for a *protectionist version of justice*. We should ask our churches, on the other hand, to declare and bind its membership by a *perfectionist version of justice*. If the state possesses the power of the sword, the church possesses the power of the keys to declare who God is, what he's done in the gospel, and everything he requires of his people. The keys of the kingdom, which we'll think about more in chapter 16, are the authority for a church to say who their members are and aren't, through the ordinances.

Table 14.1: Authority: Governments versus Churches

	Type of authority	Jurisdiction	Type of justice
Governments	Coercive	Temporal	Protectionist
Churches	Declarative	Eternal (starting now)	Perfectionist

The criteria for a perfectionist version of justice is perfection: "You therefore must be perfect, as your heavenly Father is perfect" (Matt. 5:48). The criteria for a protectionist version of justice concerns how you conduct yourself with other human beings—your neighbors: Do you give other people their due? Do you treat them fairly? Or do you harm them, exploit them, steal from them, and so forth? Do you love them as yourself? Furthermore, do you show respect and honor to the government? Do you pay your taxes so that they can do their God-assigned work?

It's these types of temporal concerns that occupy both Paul and Peter in their most extensive treatments of governments. If you glance at the quotes from Romans 13:3–4 and 1 Peter 2:14 at the beginning of this chapter, you'll see that each affirmed that God has instituted governments to reward the good and punish the bad. Does this mean that Paul and Peter intend for governments to punish every conceivable bad and to reward every conceivable good? Presumably not, unless we assume they intended for government to play God, who alone can judge all goods and all bads. Paul and Peter have a subset of goods and bads in mind.

What is that subset? Both apostles refer to the "approval" or "praise" of their pagan rulers. Pagan rulers wouldn't praise those who worship and obey Jesus. They would praise those who fulfill the temporally concerned matters that Paul mentions in his summary verse 7—paying "taxes" and "revenue"[6] and affording "respect" and "honor" to Roman officials (Rom. 13:7; also 1 Pet. 2:17). Furthermore, Paul's word for the "good conduct" that receives the king's approval is used elsewhere for practical acts of mercy for those in need (e.g., Acts 9:36; 1 Tim. 2:10; 5:10). In short, the goods and bads that Paul and Peter have in mind are the temporally concerned matters that will draw the attention of every government, whether for godly purposes or for self-interested ones, simply by virtue of the temporal tool it has—the sword.

Reacting to the broader culture's push against Christian convictions on marriage, sex, and gender, a growing number of Christians in recent years have begun asking whether God does in fact authorize governments to concern themselves not just with temporal matters but with eternal ones. Should we try to merge church and state, whether partially or completely? If the leaders are Christian, can the government promote or even enforce Christianity? Ever since the Roman emperor Constantine became a Christian in the early 300s, many Christians have believed so. Nations and empires even began to call themselves "Christian." There are lighter and heavier versions of an established church or state enforcement. Or think of a dimmer switch. You can turn it on just barely, with things like Sabbath laws or using religious language in courtroom oaths. You can turn the switch up with doctrinal tests for office or tax support for clergy of a particular

---

6   "An indirect tax levied on goods and services, such as sales of land, houses, oil, and grass" (Colin G. Kruse, *Paul's Letter to the Romans*, Pillar New Testament Commentary, D. A. Carson, gen. ed. [Grand Rapids, MI: Eerdmans, 2012], 499). Kruse quotes from Thomas M. Coleman, "Binding Obligations in Romans 13:7: A Semantic Field and Social Context," *Tyndale Bulletin* 48 (1997): 309–15.

denomination. You can turn it up all the way by criminalizing false worship or blasphemy, even executing blasphemers, as Calvin famously supported for the Trinity-denying Michael Servetus.

To make this case, Christians typically appeal to the Old Testament kings of Israel, the Ten Commandments, or some other argument from the Mosaic covenant to argue for the fusion of church and state. But is this a legitimate appeal? I can't address every click on the dimmer switch here. But if we're talking about turning the switch all the way up, the short answer is no. The Mosaic covenant was given to Old Testament Israel. It does not license the governments of the nations to enforce Christian convictions about eternity, like the first two commandments in the Ten Commandments.

It's true that every individual in government, standing before God, should acknowledge him. But just because a government is accountable to God for every action it takes doesn't mean the government has the authority to force you to believe in God. As I said, the government's jurisdiction should be limited to its actual reach, and a moral "is" does not make for a sword-wielding "ought."

Yet let's put Old Testament Israel in context. God had unique and priestly purposes for Israel. He called them to be a "royal priesthood" (see Ex. 19:6). What does a priesthood do? They mediate God's law and God's presence. Israel's job as a nation was to mediate God's law and presence to the nations by obeying his law and worshiping him (see Deut. 4:6–8). For that reason, God placed his name on Israel: "You are my people, and I am your God" (see Ex. 6:7). Tragically, Israel failed to do its job, and so God cast them out of the land.

Now, think: who has the priestly job in the New Testament? That is, who is to mediate God's law and presence and on whom does he place his name? The first word out of your mouth had better be Jesus! Okay, but who else? It's everyone who is united to Jesus by the new covenant of his blood. The church is now God's "royal priesthood" (1 Pet. 2:9). Sure enough, he places his name on the church. We're baptized into his name, and we gather in his name (Matt. 18:20; 28:19). Do a word search on "name" in the book of Acts, and you'll see the extraordinary care the apostles take on who bears Christ's "name."

In other words, this priestly job of bearing Christ's name and mediating his presence to the world doesn't go to a nation or empire. No, it passes to everyone united to Christ, the church, which is comprised of a people from every nation. To call a nation a Christian nation today or to seek to enforce the first two commandments is to go backwards to the old covenant. It's to declare a nation priestly. Yet God doesn't call nations and their governments to patrol the borders of who believes in him and who doesn't, like Israel did. He calls the church to patrol those borders through its membership. We are the "holy nation" now (1 Peter 2:9). That's why *pre-conversion* Paul sought to leverage the power of the sword and put people to death for blasphemy (Acts 26:10–11), while *post-conversion* Paul sought to leverage the power of the keys not to execute but to excommunicate blasphemers—so that they could repent and be saved (1 Tim. 1:20).

The government's job between the Old Testament and New does not change. From the Noahic covenant in Genesis 9 to today, God has called the governments of the nations to implement a protectionist form of justice. The government's job between the Mosaic covenant and the new, however, did change. Those priestly responsibilities which uniquely belonged to Israel's civil order have passed on to the church.

Besides all this, think about the Noahic covenant one more time. God promised *not* to destroy humanity for an indefinite season, in spite of our false worship. To criminalize false worship and idolatry would seem to defy God's own promise to withhold his judgment.

So how do we put all this together, and how do we decide between options (1), (2), and (3) at the beginning of this chapter? Consider Jesus's words, "Render unto Caesar what is Caesar's, and unto God what is God's" (see Matt. 22:21). I can imagine three different ways of picturing this verse, two wrong and one right. Some might say that Jesus intended to separate Caesar's things and God's things entirely, like this:

Figure 14.1: God versus Caesar: Option (1)

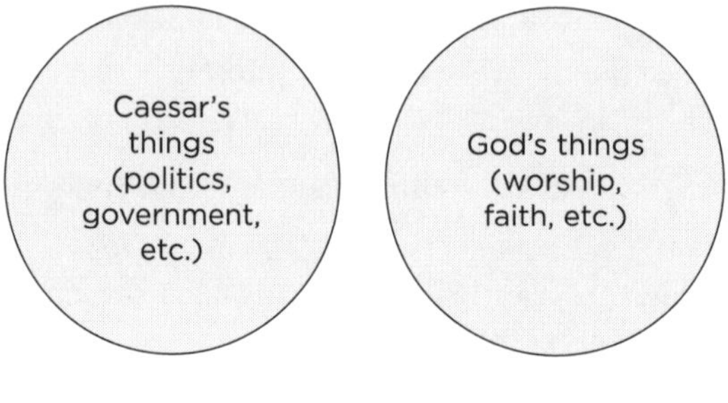

Caesar's things (politics, government, etc.)

God's things (worship, faith, etc.)

Group (3) above can tend to err in this direction, and I *would* call it a biblical error. After all, everything that belongs to Caesar also belongs to God. Caesar is made in God's image. He is accountable to God. God's coming judgment applies to Caesar and to every human government. When you, I, or Caesar step into the public square, we will represent some god and some god's version of justice, as I said above. It's only a question of whose. Insofar as Christians have a voice in government, whether as voters, officeholders, or anything else, they should seek to represent the true God alone. They should seek to influence others and pass laws in keeping with a biblical understanding of righteousness and justice.

But none of this means that the Bible calls Christians to criminalize all sin, enforce all worship, renounce religious liberty, and build a theocracy, which would be another wrong way of interpreting Jesus's words about God and Caesar. Suppose someone argued that Caesar should, if he can, promote *all* or *nearly all* of God's things, like this:

Figure 14.2: God versus Caesar: Option (2)

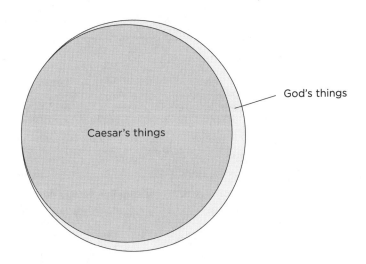

Group (1) tends in this direction. Yet that would seem to be a strange interpretation of what Jesus said. It's true that everything that belongs to Caesar belongs to God, but hardly everything that belongs to God also belongs to Caesar.

The key word, once again, is jurisdiction. Caesar, I've argued, has a temporal jurisdiction for implementing a protectionist justice. That's an important circle. But when you compare that to God's justice, which is eternal and perfectionistic, it's hardly most of the circle. Churches should speak for the whole circle. And that's a lot of circle that the government doesn't need to enforce, including eternal decisions about who God is. In fact, everything outside the government's jurisdiction we can also call the domain of religious liberty.

The jurisdictional picture that the Bible has assigned to every nation since the Noahic covenant, except for ancient Israel, looks more like this:

Figure 14.3: God versus Caesar: Option (3)

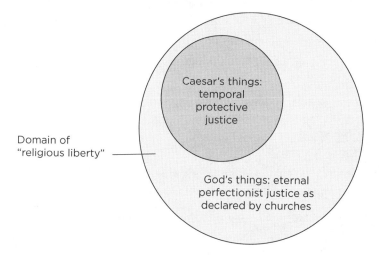

Notice that everything Caesar does is contained inside God's circle. Which means you could, if you wanted, call everything that Caesar does "religious," because it's under God, whether he acknowledges God or not. I'd even say we cannot separate the political and the religious. I would say, however, the Bible insists that we separate church and state in this sense: One has the sword; one has the keys of the kingdom. Also, one has a temporal jurisdiction and is charged with enforcing protectionist justice; the other has eternal jurisdiction and is charged with enforcing perfectionist justice. In other words, the separation of religion and politics is not the same thing as the separation of church and state. The first is impossible because your

THE GOVERNMENT (COMMAND) 217

religion always determines your politics, while the second is a jurisdictional assignment. Few people today seem to understand this distinction.

Perhaps an analogy would help for filling out the illustration for position (2) above. You might say that the Bible approaches governments like parents do a babysitter. "You're not responsible to teach our kids to love and obey us," they instruct the sitter. "You just need to keep them fed and safe, and prevent them from fighting." The babysitter is entirely "under" the parents, but the sitter's jurisdiction is limited. The babysitter knows the parents' return is imminent and will seek to fulfill the parents' will. Still, the babysitter has been given a modest job: "Your job isn't to teach the kids to love us or worship God. Just help them play well together and go to bed on time." Likewise, a good government will fear and acknowledge God. It knows a day is coming when "the kings of the earth and the great ones and the generals and the rich and the powerful, and everyone, slave and free" will experience God's judgment for how they did their jobs (Rev. 6:15–17). Still, God has given the government a comparatively modest job.

One additional reason to keep that job modest is that, unlike most babysitters, most governments oppose God (Ps. 2:1–3). Do you really think it would be wise to give God-opposers and haters the authority of the sword over worship?

In short, the separation of church and state does not prevent us from enforcing certain Christian moral convictions in the public square; but it does mean we seek to enforce only those convictions that God authorizes governments to enforce.

So, should we use the sword to insist that murder is wrong? Yes.

That marriage is between a man and a woman? Yes.

That Jesus is Lord? Every member of government should acknowledge as much, and individuals in government that don't will eventually veer toward injustice in their jobs, but no, we cannot force them to do so.

Finally, everything outside the government's jurisdiction belongs to the domain of what people have long called religious liberty.

How Do Citizens Get to Work?

In short, good governments don't try to usher in Christ's kingdom by enforcing the worship of God. Instead, they should aspire to clear the ground and make the road easy for pilgrims on their way. Their work is prerequisite and preparatory work. We shouldn't ask governments to provide salvation. They can't, and the vast majority of them will never want to anyway. Rather, we ask them, much more modestly and in ways that line up with their self-interest, to establish the necessary conditions for salvation. That way, the church can get on with its work of making disciples.

The good news is, Jesus will build his church. No, the worst governments cannot stop the Holy Spirit. Yes, God often moves underground, undisclosed to governments. But bad governments, from a human standpoint, really do make the church's work difficult. Christians should work for good governments.

How?

(1) *Pray.* Paul urges us to pray for kings and all in high positions so that we may lead peaceful and quiet lives. "This is good" and "pleasing in the sight of God our Savior, who desires all people to be saved" (1 Tim. 2:3–4). We pray for our government so that the saints might live peaceful lives and people will be saved.

(2) *Ask Scripture what God has authorized government to do.* God authorizes the government to do some things (like prosecute murder) but not other things (like enforce conversions). So before you ask, "How should I vote?" or "What should I protest?" or "What should we lobby for?" first consider what God tells governments to do. That's been the point of this entire chapter. No, Scripture doesn't speak to the specifics of law. It speaks more like a constitution, establishing basic powers and lanes. I've argued in this chapter that God has given government a narrow, protectionist lane. You might disagree on how wide that lane is. Very well. Let's have the conversation with charity and humility. Yet we have a clear criteria by which to discuss it: what does God authorize?

(3) *Engage.* For the sake of loving our neighbor and doing justice, we should not disengage from political cares. We should engage by employing whatever stewardship God has given us, whether we're a voter or the cupholder to the king. We render to Caesar what is Caesar's. In a democratic context we do this by voting, lobbying, lawyering, or running for office. Even in an empire, Paul, for the sake of the gospel, pulled the political levers he had. He invoked his citizenship and appealed to Caesar. Use such opportunities while you have them. Wherever we can build on common ground with non-Christians, we should.

(4) *Acknowledge God in the public square.* As a Christian, for instance, we should warn politicians who do injustice. Christians working in government, too, should be willing, when it serves good purposes, to point to God. "Now therefore, O kings, be wise; be warned, O rulers of the earth. Serve the LORD with fear, and rejoice with trembling" (Ps. 2:10–11). Does this mean a president can take the oath of office with his hand on the Bible? Should he invoke God in his speeches? Can a pastor open a school board meeting in prayer? Answers to questions like these will have to be judged on a case-by-case basis. As a general principle, I'm more comfortable with an officeholder speaking for him or herself rather than presuming to speak for the nation, as the words of the Constitution do. We don't put God's name into mortgages or business contracts, even though they govern the relationship. Still, I see no biblical reason for why a Christian officeholder should not use his or her pulpit to call a people to repentance (see Jonah 3:6–9).

15

The Manager (Command)

Covenantal Authorization: Adamic (Common) Covenant

*Be fruitful and multiply and fill the earth and
subdue it, and have dominion over the fish of the
sea and over the birds of the heavens and over every
living thing that moves on the earth. (Gen. 1:28)*

Other Elucidating Biblical Texts

*To the woman he said, "I will surely multiply your pain in
childbearing; in pain you shall bring forth children." . . . And to
Adam he said, . . . "cursed is the ground because of you; in pain
you shall eat of it all the days of your life; thorns and thistles it
shall bring forth for you; and you shall eat the plants of the field.
By the sweat of your face you shall eat bread." (Gen. 3:16–19)*

*[Abram] led forth his trained men, born in his house, 318 of
them, and went in pursuit as far as Dan. (Gen. 14:14)*

*You shall not oppress your neighbor or rob him.
The wages of a hired worker shall not remain with
you all night until the morning. (Lev. 19:13)*

*You shall not oppress a hired worker who is poor and needy,
whether he is one of your brothers or one of the sojourners
who are in your land within your towns. (Deut. 24:14)*

*And the Lord said, "Who then is the faithful
and wise manager, whom his master will set
over his household, to give them their portion
of food at the proper time?" (Luke 12:42)*

Masters, . . . stop your threatening, knowing that he
who is both their Master and yours is in heaven, and
that there is no partiality with him. (Eph. 6:9)

Masters, treat your bondservants justly and fairly, knowing
that you also have a Master in heaven. (Col. 4:1)

For the Scripture says, "You shall not muzzle an ox when it treads
out the grain," and, "The laborer deserves his wages." (1 Tim. 5:18)

Servants, be subject to your masters with all respect, not only to
the good and gentle but also to the unjust. For this is a gracious
thing, when, mindful of God, one endures sorrows while suffering
unjustly. For what credit is it if, when you sin and are beaten for it,
you endure? But if when you do good and suffer for it you endure,
this is a gracious thing in the sight of God. For to this you have
been called, because Christ also suffered for you, leaving you an
example, so that you might follow in his steps. (1 Pet. 2:18–21)

Job Description

To provide just or fair wages in return for faithful, honest labor.

———

BY "MANAGERIAL AUTHORITY" I mean authority in the workplace. As such, this chapter concerns the authority you possess or experience for forty-plus hours a week, whether you work in a school, a restaurant, a human resources department, a law firm, the military, a government agency, a church with multiple staff members, a football team, a magazine, a web-design firm, or a mom-and-pop road-side souvenir shop with one or two hired salesclerks. For simplicity's sake, I'm going to use the word "manager" or "boss" throughout this chapter to refer to any position in which you have oversight or management responsibilities for other people, whether your actual title is army major, shift manager, or managing partner.

Sometimes managerial authority is an authority of command. Think of a flower shop owner who can hire or fire salesclerks at will. Sometimes it's closer to an authority of counsel. Think of an army colonel who can charge a lower-ranking officer with insubordination, but must appeal to a military judge and jury to conduct the court-martial process. There is an endless variety of configurations that we could consider.

One challenge of thinking through this domain of authority is the cultural distance that separates today's employment contracts from the employment conditions of the biblical world. Both the Old and New Testaments refer to "hired workers," which is a familiar concept to us. Less familiar are ancient households, father-son apprenticeships, and slavery. For starters, ancient households included extended family, servants, concubines, and more. Hundreds of people, for instance, would have been part of Abraham's "household" (see Gen. 14:14, cited above). Whether son or servant, they depended on Abraham for their provision even as they worked for him. Family and work authority blended together.

Family and work authority also blended as sons were apprenticed to their fathers. Think of Jesus the carpenter, or James and John working as fishermen with their father.

Finally, the economies of the ancient world, from Hebrew to Roman, relied on slavery. Slaves were purchased, inherited, or taken in war. Sometimes they were treated well, almost as a professional class. Sometimes they were treated like subhuman chattel. Books and essays compare and contrast these ancient systems to the race-based systems of slavery perpetrated in recent centuries. Some argue the ancient systems weren't as bad as the slavery in the United States and the colonies of Europe. Slavery in ancient times functioned more like military service, they say, and was not race-based as we think of it. Some, however, argue the ancient systems could be just as bad as the stories we know from the sixteenth to nineteenth centuries. Crucial for our purposes is that the New Testament authors treated these structures as fixed. They focused on teaching slaves and masters alike to follow Christ whatever their structural realities and circumstances, since nearly all had no hope whatsoever of changing those circumstances. It was as if the New Testament authors meant to say, you're a mouse stuck in a laboratory maze, which you cannot change; but we'll help you to negotiate the maze. Paul encouraged slaves individually, "get your freedom if you can" (see 1 Cor. 7:21). Yet he was also a good pastor who recognized that many of his readers would invariably spend their entire lives within that system, and therefore his task was to help them follow Jesus right where they lived.

I mention all this simply because, when we turn to the New Testament for instruction on managerial authority, the primary texts we find pertain to slaves and masters, not employers and employees. The topic is unavoidable. Those are the inspired texts that God has given us, which, apparently, he regards as relevant and instructive for us. So, while we need to negotiate the cultural distance and the ethical complexities, we don't need to be afraid of such texts. We can simply ask, "God, what would you have us learn for the workplace, together with everything else the Bible says about work?"

What Is Managerial or Workplace Authority?

What is managerial or workplace authority? It's an outworking of the dominion mandate God gave to Adam and Eve. The first couple, like every human ever since, was tasked with ruling and subduing the earth. The minute they (and we) decided to undertake any project larger than farming a tiny plot of land, they needed more than each other. To build a barn, tend crops, or shepherd herds of any size requires organizing labor under a common rule. "You lead the oxen, I'll guide the plow." The Tower of Babel and its demise, among other things, demonstrated the need for a common rule—if only the rule of a shared language—for working together to build anything of consequence. Managerial authority, in other words, is a way of organizing our labor for the purpose of fulfilling God's dominion mandate and making provision for every participant. It's a necessary part of being stewards of the earth together.

If God has the right to give and take life, presumably he has the right to give the Canaanites as slaves to the Israelites, which he did (e.g., Deut. 20:10–14). Still, unlike the child who owes obedience to the parent by creation design, no human being, outside of that family relationship, owes vocational obedience to another human being. You have no right to walk up to another person and conscript their service. Therefore, Paul includes "enslavers" or "slave-traders" or "man-stealers" (depending on your translation) in his list of other sinners like murderers, the sexually immoral, and liars (1 Tim. 1:9–10). At a minimum, enslaving a person breaks the eighth commandment against stealing.

In the ideal, then, leaving aside all the scarcities and injustices associated with the fall, managerial authority depends on a kind of trade.

"I'll give you my labor and submit to your project, whatever it is, while you provide me with income or protection or sustenance." Plus, different individuals may have different gifts or talents which they can barter in exchange for income, from the musician to the ironworker (see Gen. 4:21–22).

Managerial authority, in other words, is a necessity for human beings relating to one another economically. That is why I defined managerial authority above as, providing just or fair wages in return for faithful, honest labor.

What Kind of Authority?

Notice, then, managerial authority, like civil authority, is a property of justice. It's an ethical structure, like civil authority, entailed in the grand project of fulfilling God's dominion mandate together with other people. Yet where civil authority focuses on the political, managerial authority focuses on the economic. When two people enter into such a trade—my labor for your income, provision, or protection—one party will possess authority over the other party not by intrinsic right but as part of the "deal" or "contract" the two parties have struck. "You can tell me what to do, but only if you pay me." Even the apprenticeship between father and son, the expectations of the ancient patriarchal household, and slavery presume such contracts. Masters, for instance, are expected to provide and care for their slaves, presumptions that the Old Testament law sought to make explicit (e.g., Ex. 21:7–11, 20–27). When their Egyptian masters deprived the Israelite slaves of the straw for making bricks, the Israelites cried out against this injustice.

So it is in our employment-at-will work contracts today. Both the obedience required by the manager as well as the obedience given by the worker depend on what's fair, due, right, or just. They depend on each party fulfilling their end of the bargain and giving the other what's due to them. The apostle Paul, for instance, observes, "You shall not muzzle an ox when it treads out the grain," and, "The laborer deserves his wages" (1 Tim. 5:18). To refer to what the laborer deserves is to appeal to what is just. Other translations (e.g., CSB) say the worker "is worthy" of his wages. Something about the laborer is worthy of being paid. It is the laborer's due. God inserted the same principle into the Levitical law: "You shall not oppress your neighbor or rob him. The wages of a hired worker shall not remain with you all night until the morning" (Lev. 19:13). An Israelite could not withhold someone's wages even overnight, lest he risk robbing or oppressing the worker.

Elsewhere, Paul commands masters to "treat your bondservants justly and fairly, knowing that you also have a Master in heaven" (Col. 4:1). The Roman Empire might have granted church members the ability to own slaves. Yet make no mistake: God's rules of right still applied. He's the master's Master, after all. The world may devalue and dehumanize them, but God's people were to treat slaves as fully human—justly and fairly. Some authors have speculated that Paul didn't want to make politically revolutionary material explicit in his letters in order to avoid immediate Roman reprisal, knowing that the call for biblical justice would accomplish this work among God's people soon enough. I don't know. He does at least imply that Christian masters should grant Christian slaves their freedom, as he insinuates with Philemon, calling the slave Onesimus "no longer . . . a bondservant but . . . a beloved brother" (Philem. 16).

Certainly, Paul wanted Christian masters to treat all slaves, Christian or no, with fairness as fellow human beings, unlike so much slavery in the ancient world: "stop your threatening," says Paul, "knowing that he who is both their Master and yours is in heaven, and that there is no partiality with him" (Eph. 6:9). By God's standards, in other words, that slave is your equal as you stand before one heavenly Master. And that Master is not partial to you in comparison to him. So, whatever the political and economic structures happen to be, Christians have a job to do: treat their fellow human beings as equals and afford them the rights of their humanity.

Now, again, my purpose here is not to work out all the ethical complexities of slavery in the Bible and how we might compare it to the structures of slavery in recent centuries, which is inherently sinful if for no other reason than its being race-based. My quick take is, Scripture took what was a given in the ancient world and would not be eradicated anytime soon and shoved it hard in a humanizing direction that would ultimately undermine it. Which is to say, the idea of one human being owning another stands against creation design and against God's purposes for humanity, even if he allowed a highly regulated version of it in Israel for a period for purposes of provision and judgment.

The point of this chapter is to make an argument from greater to lesser. Masters had far more authority over their slaves than any manager or boss does today. Yet if Scripture commands masters to treat slaves fairly and justly, because God shows no partiality to the master, how much clearer this lesson should be for our modern-day voluntary employment contracts. Whether we possess an authority of counsel or of command, our relationships with employees under us are structured by ethical demands. We *owe* them fairness and justice. God is not partial to the pastor over the church secretary, the shop owner over the salesclerk, the officer over the soldier, the factory foreman over the factory worker, the principal over the teacher, the editorial director over the editorial assistant. If anything, he holds the manager to a higher ethical standard: "Everyone to whom much was given, of him much will be required, and from him to whom they entrusted much, they will demand the more" (Luke 12:48).

We owe those under us justice in what we pay them. How we speak to them. How we correct them. How we look for opportunities to help them flourish and grow. How we help them discern their strengths and compensate for their weaknesses. Treating those under us as God-imagers in all these ways is fair and just. A worker is worthy of his wages; and by implication he's worthy of being treated as a God-imager. Those under us are our stewardship.

Why Managerial Authority?

What's the purpose of managerial authority? As we've discussed so far, it exists for the sake of fulfilling the dominion mandate and, second, for purposes of provision.

Aside from sin generally and self-worship specifically, God's curse, which translates into economic terms as a scarcity of resources and death, is the perennial foe which all our employment and economies must work against. Even the author of Ecclesiastes, who purchased slaves to build houses and vineyards, gardens and parks, pools and forests, herds and flocks, found the curse undefeatable. Everything returns to death and proves to be meaningless. What is our reward for a hard day's work? It kills us: "He who digs a pit will fall into it, and a serpent will bite him who breaks through a wall" (Eccl. 10:8).

Still, along the way, God's common grace causes the sun to shine and the rain to water the earth, so that crops grow, economies are built, and people are fed. Good authority in the workplace maximizes this potential. It builds cities, conducts symphony orchestras, and accomplishes scientific breakthroughs. How remarkable that undernourishment in developing countries decreased from more than 34 percent in 1970 to 12.9 percent in 2015.[1]

A third answer to the question of "why" is worth mentioning: Good authority in the workplace serves the purposes of training. I cannot think of a good biblical prooftext to make this point, but the overall structures of apprenticeship in the biblical world surely reinforce it. It's why parental and managerial authority can be somewhat blurred within a patriarchal structure. Even as parents train the children to subdue the earth, so a godly manager undertakes an aspect of that parental job. A good editorial manager trains the editors under him, a good senior pastor the associate pastors working with him, a good sales leader the sales team, a good teacher the junior teacher working with her.

As with all authority, any authority you possess in the workplace should reflect how God uses authority in creation and how Christ used it in redemption. It should be used to author life and opportunity and growth in others.

Finally, there's a fourth answer to the question of why we need managerial authority: it provides opportunity for the witness of the saints. This is implied in Paul's instruction to Philemon, the master, and it receives particular emphasis in the apostles' instructions to slaves, as when Peter exhorts them to endure suffering by following in the footsteps of Christ, who left us an example (1 Pet. 2:21). Paul hints at the same thing when he relativizes the significance of every station one might possess, whether circumcision, slavery, or marriage, in comparison to knowing and serving Christ (1 Cor. 7:17–35). The lesson here is, a Christian should be more concerned about his or her witness than with job, marital status, or political

---

1   https://www.washingtonpost.com/world/2018/09/11/decades-global-hunger-was-decline-now
     -its-getting-worse-again-climate-change-is-blame/.

station. This in turn yields a *prima facie* duty to submit to one's employers by working hard for them.

When I worked in journalism, I had a boss who treated me and my colleagues unjustly. I was the managing editor of a magazine. He was the publisher and owner. He would shout, belittle, and insult us. We felt like we lived on the side of a volcano, ever leery of a sudden eruption. I loved the days when he was absent from the office. Though I left that job over two decades ago to attend seminary, he still shows up in a bad dream now and then.

Yet what is my biggest regret from that job? It's the fact that I didn't do a better job for this man. I'd give myself a passing grade for my work at the magazine—maybe a "B." Yet I wish I had done "A" level work. Why? To get ahead in the field? No, I left the field of journalism. Rather, he knew I was a Christian, and excelling in my work would have made my testimony even sharper in his mind—the testimony of a Christian doing exceptional work and absorbing his injustices with grace. That, I think, would have testified against his injustice and for Christ even more loudly. After all, wasn't Christ's work excellent and life-giving amid all those who persecuted him?

What Are the Limits of a Manager's Authority?

I've already touched on some of the limits of a manager's authority. There's some threat of a manager veering into lanes he or she should not be in, such as imposing religious or family requirements. I had a friend who worked for a global management consulting firm that discouraged marriage and family life because they interfered with its employees' ability to give themselves more fully to the job.

The more common limit worth mentioning simply brings us back to questions of justice and fairness. A manager must never be unjust or un-righteous either with or toward an employee. This covers a lot of matters, from humiliating or threatening employees, to making sexual advances, to underpaying and overworking them, to many other possible wrongdoings. The general principle at play here is, a bad manager can easily exploit a worker's financial needs and vulnerability for personal gain, particularly in a world of scarce resources and poverty. This is the opposite of what God intends.

How a Manager Gets to Work

Instead, every workplace boss or manager should undertake the work of oversight by meditating on Paul's words, "because you know that you also have a Master in heaven." Good authority in the workplace begins with the fear of the Lord. You're accountable to God for how you treat those under you. And remember, God is not partial to you just because you're the boss. Your authority is a stewardship, and you will be judged for how you use that stewardship. You might be *over*, but you are also *under*.

Then, in light of that fact, treat those who work for you in a way that is right and fair:

- Don't be dishonest, unkind, harsh, exploitative, oppressive.
- Remember they are human beings, who need to live full lives because God has given them other stewardships, too.
- Pay them in a manner that's worth their work.
- Help them get better at their jobs. Train them.
- Give them opportunities to succeed, and root for their success, not just for your sake but also for theirs.
- Call out their mistakes, but not every time.
- Delegate where you can; take a few risks. Give them a chance to write the memo, chair the meeting, host the dinner, design the room, teach the class.
- Don't micromanage, which undermines initiative and project ownership and teaches people not to work hard.
- Be aware of their weaknesses and sometimes protect them from themselves, so that they don't try to lift something that's too heavy for them to lift.
- Remember they are sinners, who will be tempted to sin, whether through laziness or deceit or maybe even stealing. Establish structures and build relationships to minimize temptations.
- Be generous, including the generosity of absorbing their mistakes and taking the blame when you can.

Ancient Israel at its height offers a beautiful picture of good management and governance: "Judah and Israel lived in safety, from Dan even to Beersheba, every man under his vine and under his fig tree, all the days of Solomon" (1 Kings 4:25). Good management and governance helps people to flourish. It's a picture of what Adam should have been in the garden, and what husbands and parents can be in the home, and what you should be in the workplace, with whatever authority you've been given.

So the question for you and me is, how can we help our workspace, and especially those under us, to flourish?

16

The Church (Command)

Covenantal Authorization: New (Special) Covenant

Truly, I say to you, whatever you bind on earth shall be bound in heaven, and whatever you loose on earth shall be loosed in heaven. Again I say to you, if two of you agree on earth about anything they ask, it will be done for them by my Father in heaven. For where two or three are gathered in my name, there am I among them. (Matt. 18:18–20; see also Matt. 16:13–20)

And Jesus came and said to them, "All authority in heaven and on earth has been given to me. Go therefore and make disciples of all nations, baptizing them in the name of the Father and of the Son and of the Holy Spirit, teaching them to observe all that I have commanded you. And behold, I am with you always, to the end of the age." (Matt. 28:18–20)

Other Elucidating Biblical Texts

When you are assembled in the name of the Lord Jesus and my spirit is present, with the power of our Lord Jesus, you are to deliver this man to Satan for the destruction of the flesh, so that his spirit may be saved in the day of the Lord. . . . For what have I to do with judging outsiders? Is it not those inside the church whom you are to judge? (1 Cor. 5:4–5, 12)

For such a one, this punishment by the majority is enough. (2 Cor. 2:6)

But even if we or an angel from heaven should preach to you a gospel contrary to the one we preached to you, let

him be accursed. As we have said before, so now I say
again: If anyone is preaching to you a gospel contrary to
the one you received, let him be accursed. (Gal. 1:8–9)

Job Description

To go into all nations and establish embassies of a new creation and heavenly kingdom by making disciples of Jesus, gathering them in his name, and teaching them to live in his image.

———

MY INTEREST IN THIS CHAPTER is not the authority of individual members, but the authority of a whole church acting together or jointly. As a *congregationalist*, I believe that the Bible explicitly gives the congregation final say in matters of membership, discipline, and doctrine. By implication, this means that congregations are responsible to elect (or remove) their leaders or be involved in any decision that significantly impacts the nature, integrity, or mission of the church. As an *elder-led* congregationalist, I believe the elders or pastors should lead the church in its use of authority. We'll consider their leadership in the next chapter.

If, however, you believe that the elders or pastors have the final say in a church instead of the whole congregation, that does not need to distract from our purposes here. What I say about the congregation as a whole you can apply to the pastors or elders.

What Is Church Authority?

In Matthew 16, Jesus famously gave the apostle Peter—and by implication all the apostles—the keys of the kingdom for binding and loosing on earth what is bound and loosed in heaven (vv. 13–20). Then in chapter 18 he extends that same authority to gathered congregations (vv. 15–20).

What is the authority of the keys? It is the authority to make official pronouncements on behalf of God's heavenly courtroom. More specifically, it is the authority to pronounce judgments on the *what* and the *who* of the gospel: on confessions and confessors.

Think of Jesus saying to apostles, "Who do you say that I am?" Peter answers, "You are the Christ, the Son of the living God" (Matt. 16:15–16).

Jesus then affirms Peter's answer on behalf of his Father in heaven. He also tells Peter that he's going to build his church on confessors like him who confess the right confession. That's what churches are built on, after all: confessors confessing the right gospel confession.

The interchange is similar to what occurs in a church membership interview in my church. The pastor asks the prospective member, "What is the gospel?" The person answers. Then the pastor has a choice about recommending the person to the elders and to the church. If he does, the elders and church will then affirm the man on behalf of heaven, like Jesus did with Peter.

Did you follow all that? To exercise the keys of the kingdom, which are first mentioned in Matthew 16, involves affirming a gospel *confessor* and a gospel *confession* on behalf of heaven, just like Jesus did with Peter.

Then in Matthew 18 Jesus hands those keys to the gathered congregation, but here he talks about the keys in reverse. A member of a church may be confessing the right confession, but his or her life contradicts that confession. Jesus tells the church to remove that member as an act of discipline: "If he refuses to listen to them, tell it to the church. And if he refuses to listen even to the church, let him be to you as a Gentile and a tax collector" (v. 17). The church is the final court of appeal. And by what authority can a church remove a member like this? By the authority of the keys. The next verse reads, "Truly, I say to you, whatever you bind on earth shall be bound in heaven, and whatever you loose on earth shall be loosed in heaven" (v. 18).

Paul also presents the church as the final court of appeal. He tells the church in Corinth to remove a man guilty of incest as an act of discipline "when you are assembled in the name of the Lord Jesus and my spirit is present, with the power of our Lord Jesus" (1 Cor. 5:4). Notice he doesn't say the power of the Lord Jesus is present in the Thursday night elder meeting or with the bishop. He says it is present when the congregation is gathered in Jesus's name (see also Matt. 18:20).

In short, churches possess the keys of the kingdom to say, "Yes, that is/is not the true gospel confession," and "Yes, that is/is not a true gospel confessor." In the most prosaic terms, it's how they agree upon a statement of faith and decide who belongs in the church membership directory.

What Kind of Authority Is Church Authority?

Christians have long said the church's authority is *declarative*, by which they mean to distinguish it from the state's authority, which is *coercive*. That's true so far as it goes, but what kind of declaration is it? There are many kinds of declarations: romantic declarations; friendship declarations; the declaration of the Olympic official who says every four years, "Let the games begin"; a pastor's declaration when he says, "I now pronounce you man and wife"; or a judge's declaration when he says, "Not guilty." The church's declaration is most like the last two examples. It accomplishes something public and legal, though "legal" from the perspective of Christ's kingdom.

Think about a judge's declaration when saying "guilty" or "not guilty." The declaration doesn't *actually* make the law what the law is. Nor does it make the person *actually* innocent or guilty. But the judge's declaration functions on behalf of the legal system to render a particular interpretation of the law as the binding interpretation, and it functions on behalf of the legal system to render a person innocent or guilty. Once the gavel hits the desk, the courtroom bailiff will either let the defendant go free or escort the defendant to a jail cell. Publicly, the judge's declaration accomplishes something. It binds or looses the defendant on behalf of the legal system.

So with the congregation's use of the keys. It represents a church's way of publicly saying, "This is the gospel we believe in," and "These are the people we recognize as gospel believers and citizens of the kingdom of heaven." If a judge speaks on behalf of a nation's legal system, the church speaks on behalf of another legal system—the kingdom of heaven.

In that sense there's a difference between you sharing the gospel with your next-door neighbor, and the preacher sharing the gospel from the pulpit on Sunday, even if he uses the exact same words. Both of you are speaking with the authority of the Bible. But when he speaks the gospel on behalf of the church, he's also speaking with the authority of the church. It's how the church says, "This is the gospel we believe in and that binds us together as a congregation."

Why Church Authority?

Christians today tend to give little attention to the idea of church authority, just like we give little attention to church membership and discipline. Many churches don't practice these things. After all, can they really be that important?

THE CHURCH (COMMAND) 237

(1) *Church authority is important because it tells us* who *and* what *on planet Earth represents King Jesus and his kingdom.* It shows us where to go to start looking for God's new creation.

Think about it. With the nation of ancient Israel, you could recognize the nation in all the typical ways you might recognize a nation and its citizens: a land, a king, an army, and all that. Yet these people disobeyed God, and so God said he would remake them as a new Israel by forgiving their sins and by placing his Spirit within them so that they wanted to obey God's law. Christ then came and united that new Israel to himself by the new covenant in his blood.

The trouble is, the work of forgiveness and God's Holy Spirit is invisible. How do we know who belongs to this new heavenly kingdom? Do I belong? Do you belong? Do we or our non-Christian neighbors recognize us as belonging?

Answering those questions is why church authority exists. Church authority is necessary for making the invisible universal church visible and local. It's necessary for saying who on earth represents King Jesus. Someone has to say, "Yes, this is one of the members," and "That right there is the doctrine we believe in."

As I said a moment ago, different denominations recognize different people as possessing the authority to do that. Some say the pastors or elders; some the presbytery; some the bishop; and some, like me, the whole congregation. But the point is, every denomination agrees that somebody has to exercise this declarative authority. Somebody holds the keys, even if we disagree on who.

(2) *Church authority creates the local church.* Really, this is another way of making the last point, but it's worth highlighting on its own. Protestant churches are formed in two steps:

- Step 1: someone preaches the gospel so that people hear, repent, and are saved.
- Step 2: those Christians then organize by coming together and declaring themselves a church through baptism and the Lord's Supper. They "gather" and "agree" with one another, two ingredients that Jesus says are essential to making a church a church (Matt. 18:19–20). For several centuries, many Christians have called this agreement a church covenant.

Once a church is planted, it now constitutes an outpost of God's new creation or an embassy of the kingdom of heaven. An embassy is the place you go to hear from another kingdom, its people, and its government. It's where you should begin to experience a nation's culture and hear its language. So with the local church. Its culture should be characterized by Jesus's beatitudes and Paul's fruits of the Spirit; its language characterized by the gospel, as in, "I forgive you, brother."

(3) *Church authority is also essential for the sake of Christian assurance and growth.* Being baptized "into the name" of Christ and regularly receiving the Lord's Supper together with Christ's body offers the public assurance of our salvation. God never intended our sense of assurance to be entirely internal, but also external. When brothers and sisters receive you into church membership, that's Jesus's way of using other people to say, "We think you're a Christian."

That same recognition helps us to grow in the grace of following Jesus. It tells you and me whom we're responsible for discipling and encouraging and correcting, when the occasion arises.

Here's an illustration I often use: One evening two single men from my church joined my family for dinner. One had had an abusive dad, the other an absent dad. On that evening, one of my daughters was misbehaving, which annoyed me. Yet in that moment, it occurred to me that I needed to respond to her kindly and not harshly for several reasons: for God's sake, for her sake, and finally for these young men's sake. At church, they had heard lessons about being a godly father. The sermons and Sunday school lessons, you might say, offered them an outline, like in a coloring book. Yet sitting in my home, watching me respond to a misbehaving daughter offered these young men an opportunity to watch me color in that outline. Why would they look to *me* for that purpose? Simply because our church had formally recognized me through baptism and the Supper as a Christ-follower and kingdom citizen. The church had given me the "I'm with Jesus" name-tag and the team jersey.

Now suppose I had treated my daughter harshly. Such behavior would have taught them that Christian dads are no different than non-Christian dads. Suppose, however, they corrected me, or asked the pastors or other members to correct me, even to the point of church discipline. Such discipleship or discipline in my life would serve to correct their impression of

Christian dads. "Oh, I see, Christian dads should be different. The church won't stand for such behavior." In other words, the exercising of church authority, both in membership and possibly in discipline, would help these young men better understand Christlikeness and grow in grace themselves. It would also give integrity to the church's preaching.

(4) *Church authority is essential for the sake of Christian witness.* When the church looks just like the world, we provide an unattractive witness. As I've heard our pastor friend say on a number of occasions, if there's a known adulterer in your church choir, you might as well cancel your Tuesday night evangelism program. Church authority marks off the people of God, and it helps them to be distinct like salt and bright like light.

What Are the Limits of Church Authority?

Another way to describe the authority of the church is to say it's priestly (see 2 Cor. 6:14–7:1). Just as the priests of ancient Israel regulated membership in the people of God and their ability to approach the temple through sacrifices, so the whole congregation, together with its pastors, acts as priests and temple. We exercise our priestly function by teaching God's word and by guarding the membership through the ordinances.

What that means is, the church's authority is limited to these priestly functions concerning the *what* and the *who* of the gospel. Its authority is not kingly, like the civil government's is. Christians might pick up the sword of state as individual members of the church, but the church itself must never pick up the sword of state *as the church*. It can render judgment upon its own members, as when Paul removes two blasphemers or tells the Corinthians to remove an adulterous man (1 Tim. 1:20; 1 Cor. 5:2, 5). But it has no authority over non-members or over a nation as a whole.

Further, the church's authority is limited to declaring the word of God and not statecraft, except when a matter of statecraft is addressed in explicit fashion by the Bible or is clear "by good and necessary consequence," a good phrase I borrow from the Westminster Confession.

By the same token, churches must not require their members to adhere to any particular doctrinal position—they must not bind consciences—on any matter that's not addressed in Scripture. They should not divide themselves over the countless life and lifestyle decisions that Christians must make, except when such choices oppose the word of God. Just as the authority of the civil government must be paired with a strong doctrine of *religious freedom*, so the authority of the church must be paired with a strong doctrine of *Christian freedom* (see Rom. 14). Just as everything outside the walls of the government's domain belongs to the fields of religious freedom, so everything outside the walls of the church's domain belongs to the lands of Christian freedom. This is not to say that the principles of Scripture don't apply in these lands. Churches should indeed instruct the consciences of members, preparing them to live in these lands. Yet then it should leave every individual conscience free to apply the Bible's principles as each person sees fit.

As a congregationalist, I don't believe one church can exercise formal authority over another church. But I do believe healthy churches frequently interact with one another and seek one another's wisdom in all types of matters. In fact, I've argued at length that such a strong doctrine and practice of catholicity is the biblical pattern. (See my book *One Assembly* [Crossway, 2020], ch. 3.)

Anecdotally, my sense is that abusive churches and church leaders tend to be those that spurn either the authority of the whole congregation or the authority of something outside the church, like a presbytery. In other words, the cases of abuse or scandal that hit the news are often independent, pastor-or-elder-ruled churches. While rare in two thousand years of church history, such churches have become common since the 1960s and '70s. It's no surprise. Pastors can make decisions quickly and efficiently, without all the hassle of either the congregation or the presbytery slowing down decisions or acting as a check.

How the Church Gets to Work

The church then gets to work by gathering weekly to preach the Bible and affirm one another's membership in Christ through the ordinances. The invisible church becomes visible—as in, you can see it with your eyes— in these gatherings.

Plus, exercising the authority of binding and loosing occurs with integrity when church members work to know and encourage one another throughout the week. This doesn't mean every member is responsible to know every other member. It means each member knows maybe five to fifty fellow members, and the whole thing hangs together like a spider web.

When you touch any one part, the whole thing vibrates: "If one member suffers, all suffer together; if one member is honored, all rejoice together" (1 Cor. 12:26).

If you call yourself a Christian, you should be a member of a church, which in turn means you have a job to do. Your job is to guard the gospel and to protect gospel citizens. You're responsible to address the pastors should they begin to teach false doctrine, and you're responsible to get to know your fellow members so that you might help them walk in faithfulness. By this token, you should let them get to know you, so that they can help you. Finally, your job is to be an ambassador for Christ's kingdom by sharing the gospel with those who are not yet citizens of Christ's kingdom. You should share the gospel in your own city, and you should work with your church to send other ambassadors to nations around the globe. No national borders have the authority stop the spread of this kingdom.

So ask yourself, when was the last time you encouraged or corrected a fellow church member? Likewise, when was the last time you invited a brother or sister to speak directly to you? Are you growing in your knowledge of the gospel, so that you can protect it? And when was the last time you shared the gospel?

17

The Elder (Counsel)

Covenantal Authorization: New (Special) Covenant

So I exhort the elders among you, as a fellow elder and a
witness of the sufferings of Christ, as well as a partaker in
the glory that is going to be revealed: shepherd the flock
of God that is among you, exercising oversight, not under
compulsion, but willingly, as God would have you; not for
shameful gain, but eagerly; not domineering over those in
your charge, but being examples to the flock. (1 Pet. 5:1–3)

Other Elucidating Biblical Texts

Pay careful attention to yourselves and to all the flock,
in which the Holy Spirit has made you overseers,
to care for the church of God. (Acts 20:28)

We ask you, brothers, to respect those who labor among
you and are over you in the Lord and admonish you, and
to esteem them very highly in love. (1 Thess. 5:12–13)

If anyone aspires to the office of overseer, he desires a noble task.
Therefore an overseer must be above reproach . . . (1 Tim. 3:1–2)

Remember your leaders, those who spoke to you the
word of God. Consider the outcome of their way
of life, and imitate their faith. (Heb. 13:7)

Obey your leaders and submit to them, for they are keeping
watch over your souls, as those who will have to give an
account. Let them do this with joy and not with groaning,
for that would be of no advantage to you. (Heb. 13:17)

Job Description

To teach and exemplify, for a church, Christ's new creation and kingdom life, giving oversight to an entire church body and shepherding
its members.

———

THE TEMPTATION FOR SOME Christians when addressing the topic of
church government is to emphasize either the elder's authority or the congregation's authority. Yet we must address both, give each their due, and
explain how they work together. Most organizations, after all, have more
than one type of authority, such as the authority of the shareholders, the
board of directors, and the CEO.

In the previous chapter, I argued that the congregation possesses the
authority of the keys, which means that the whole congregation, when
gathered together, has the authority to render judgment on the *what* and
the *who* of the gospel—confessions and confessors. Pastors or elders then
possess the authority to teach the church and oversee the church. Among
other things, this includes leading the church when it uses the keys.

As I have throughout this book, I will continue using the terms "elder,"
"pastor," and "overseer" interchangeably, since Scripture does, keeping in
mind that the word for "pastor" is typically translated as "shepherd" (e.g.,
Acts 20:17, 28; Titus 1:7; 1 Pet. 5:1–5; see also, Eph. 4:11). Sometimes
churches call one group of men elders and another group pastors. Yet this
creates two offices where the Bible has only one. So with any distinction
that exists between bishop and pastor.

What Is the Authority?

Ever since God removed himself from Adam and Eve's presence, God's
people have lived by faith, not by sight. Gratefully, God still speaks. We may
not encounter him with our eyes, but we can with our ears.

That means the Christian life and our church gatherings center on God's word, the Bible. The Bible teaches us how to know and follow God in the fellowship of the church. It's how we know anything with certainty. Though I haven't dedicated much space to the authority of Scripture in this book, it alone is the absolute and perfect authority for what to believe about God, salvation, and how to live before God. It's the "norming norm" for all our doctrines and practices. Therefore, the church *gathers* to hear the Bible and *scatters* to live out and share the Bible, letting it reverberate into every area of members' lives.

That's why, in the previous chapter, I tied the church's authority to the Bible. I said that churches must not require their members to believe or practice anything that is not taught in Scripture or deduced from it "by good and necessary consequence."

Yet all this raises another question: whose interpretation and teaching of the Bible will count as a church's interpretation? One member may have one interpretation; another person another. If the judgments of the church as a whole bind every member, whose interpretation binds the church as a whole?

Answer: the elders. They're the ones who say, "Church, these are the doctrines we believe." The congregation then replies and formally affirms, "Yes, those are the doctrines we believe," making those doctrines official. The congregation makes the final judgment in matters of doctrine and membership, but the elders lead or tell the congregation which judgments to make.

The elders' authority is an authority of counsel, as we discussed in chapter 11. They cannot excommunicate the church or members of it. Yet their teaching and counsel binds the members together. God intends for members to "obey" and "submit," to use the language of Hebrews 13:17, when their leaders say, "This is the doctrine we believe" or "We should receive this person as a member." The pastors cannot enforce their pronouncements, but Jesus will back up the elders. As such, church members should feel the weight of elder pronouncements on their consciences.

For instance, Paul plays the part of a pastor when he tells the church in Corinth to remove a man as an act of discipline. In one verse, he tells the church, "I have already pronounced judgment" (1 Cor. 5:3). Yet that doesn't mean the deed is done. He then exhorts the church to pronounce the same judgment: "Is it not those inside the church whom you are to judge?"

(v. 12). The Corinthian congregation is under obligation to obey Paul, but the final decision still remains in their hands. This process, whereby Paul renders a judgment but then asks the congregation to render that same judgment, gives the Corinthian church a training opportunity. Paul doesn't infantilize them by doing all the work himself. He wants them to mature toward spiritual adulthood by calling them into his own work. He's like a parent teaching a child to walk on its own.

To be sure, elders can err, which is one more reason the congregation remains the final court for rendering judgment and the keys of discipline remain with them. Paul tells the churches in Galatia that they should reject even an apostle or an angel from heaven who preaches a wrong gospel to them (Gal. 1:6–9). Jesus won't give any bonus points on the last day to a congregation who submits to a false teacher or a wolf.

What Kind of Authority?

One of the most prominent metaphors for an elder in the New Testament is "shepherd," which is what the word "pastor" means. In the Old Testament, the title belonged principally to the kings of Israel (e.g., 2 Sam. 5:2; 7:7; Ezek. 34:23; cf. Isa. 44:28). Since these shepherds proved faithless (e.g., Jer. 23; Ezek. 34), Jesus came as the good shepherd. He knows his Father's sheep and keeps all of them (John 10:11, 14, 27–29). An elder's job, then, is to be an undershepherd of the good shepherd. Like Jesus, they should work to know and keep the sheep by leading, feeding, and protecting them. Paul instructs, "Pay careful attention to yourselves *and to all the flock*" (Acts 20:28a; also, Eph. 4:11; 1 Pet. 5:1).

Furthermore, shepherds possess oversight, analogous to an Israelite king's oversight over the nation. Paul continues: "Pay careful attention to yourselves and to all the flock, in which the Holy Spirit *has made you overseers*" (Acts 20:28).

Yet that oversight exists for the purposes of ensuring that the congregation is being built up upon the word of God and its doctrines. Paul one more time: "Pay careful attention to yourselves and to all the flock, in which the Holy Spirit has made you overseers . . . *from among your own selves will arise men speaking twisted things, to draw away the disciples after them*" (Acts 20:28, 30). The elders' task, in other words, is to lead the congregation as a whole and each member individually toward the green pastures of God's word, protected from the jaws of wolves who would devour them with false teaching.

In short, elders have the authority to teach and the authority of oversight, and those two things are closely related. Elders teach us to know and apply the Bible's content individually; and they lead us to know and apply the Bible in our corporate life together. Let's unpack each of these:

(1) *Authority to teach.* If we look at Paul's list of elder qualifications in Titus 1 and 1 Timothy 3, nearly every qualification applies to every Christian. Every Christian, for instance, should aspire to be sober-minded, temperate, not a drunkard, faithful to one spouse, and so forth. Paul lists only two qualifications here that apply to elders alone: "not a recent convert" and "able to teach." The ability to teach doesn't so much refer to the elder's gifts of charisma or rhetorical power, but more to the quality or "soundness" of his teaching. He teaches "what accords with *sound* doctrine" (Titus 2:1). He "holds firm to the trustworthy word as taught, so that he may be able to give instruction in *sound* doctrine and also to rebuke those who contradict it" (Titus 1:9). He follows "the pattern of the *sound* words" taught by the apostles (2 Tim. 1:13). The word "sound" shows up nine times like this in Paul's pastoral letters (1 and 2 Timothy and Titus). The point here is, an elder "rightly handles the word of truth" (see 2 Tim. 2:15).

In other words, an elder's ability to teach doesn't mean he can step into the pulpit and enthrall a thousand people with his wisdom and wit. It means that, if you're struggling to understand the Bible or how to handle a tough life situation, you can stop by his house and ask him for help, and you'll receive sound biblical wisdom. You trust that, when he opens the Bible, he doesn't say crazy things from it. He provides you with a faithful understanding of it.

When a church installs men as elders, they're affirming these men as the ones who will provide the church with its authoritative interpretation of God's word. Some of those men might teach from the church pulpit, some from the counselor's chair, some over coffee. But the point is, that's what you'll get from them—faithful Bible teaching. And the fact that they possess the office of elder means the whole church recognizes them as trustworthy in this.

(2) *Authority of oversight.* Peter, like Paul, closely associates the work of oversight with shepherding: "shepherd the flock of God that is among you,

exercising oversight" (1 Pet. 5:2). Notice, the shepherd is to be "among" his sheep. He knows them. He's with them. Also, he and his fellow elders aspire to know and pay careful attention not to some of them but to all of them. Paul one more time: "Pay careful attention . . . to all the flock" (Acts 20:28). By paying careful attention, he knows what the flock struggles with, where they're tempted, and what weaknesses wolves might exploit.

An elder's position, then, is one of oversight or leadership. It's a position to which the flock should "submit" (Heb. 13:17). That doesn't mean the elders have the authority to tell you whom to marry or which job to take or which house to buy. The scope of that oversight is limited to decisions concerning the church as a whole or that are pertinent to its life together, particularly what is taught. They'll make decisions about the preaching schedule, any small group or Sunday school curriculum, what the church does when it gathers, what songs it sings, how to approach counseling, whether to plant a new church or to build a bigger building when the room is full, whom the church should support as a missionary, and more.

Of course, the Bible does not explicitly address the countless decisions a church must make in its weekly life together. That a church should send missionaries? Yes. Whom exactly it should send? Of course not. That a church should collect the offerings of its members for gospel work? Yes. Whether it should use extra space in its budget to hire another associate pastor or to replace the church building's aging boiler and roof? No. The congregation relies on the oversight of the elders, with the aid of the deacons, for these kinds of biblically informed but wisdom-dependent judgments.

Sometimes churches will attach adjectives to pastoral job titles—executive pastor, missions pastor, young adults pastor, youth pastor. Yet they should not miss this fact: if the noun in a man's title is elder or pastor, he is most fundamentally a pastor with oversight over the whole flock. This is one thing that distinguishes a pastor or elder's authority from a deacon's. Acts 6:1–7, if we take it as instructive for the office of deacon, as I do, implies that deacons possess an administrative authority over specific areas in the life of the church. A deacon might be responsible for facilitating a nursery schedule, a church website, its parking procedures, a church benevolence fund, or food distribution to widows. But deacons undertake this work at the behest of the elders, who possess authority over the whole flock and over the flock's spiritual progress in particular.

The metaphor of a shepherd is a distant one for most people in the world today. Yet it's a beautiful one that sets transcendence down inside of immanence, like a man nestled among his sheep. It pictures "the benevolent use of authority," as one author puts it, or a "subtle blend of authority and care," says another.[1] Meditating on a shepherd's work, the first author continues:

> Some situations require militant protection and discipline, others beckon for gentle nurture. The shepherd ruler of Psalm 2 rules with an iron rod. The shepherd ruler of Isaiah 40 tenderly carries the nursing ewes. The shepherd image is especially useful for *holding in tension* these essential features of leadership. Authority without compassion leads to harsh authoritarianism. Compassion without authority leads to social chaos.[2]

Of course, the best picture of a transcendent authority who leans with compassion toward immanence is God himself: "I myself will be the shepherd of my sheep, and I myself will make them lie down, declares the Lord GOD" (Ezek. 34:15; see also Ps. 23). The elders of our churches have the privilege of reflecting him, even as they prepare to give an account to him (Heb. 13:17).

Why Such Authority?

Why does Scripture give authority to elders? There are a number of ways we could answer that question.

For our purposes, I want to focus on the example elders set. Peter charges elders not to be "domineering" but to be "examples to the flock" (1 Pet. 5:3). The author of Hebrews, likewise, enjoins the congregation, "Remember your leaders, those who spoke to you the word of God. Consider the outcome of their way of life, and imitate their faith" (Heb. 13:7). An elder's office, as much as anything, is about recognizing him as an example in life and doctrine. To give him the office is to say, "Church, here is a man you should follow. Listen to what he teaches. Watch how he lives. When it comes to following Jesus, be like him."

---

1 Timothy Laniak, *Shepherds after My Own Heart: Pastoral Traditions and Leadership in the Bible*, New Studies in Biblical Theology 20 (Downers Grove, IL: InterVarsity Press, 2006), 247; the latter quotation is from Derek Tidball, quoted in Laniak, 247.
2 Laniak, *Shepherds*, 247.

The elder's authority, in other words, doesn't depend on differences of class but of maturity. He's not a member of the aristocracy or possessor of blue blood. He's not a medieval Roman Catholic priest whose soul has been emblazoned by the Holy Spirit of God. Martin Luther rightly observed, "There is really no difference between laymen and priests . . . except that of office and work, but not of 'estate'; for they are all of the same estate."[3] Rather, an elder or pastor is more like a parent with a child. His job is to call the members *up* and *into* maturity. He works to reduplicate himself in all those places in which he imitates Christ (see 1 Cor. 4:16; 11:1).

His office, then, is about character recognition. That's why Paul spends most of his time talking about an elder's character. Sometimes Christians are surprised when they search for an elder's job description in the Bible only to discover that the authors are more systematic in describing an elder's character (1 Tim. 3:2–7; Titus 1:6–9). Also interesting is the fact that these descriptions of an elder's character point to attributes that, as I said, should characterize every Christian. Why doesn't Paul require something more extraordinary of elders, such as "demonstrated track record in leading large organizations," "started seven orphanages," or "launched a revival?" The reason, it would seem, takes us right back to the idea of an elder being an example. The New Testament spends more ink on the qualifications than on the job description because the qualifications *are* the job description. Other than being able to teach, his life should be something that other Christians can copy.

An elder works by calling people to imitate his ways. So says Paul to the Corinthians: "I urge you, then, be imitators of me. That is why I sent you Timothy, my beloved and faithful child in the Lord, to remind you of my ways in Christ, as I teach them everywhere in every church" (1 Cor. 4:16–17).

Speaking figuratively, a pastor demonstrates how to use the hammer and saw, then places the tools into the members' hands. He plays the piano scale or swings the golf club, then asks the members to repeat what he has done. He says to his church, "Let me teach you the way of the cross. Now watch me walk it. Here's how you endure suffering. Here's how you love obstinate

---

3 Martin Luther, "An Open Letter to the Christian Nobility of the German Nation," in *Works of Martin Luther*, The Philadelphia Edition, 6 vols. (Grand Rapids, MI: Baker, 1982), 2:69.

teenage children. Here's how to love your wife when she receives the cancer diagnosis. Here's how you share the gospel in a difficult work environment. Here's what generosity and justice look like, even when people don't like you. Here's how to follow Jesus when money is short. Let me show you how to be valiant for the truth and tender toward brokenness."

Members, then, consider all this and imitate the elders' faith and their way of life.

The fact that setting an example is central to an elder's work is one reason why churches should seek to affirm a plurality of elders and not rely on just a solo pastor. If the work of an elder is to present a way of discipleship for every Christian, churches benefit from having more than just one. We learn from watching the men in full-time vocational ministry. Yet we also learn from the elder who works full-time as a teacher, at the factory, or in finance. Men in different vocations give us the opportunity to see how godliness might look in different spheres. The man working in finance demonstrates what it looks like to follow Jesus when you're wealthy; the one cleaning the building what it looks like to follow him when you're living paycheck to paycheck. So also with many other differing life circumstances and personality types.

Not only that, the shepherding work of the elders sets an example for the older women in the church, who in turn should devote themselves to discipling the younger women. Paul, like the Bible as a whole, believed that God created male and female wonderfully and differently. While a group of qualified men will possess oversight over the congregation as a whole, those men should seek the counsel of the "mothers" of the congregation, as Paul implies with Timothy (1 Tim. 5:2; see also Acts 18:26). Pastors also "teach" the older women to in turn "train the young women" in the way of godliness (Titus 2:3–5). One-on-one shepherding ministry then, typically, travels along gendered lines, men to men and women to women.

Why does an elder have authority? To teach and demonstrate an example of godliness, because by that he will save himself and his hearers (1 Tim. 4:16).

What Are the Limits of an Elder's Authority?

The limits of an elder's authority map over the limits of the congregation's authority. Like the congregation's authority, his authority is not coercive but declarative. And like the congregation's authority, his authority centers entirely on the Bible and can only go where the Bible goes, no further. An elder with no Bible is an elder with no authority. The elder's job, recall, is to lead the church to do *its* job. The church's limits are also the elder's limits.

Good pastors, therefore, will quickly acknowledge the fallibility of their wisdom relative to the Bible's perfect wisdom. It is one thing to teach the Bible faithfully; it's another thing to apply the Bible to the diverse circumstances of daily life. Pastors involve themselves in both teaching and applying, but good pastors recognize the difference between these two things. For instance, there is a qualitative difference between teaching the church, "Paul tells us to raise our children in the training and instruction of the Lord" (see Eph. 6:4), and saying to them, "Here's how to think about movies and video games or schooling options." There's a difference between "Jesus instructs us to make disciples" (see Matt. 28:19) and "Here's a method for evangelism." Teaching a church to follow the Bible necessarily involves both kinds of statements. Both kinds are important. Members need not just principle statements but practical guidance, because life is lived in the practical domain. Still, a good pastor weights these kinds of statements differently. He doesn't treat his wisdom as God's.

Personally, I'll offer some type of verbal cue to indicate the different weights. I'll say something like, "I could be wrong"; or, "I don't mean to bind your conscience, but I do mean to put a little pressure on it"; or, "Now, I'm drawing that counsel out of the wisdom bucket, not the law or biblical truth bucket"; or, "You might not be sinning to do that, but I think you might be unwise."

Paul, too, seems to recognize the need for different weights when he says, "'All things are lawful,' but not all things are helpful" (1 Cor. 10:23); or, "admonish the idle, encourage the fainthearted, help the weak, be patient with them all" (1 Thess. 5:14).

The point is, a pastor needs to be an expert in moral weighting. That's essential to the job. Sometimes biblical application is clear and direct. Sometimes indirect. Sometimes implied. Sometimes suggested. Sometimes possible. Sometimes perhaps. Sometimes "if you think it's best." The pastor who treats everything he says as black or white is a pastor who, ironically, confuses his wisdom with God's and undermines the supremacy of Scripture.

Pastors must therefore realize that one of their jobs is to be staunch advocates for Christian freedom (see Rom. 14). Their job is to teach the congregation how to "welcome" one another in disputable matters, and not to "pass judgment" on each other in matters of conscience (Rom. 14:1, 3, 4, 10). Part of teaching the Bible is helping the church to recognize what the Bible binds and what it doesn't bind, but then being gracious toward those who see things differently.

Let me go just a little bit deeper on this point. Legalism or self-justification is native to all human beings. Becoming a Christian means repenting of such self-justification and seeking our justification in Christ. Yet the old sinner nature still shows up in camouflage. Even as Christians, we still like to make rules, feel good about ourselves because we keep the rules we make up, and then put ourselves over others because they don't keep our rules. Only now, we fool ourselves into thinking we have the warrant of Scripture behind us, because we're able to make some tenuous connection from our rule to the Bible. All this is why Pharisaism is a perennial temptation not just for non-Christians, who have their own made-up rules, but for Christians as well.

A pastor's job, then, is to destabilize or even demolish the massive edifices of human morality. He reminds his church members not to impose their wisdom and fear and moral deductions on one another. The good pastors I've known even display a little bit of impiety, at least the kind of impiety that refuses to kowtow to the manmade "religious" expectations of the day. They deftly use humor, even sarcasm, to melt a church's sacred cows.

The need for dexterous moral weighting is especially crucial amid the growing number of political and ethical controversies of the day. On the one hand, pastors should be the first to stand up for biblical truth when it's clear. On the other hand, pastors should be the first to stand up for Christian freedom when a matter is not clear, so that our unity is built around Scripture, not the wisdom of man. Christians err by faithless compromise. They also err by prosecuting what shouldn't be prosecuted and by endlessly dividing. A good pastor keeps his eyes on both risks.

A last word on the boundaries of pastoral authority pertains to the manner of his instruction. Insofar as his authority is declarative, not coercive, he relies on the power of the declaration of the Bible, not on any other kind of power to coerce or cajole or manipulate or pressure or force people to agree with him or do what he wants. He doesn't even rely on the power of his personality. He relies on the word and the Spirit.

Think of the apostles in Acts 6. They ask the church to find men who could help repair the division in the church as certain widows were being neglected in the distribution of food. As for the apostles themselves, "But we will devote ourselves to prayer and to the ministry of the word" (Acts 6:4). The word and prayer give a pastor all the power he needs, and it's a power that demolishes the strongholds of disobedience (2 Cor. 10:3–6).

On the other hand, a Pharisaical or abusive or oppressive pastor characteristically . . .

- makes dogmatic prescriptions where Scripture is silent;
- relies on intelligence, humor, charm, guilt, emotion, or threats rather than on God's word and prayer;
- plays favorites;
- punishes those who disagree with him;
- employs extreme forms of communication (temper, followed by silent treatment);
- recommends courses of action that always, somehow, improve his own situation, even at the expense of others;
- speaks often and quickly;
- seldom does good deeds in secret;
- seldom encourages;
- seldom gives the benefit of the doubt;
- emphasizes outward conformity rather than repentance of heart;
- is a glory seeker and not a glory-to-God giver.[4]

Such men should not be pastors, but should be removed from that office. If you cannot remove them, you should leave the church and find one where you can trust the men to keep their eyes on God, not themselves.

How an Elder Gets to Work

How then does an elder get to work? His work begins in his personal life through attending to his knowledge of the Bible, prayer, and improvements of character. His training should take him into deeper and deeper meekness,

---

4 These bullet points are adapted from Jonathan Leeman, *Church Membership: How the World Knows Who Represents Jesus* (Wheaton, IL: Crossway, 2012), 118–19.

humility, and purity of heart. His aspiration to serve as an elder, which is good, says Paul, is an aspiration to love and serve others (1 Tim. 3:1). Along these lines, if a man spends all week wrapped up in talk about politics, culture, and sports, don't be surprised if his sermons on Sunday feel a little thin. An elder should work to seek first the kingdom of heaven all week.

To ordain a man as an elder is not so much to *make* an elder but to formally *recognize* what a man is already doing. The elder and the church recognize that "Joe" is faithful in the home and faithful in the church. He's quick to point people to the Bible, and he's trustworthy with the word. Members of the church tend to gravitate toward him at the end of the services, not because he exhibits the marks of worldly popularity but in the same way someone who is sick might draw toward a doctor. The spiritually sick seek him out.

For his part, Joe doesn't merely gravitate toward people who look just like him, but to the sick and hungry and teachable and impressionable no matter what they look like: young or old, minority or majority, man or woman, popular or pathetic. A church ordains a man when they see this kind of activity.

Beyond all this, a pastor is a man who lives by the gospel. His character is "above reproach." Yet he's as unimpressed with his own character as anyone else in the church is unimpressed with their own. He knows he's a sinner. He knows he's saved by grace alone. He knows everything good he has is a gift (1 Cor. 4:7). Therefore, he doesn't lord it over others but is filled with compassion, patience, and forbearance.

It's often said that good elders smell like sheep. Yet if they smell like sheep it's because they smell like Jesus. Spend time with a godly elder and somehow you walk away feeling corrected and encouraged, challenged and built up, convicted and inspired, exposed and loved. I praise God for the men who have had this effect on me, and I could name dozens. I pray that you can, too.

Conclusion

Equality, the Fear of God, and a Reward

I WANT TO CONCLUDE THIS BOOK with a final reflection, an exhortation, and a word of hope.

The reflection is on the topic of equality. Genesis 1 and 2 teaches that every human being was created equally in God's image. And the book of Revelation pictures us worshiping equally around his throne. Not only that: the gospel declares that, even now, "There is neither Jew nor Greek, there is neither slave nor free, there is no male and female, for you are all one in Christ Jesus" (Gal. 3:28). Our present generation's impulse to affirm equality is, at its best, good, humane, creation-affirming, and redemption-aspiring.

As I said earlier in the book, Christianity offers a radically egalitarian perspective in affirming both our creational equality and our equally shared redemption in Christ. There's a sense in which good authority always aims at a kind of equality. I don't mean to suggest we will ever be equal with Christ. We won't. Still, Christ commands us to make disciples so that we might share in his reign. Astonishingly, the Bible even uses the language of a redeemed humanity reigning *with* God (in 2 Tim. 2:12; Rev. 20:6—literally, "be kings with").

Good and Bad Versions of Equality

Yet just as there are both satanic and godly versions of authority, so there are both satanic and godly versions of equality. The satanic version is a product of Genesis 3: "You will be like God." You are God's equal. You may define and create the universe for yourself. Your basic instincts and desires are good.

This satanic version of equality operates by power. It is defined on the self's terms. It looks inward, lists the self's assets and virtues, and then asserts itself by comparing itself to others. "I'm as smart as he." It possesses a strong sense of entitlement. It lives by making demands. "I deserve this. I have a right to that." Ultimately, satanic equality yields a war of all against all as everyone makes their demands.

Satanic equality has little to no room for assigned roles, responsibilities, differences, and, most of all, hierarchies. It seeks to level all hierarchies because the self's sense of the self is rooted in the self and can therefore tolerate few externally imposed limitations. In one moment it praises "difference," but in the next moment it smothers any and all differences because difference always looks like a threat to equality. So it tends to sameness, androgyny, conformity.

Satanic equality follows short-term thinking. It promises immediate gain: you will be like God. Therefore, it despises any role for submission or talk of constraint. It lives on continual self-assertion.

It is atomistic and therefore insensitive to the concerns of others since identity is rooted in the self. It is self-righteous and self-justifying, always convinced that its arguments are correct. Ultimately, so much self-assertion destroys relationships. It might talk about group identity, but the basic instinct here is employing groups and group identities for pragmatic and finally selfish purposes. Groups serve to exalt and empower the self.

Godly equality, on the other hand, shows up two chapters earlier in Genesis: "So God created man in his own image, in the image of God he created him; male and female he created them." This equality is untroubled by the distinction between male and female, or, by implication, by any other differences God might have ordained among image-bearers. Godly equality is rooted in the gift of God's image. Image-bearers are equal by virtue of his image.

Godly equality also depends on God's word and his work of redemption. It's defined on God's terms. In the face of this world's inequalities, it is discovered by faith. Its default mode is not power but humility, a humility that allows it to speak with all the strength of someone who has heard God speak, even when outward comparisons fail. It begins with listening: "Who does God say that I am?" It asks questions and seeks out its responsibilities: "God, what would you have me do?"

Godly equality feels no threat from God-given roles, responsibilities, or even hierarchies. It delights in difference, trusting that every God-assigned distinction possesses purpose and contributes to the countless refractions of his glory. It doesn't assume that God's assignments of different steward-ships and stations, responsibilities and roles, undermines equality. Rather it views them as so many parts of one body, each part purposed with doing the work of the whole body. It follows long-term thinking, and ultimately reinforces equality under and in the rule of God.

Therefore, godly equality maintains room for sacrifices, constraints, and the call to submission. God, after all, gives a job to everyone. And with every job he establishes a set of rules, procedures, and jurisdictional boundaries. Every one of us must drive within our lanes, whether we're a leader or a follower. Every one of us must keep the speed limit, and drive in the direction in which God tells us to drive. We must all submit to him and to his law. Leaders lead and followers follow—all in submission to him. There is, in that sense, no difference between leading and following for a human. To lead according to God's law is to follow according to God's law. They are the same, because his law is one.

Godly equality can maintain room for difference, whether hierarchi-cally defined or not, because everyone and everything serves God. All must submit to him or receive the fire of his judgment if they do not. Yet to live by his law, says the psalmist, is blessing. It creates a community of peace, harmony, shalom, where individuals bear fruit like trees planted by streams of water.

Godly equality is more sensitive to the needs of others. It recognizes the bond shared among all humanity by virtue of our common creation in God's own image. It possesses a humble posture toward others, recognizing that everything a person possesses comes from above. It points to groups and group identities for theological purposes. If God has created something, it is good and should be celebrated because it will teach us about him.

The point, finally, is not that equality is good and authority is a necessary evil that we have to endure until we don't need it anymore. Good equality depends upon good authority. Remember what I said in chapter 1: authority exists because something good, true, beautiful, holy, and righteous exists worth protecting and even worshiping. And remember what I said in chapter 13: even as my children must internalize my discipline, so that I no longer have to rule them, so the redeemed must internalize the rule and law and authority of God. Only then will we be equally in his rule and under his rule.

Observe what happens when Christ delivers the kingdom of God to God the Father: "When all things are subjected to him, then the Son himself will also be subjected to him who put all things in subjection under him, that God may be all in all" (1 Cor. 15:28). God's rule will envelope and incorporate all things, so that we'll all be under his rule, in his rule, and sharing his rule.

The Fear of God

Where then do we go from here? How do we begin the project of pursuing a godly authority and a godly equality?

Look one last time at David's final words: "When one rules justly over men, ruling in the fear of God, he dawns on them like the morning light, like the sun shining forth on a cloudless morning, like rain that makes grass to sprout from the earth" (2 Sam. 23:3–4). Notice that just rule begins with the fear of God. A fear of God is the beginning of wisdom and justice. It's the beginning of an authority that protects the vulnerable, strengthens communities, promotes human flourishing, and will finally save the world.

As I said at the beginning, I can offer you principles for how good authority works. I can reason with you page after page from the Bible, explaining and illustrating to the best of my ability. You can read along and decide you agree with this or that point, and maybe even be persuaded of something you didn't believe before. But if you don't fear the Lord, you won't finally rule or lead or exercise authority well and justly.

If your God is small; if he's of little account; if you have no concern about his wrath; if his holiness rests lightly on you and you never give thought to standing before him on that final day of glorious and awful judgment, in which God's people will be vindicated and God's enemies condemned; if you're not confident in his sovereign rule over all things, even the lot that is cast into the lap; if you're not building your life on the victory of Christ's already-accomplished victory over sin and death and Satan; if you don't trust God's character, that he's good and loving; if you don't know deep in your gut that he holds this universe together by the word of his power, and that from him and through him and to him are all things, and that the nations are a drop in the bucket before him, dust on the scales, and that the earth is a footstool for his feet; if, that is to say, you don't fear God, you will not rule or use your authority well—not in the home, church, workplace, or nation. To the extent that you do use it well even though you reject him, it will be his grace alone that does good through it. The good you do will, in that sense, be in spite of you.

Therefore, survey one last time the different areas of authority in your life. What are your goals? What are you trying to accomplish? Build up others, or yourself? That's a good practical question to ask yourself.

More crucially, ask yourself, who is your God? What is he like? If you tell me your answer to those questions, I can tell you the most important things about how you use your authority.

Our Reward

Fearing God means we will look to him for our reward, a reward that awaits us on the last day. For instance, consider what Peter says to the elders of a church: "Shepherd the flock of God . . . eagerly, not domineering. . . . And when the chief Shepherd appears, you will receive the unfading crown of glory" (see 1 Pet. 5:2, 3, 4).

I believe we can assume a similar promise applies to all people who use their authority for the glory of God and the good of others.

What will enable you to step into positions of leadership and use your authority in a way that does good to others even at cost to yourself? The larger answer is faith, love, and hope, yet here I want to emphasize the hope of an eternal reward. You must want what Christ's heavenly city affords more than the treasures of this world (see Heb. 11:16; Rev. 21:24).

Every morning, my heart returns to the default setting of selfishness. That means I wake up and am tempted to use my authority—in my marriage, my parenting, my work, my church—for the rewards I can get in the here and now. Then the Spirit speaks through the new man in me: "Don't work for a perishable wreath, but an imperishable one" (see 1 Cor. 9:25).

It's that hope, the hope of knowing God's pleasure, that will enable us to work hard and sacrifice more, and to use our strength to make ourselves most vulnerable for those we lead.

"Humble yourselves, therefore, under the mighty hand of God so that at the proper time he may exalt you" (1 Pet. 5:6).

Postlude

A Prayer of Praise

AT THE BEGINNING OF THIS BOOK, I said that I hoped to help us look into the face of the one who kept the entire law and exercised his authority perfectly. Then I offered a prayer of confession. It seems appropriate, then, to conclude with a prayer of praise to him.

Lord Jesus,

Our hearts long to see perfect beauty and love, and we behold them in your authority.

You came as a king to rule as Adam, David, and none of us could. You proved yourself the greater David by undertaking the work of a priest and sacrificial lamb. You defeated our greatest enemies by bearing our sin on the cross and rising from death. You showed your sovereignty as the suffering servant. Therefore, all authority in heaven and on earth rightly belongs to you.

You, incarnate Son of the Father, submitted to God, reflecting and enacting his supremacy over creation. You worshiped no other gods, had no other idols, never took his name in vain, found your rest in him. You honored your parents. You never murdered or hated; never committed adultery or lusted; never stole or coveted; never lied, embellished, or equivocated. In all these ways you showed us what God is like. You ruled as the perfect God-man, the firstborn brother who leads adopted sons and daughters to do likewise.

You are generous beyond measure. You came to share your rule and glory with a people, creating, forgiving, saving, and raising us up that we might reign with you for eternity. Why would you give so much to a rebellious people like us? Why would you entrust power to those who have misused it? Yet you gave and gave and continue to give. While we are glory-hoarders, you are a glory-sharer.

You are humble beyond reckoning. You possess all knowledge and all power, yet you did not consider equality with God something to be grasped but emptied yourself. You put on weakness. You sought and grew in wisdom. You opened God's word and meditated upon it day and night, so that you became like a tree planted by steams of water who bears the fruit of life.

You are courageous beyond comparison, and kind like no other. You fear no threats, nor are anxious about anything. Instead, you made yourself vulnerable for our sakes. You paid the cost of our salvation. You absorbed the evil one's arrows so that we might be kings and might sing as we rule. You are the Shepherd who guides us into green pastures, carries us when we are weak, and prepares a table for us in the presence of our enemies. You dawn on us like the morning light, like the sun shining forth on a cloudless morning, like rain that makes grass to sprout from the earth.

You, the image of the invisible God, the radiance of his glory, the imprint of his nature, are beauty. Like the perfect face, your rule is perfectly balanced, perfectly composed, perfectly resplendent. It's gentle and mighty, loving and fierce, conscientious and wise, empowering and correcting, demanding and giving, forgiving and just, righteous and good. It inspires desire, affection, and love. It makes us want to rule like you rule, so that all things may be in subjection to God, and that God may be all and in all.

All glory, dominion, majesty, and praise to you.

Amen.

General Index

Abigail, 155
Abraham, xvii, xviii, xix, 5, 169, 206, 223
abuse. *See* authority: abuse of
Adam, xvi, xvii, xviii, xix, 9, 18, 22, 35,
　　67, 70, 71, 92, 97, 99, 170, 171, 176,
　　182, 183, 186, 200, 221, 224, 231,
　　244, 263; *see also* covenant: Adamic;
　　Eve
affirmation. *See* authority: and
　　affirmation
Ahab, 5
Alexander (NT person), 162n5
Alles, Major General Randolph "Tex,"
　　story of, 136–38
Amnon, 126
Amy, story of, 31–42, 43, 75, 143, 144
"Anakin Skywalker" (fictional character),
　　6, 10
Angela, story of, 17–29, 31, 43, 70, 158
anti-hero, 4
Arendt, Hannah, 186
authority
　　abuse of, xv, xvi, 3, 6, 9, 32–44, 50, 56,
　　　64, 79, 80, 102, 104, 123, 154, 174,
　　　182, 185, 209, 240
　　and accountability, xviii, 3, 8, 10, 11,
　　　12, 70, 72, 91–98, 105, 125, 151,
　　　160, 202, 208, 213, 215, 230
　　and affirmation, 51, 124, 128–29, 134,
　　　187, 201
　　authorization of, 9, 25, 78, 149, 150,
　　　167, 169, 183, 197, 221, 233, 243

bad, 6, 7, 8, 9, 10, 12, 13, 29, 37, 57, 58,
　　72, 75, 97, 114
bottom-up, 107–10
and church, 3, 4, 6, 7, 8, 17, 21, 24, 26,
　　31, 31–34, 36, 38, 39, 41, 51, 52–54,
　　57, 61–64, 67, 70–72, 75, 77, 82–86,
　　86n4, 94–96, 101, 104, 106–7, 110,
　　116–17, 129, 138, 140, 143, 150–51,
　　152n2, 153, 154–57, 159–61, 162n5,
　　163–64, 168, 169–72, 174–75, 178–
　　82, 187–88, 190–91, 193, 198–200,
　　206–7, 210, 210n5, 211–14, 216–18,
　　222, 226–27, 233–41, 243–54,
　　254n4, 255, 261; *see also* authority:
　　and elders
and command, 13, 25, 27, 29, 58, 64,
　　66, 67, 69, 71, 77, 78, 79, 80, 82,
　　100, 113, 121–22, 132, 136–39,
　　149–65, 174–75, 178, 180–93,
　　197–219, 221–31, 233–41, 257
and conscience, 62, 66, 78, 82–83,
　　85–86, 125, 153–56, 161, 239, 240
and cost, 11, 44, 49, 53, 80, 96,
　　131–46, 177, 261, 264
and counsel, xviii, 13, 32, 33, 36,
　　38, 51, 80, 83–84, 95, 96, 98, 114,
　　118–20, 146, 149–65, 167–82, 188,
　　190, 222, 227, 243–55
definitions of, 24–27
and discipline, xviii, 9, 19, 20, 70, 79,
　　81, 96, 97, 121–30, 135, 141–43,
　　153, 154, 155–57, 160, 163, 180, 184,
　　187–93, 234–39, 245–46, 249, 260

Scripture Index

9Marks

Building Healthy Churches

9Marks exists to equip church leaders with a biblical vision and practical resources for displaying God's glory to the nations through healthy churches.

To that end, we want to see churches characterized by these nine marks of health:

1. Expositional Preaching
2. Gospel Doctrine
3. A Biblical Understanding of Conversion and Evangelism
4. Biblical Church Membership
5. Biblical Church Discipline
6. A Biblical Concern for Discipleship and Growth
7. Biblical Church Leadership
8. A Biblical Understanding of the Practice of Prayer
9. A Biblical Understanding and Practice of Missions

Find all our Crossway titles
and other resources at
9Marks.org.

Also Available from 9Marks

For more information, visit **crossway.org**.